Occasional Paper No 47

The Cultural Heritage of the Indian Village

edited by
Brian Durrans
and
T. Richard Blurton

British Museum
1991

BRITISH MUSEUM OCCASIONAL PAPERS

Publisher: The British Museum.
Great Russell Street, London WC1B 3DG

Production Editor: Johanna Awdry

Distributors: British Museum Publications Limited
46 Bloomsbury Street, London WC1B 3QQ

Occasional Paper No. 47, 1991:
The Cultural Heritage of the Indian Village
Edited by Brian Durrans and T. Richard Blurton

ISBN 0 86159 047 3

ISSN 0 142 4815

Orders should be sent to British Museum Publications Ltd.
Cheques and postal orders should be payable to
British Museum Publications Ltd and sent to
46 Bloomsbury Street, London WC1B 3QQ.
Access, American Express, Barclaycard/Visa cards are
accepted.

Printed by Electromec Offset Ltd, London

CONTENTS

INTRODUCTION

Beyond its many physical forms, the Indian village is a powerful symbol of social continuity and interdependence. To critics this is interpreted as inertia or reaction; for admirers, like Gandhi, it has meant traditional self-sufficiency from which a humane future might evolve. For generations of India's rural majority, any such abstractions begin and end with the particular advantages and disadvantages of home.

Behind its symbolic meaning the realities of Indian village life are more dynamic, variable, complex and externally oriented than is commonly supposed. It is with these realities that the ideas and findings set out in this Occasional Paper are primarily concerned. Originally presented in 1982 at a symposium at the Museum of Mankind entitled The Cultural Heritage of the Indian Village, they have subsequently been reviewed by their authors, each of whom has explored a specific aspect of village culture. Held during the Festival of India in Britain - the first and perhaps the most successful of such festivals - the symposium was associated with the British Museum's two Festival exhibitions: From Village to City in Ancient India (Department of Oriental Antiquities) and Vasna: Inside an Indian Village (Department of Ethnography). (See Durrans, B and R Knox, India: Past into Present, London 1982.)

No editorial line has been imposed on the following papers regarding the use or assessment of 'ethnographic parallels' from the remote past; some authors favour them explicitly, while others are more concerned with presenting empirical evidence. In our view, what really matters is that the factual content of the archaeological data should be recorded as accurately and comprehensively as possible and that its interpetation should be open to ideas derived from different sites, periods, cultures or communities (what Dhavalikar describes in his paper as 'general comparative analogy' [p. 29]). It would be redundant to proselytize for ethnographic parallelism as a mode of interpretation, for there is now a large literature in which Indian scholars and others use admirably broad strategies to explore various aspects of social life and its development. By placing archaeological studies alongside ethnographic or sociological ones, we simply suggest that these categories can usefully inform each other, without being dogmatic about levels of degree.

The archaeological contributions of Thapar, Joshi, Chakrabarti and Dhavalikar present a varied menu of empirical facts and interpreted meanings. Most focus on the northern part of the subcontinent. Thapar assesses work on one chalcolithic and two neolithic sites in northern and northwestern India. Most notably, excavations in the Belan valley indicate a local autonomous evolution of neolithic culture and have exposed much evidence for wider comparison. The forms and arrangements of huts and corrals find parallels not only in neolithic cultures elsewhere, but also in 'transitional' cultures, or those engaged in both cultivation and foraging, from the recent past or the present in India itself.

Settlement patterns are also discussed by Joshi, with respect to Harappan and pre-Harappan evidence in the Punjab of the first three millennia BC. Again, there is strong evidence for local autonomy in the transition from pre-Harappan to Harappan culture, and for complexes of villages and urban centres constituting distinct economic zones. Such zoning was a response to the fragmentation of cities and to a spread of population eastward and from larger river valleys to smaller tributaries.

Following or fuelling these broad developments of new economic systems and settlement patterns were particular technologies, pre-eminently food-production, pottery and tool-manufacture. Chakrabarti focuses on a later technology - metalworking - to review the published geological, historical and ethnographic evidence for the use of different metals in the proto- and early historical period. He also notes that the pre-industrial iron smelting tradition now survives in India only in part of Bihar. The previous general dependence of ironworkers on local ores is itself a clue to the long practice of this technology throughout the subcontinent. Chakrabarti suggests that modern pre-industrial furnaces and such existing techniques as lost-wax casting may supply 'further inferential evidence' for a better understanding of excavated material.

Especially fruitful prospects for interpreting archaeological evidence in terms of wider patterns of meaning can emerge when intensive work on particular sites extends to careful exploration of local traditions or ways of life in the immediate vicinity. This is what Dhavalikar presents in his case-study of the important Maharashtran site of Inamgaon.

A different frame of comparison - this time between textual precepts and observed data from various periods - is adopted by Khare in his resourceful analysis of Indian hospitality, which here serves as a bridge from more archaeological to more ethnographic contributions. Khare demonstrates the importance of cultural rules of sociability, expressed in terms of reciprocity and access to space and food, and focused on domestic arrangements. We are reminded that the effective structure of the Indian (as any other) built environment is constituted as much by ideas as by walls.

The remaining papers refer to particular parts of the subcontinent, although the itinerant ascetics whose ornaments are analysed in Burghart's paper belong to a sect which is widespread throughout much of northern India. Although their practice is extreme, the Ramanandi renouncers articulate values with deep resonance in Hindu India and serve as a reminder of ideological unity, as well as the persistence of the most ancient traditions beneath the surface fissures of modern cultural life. Although rejecting settled existence, they cannot survive, paradoxically, without it, for it is village or small town devotees who sustain them as they wander through India.

Most of the 'ethnographic' contributions examine the rich cultural traditions of Gujarat (also the focus of the Vasna exhibition), while the remaining three are concerned with Bihar, West Bengal and Tamil Nadu respectively. Dowry is a controversial subject in much of India, but in her study of this institution in rural Kutch Elson reveals its positive role in symbolising ethnic distinctions and in partly compensating the bride for patrilocal residence. Like the embroidered costumes of Kutch, the votive terracottas of certain Gujarati communities are a medium through which traditional tribal beliefs are expressed. But as Shah describes, devotees are locked into a larger economic sphere even in the pursuit of their own traditions.

Still wider networks of contact and influence are traced in Donley's comparison of architecture in Gujarat and the Lamu archipelago, off the East African coast. Her key argument is that house forms reflect the social and religious functions of domestic space and ultimately cultural definitions of gender and status. This approach is neatly complemented by Pramar's survey of how traditional Gujarati architecture encodes relations between town and country.

Mainstream village life has long been integrated into larger political and moral systems through such means as administration, religion and caste. However, external political interests have had instrumental objectives; far subtler in the spread and maintenance of shared values are popular activities of the kind that Jain describes in his study of scroll-paintings which travelling narrators use to entertain village communities in Gujarat. Local and topical references enhance a sense of participation in performances which mix recreation, education and the acquisition of supernatural merit. Even stronger involvement is experienced in the creation of images for the Kali-puja of West Bengal. Robinson describes a system of competitive dramatic expression in which popular and local values mediate pressures for change. A 'folk' artform developed under middle-class patronage, but its devotional content found itself channelled into relatively autonomous inter-group rivalry. The Kali-puja eclectically incorporates symbols of industrial or Western origin for its own ends, in defiance of both middle-class and traditional values. Eastern India is also the setting for Singh's surprisingly optimistic interpretation of contemporary Munda life and religion. The situation for tribal communities continues to change quickly, often catastrophically. The undoubted changes which Singh chronicles, while initially destructive, suggest that catastrophe is not inevitable.

Finally, Huyler, like Shah, examines the tradition of producing low-fired terracotta votive sculpture. In this paper, however, the locale shifts to Tamil Nadu, and the practice of making large-scale sculptures which are incorporated into the shrines of the deity Aiyanar. He rightly reminds us that the vast majority of India is rural (still some 70% out of a population in excess of 800 million). If we needed any other justification for the holding of the original symposium and subsequently the publication of its proceedings, we would do well to remember this fact. Only in recent decades have scholars fully realised the extent to which the village, as well as itinerant tribal life, have acted as reservoirs for later urban cultural and religious developments. It is within this context that the expansion of Indian village studies assumes a central importance. This publication in a small way is intended as a contribution to this end.

The editors wish to thank all those who made this publication possible. The contributors themselves are not only blameless for the delay in its appearance but have also responded patiently to our various queries and suggestions. We also wish to thank Peter Khoroche, who advised us concerning the use of diacritical marks for the Sanskrit words, and Rebecca Jewell, who added them to the camera-ready copy.

We gratefully acknowledge the support of the Charles Wallace (India) Trust whose backing for the symposium made it possible for the valuable contributions from India to be presented. We also acknowledge the Trust's generous support of this publication. Finally, every effort has been made to obtain permission for the quotation in Khare's paper from Prakash Tandon's Punjab Century, but without success. If any question arises concerning the use of this, or other quoted extracts in this Occasional Paper, the publisher apologises for any error inadvertently made, and will be pleased to make necessary corrections in any future editions.

Brian Durrans
T. Richard Blurton

RECENT ARCHAEOLOGICAL DISCOVERIES: PROBLEMS AND PROSPECTS

B K Thapar

During the last decade there has been a considerable amount of problem-oriented fieldwork carried out in India, particularly with respect to neolithic and chalcolithic cultures. This clearly necessitates a re-appraisal of the contexts and importance of these cultures. This paper will consider three of the excavations which have opened up exciting new fields of archaeological research. Of these, two relate to the neolithic - one each in Kashmir and the Belan valleys - and one to the chalcolithic in the copper-belt of Rajasthan.

The cultures of the Indian neolithic have so far been recognised in six different geographical regions:

i) Northern, covering the Kashmir valley;

ii) Belan valley, covering the Vindhya plateau, in Allahabad, Mirzapur, Rewa and Sidhi Districts;

iii) Northern Bihar, covering Saran District;

iv) Northeastern, covering Assam and the sub-Himalaya regions;

v) Central-eastern, covering the Chhota Nagpur plateau with its peneplains;

vi) Southern, covering peninsular India.

In each region at least two sites have been excavated with the explicit aim of understanding the specific character of the culture. Further, the Southern region has been extensively investigated with over a dozen sites from Karnataka, Andhra Pradesh and Tamil Nadu having been excavated to varying degrees. Among the neolithic cultures of these six regions, recent work at the first two - the Kashmir and Belan valleys - has added significantly to our existing knowledge, both in terms of material culture, and also as far as subsistence is concerned.

Kashmir valley

Neolithic culture in the Kashmir valley is represented by nearly three dozen sites, all of which are located on the elevated flat terraces of Karewa clay, which often overlook streams and lakes. Pollen diagrams based on samples from the Haigram lake, not far from Srinagar, have provided evidence for a three-stage disturbance of natural vegetation, as shown by the decline and re-appearance of pine forests. The clearance of pine forests at one stage in the sequence is thought to have been related to the farming experiments of the neolithic settlers in the valley. Of these sites, only two - Burzahom and Gufkral - have been systematically excavated. The former (the name literally means 'the place of the birch') is situated 16 km northeast of Srinagar. The site was initially excavated in 1935 by De Terra and Paterson (De Terra and Paterson 1939) and during 1960-71 by T N Khazanchi (Khazanchi 1976, 1977). These excavations yielded a threefold sequence of cultures, beginning with the neolithic, followed by a megalithic and then an historical phase. The current excavation at Gufkral (literally 'the cave of the potter'), while confirming this same sequence, has added new dimensions to the neolithic culture, and has demonstrated three phases of evolution, known as Periods IA, IB and IC. The earliest of these periods is aceramic - this being the first time that this neolithic phase has been identified in India. The characteristics of these three phases are outlined below.

Period IA - this was aceramic. The subsistence economy of the site seems to have been based on specialised food gathering and cereal farming; wheat, barley and lentils have been identified. Stock raising was also important, as evidenced by the find at Gufkral of the bones of wild animals (ibex, bear, sheep, goat, cattle, wolf and Kashmir stag) and also those of domesticated animals (sheep and goat). This evidence for domesticated animals confirms that which is known from Burzahom, and although there is no direct evidence for the existence of cereals at Burzahom, palynological studies carried out near the site have revealed the existence of the type of weeds which are usually associated with the cultivation of wheat and barley. The analysis of the bones of the domesticated goat reveals the absence of old animals, and a contrasting predominance of immature specimens; this suggests herd management.

The inhabitants lived in underground pits which are usually circular or rectangular in plan; less frequently are they oval or square. The pits were cut into the loess and often had their floors painted with red ochre. As protection against bad weather the pits had birch covers supported on wooden posts, as is indicated by the presence of post-holes around the tops. Close by to these were found other, shallower pits, which seem to have been used as storage bins and also as hearths. Tools were made of both bone and stone - the former consisting of points, needles, and scrapers, and the latter of axes, drills, picks, pounders, querns and mace-heads. The stone tools were made of Himalayan trap, while the bones were of the bone of various animals, but including goat, sheep - and stag (this was used though only when the bones were in the green stage).

Period IB - in this period pottery first appears. In addition to the domesticates known from the previous period, cattle and dogs are now recorded, as also are common peas. In this period the percentage of bones of domesticated animals, as against wild ones, shows a steady increase; this feature continues also in the next phase. The animals hunted during the various stages of the neolithic are invariably found to belong to the herbivores.

The items of cultural equipment noted in the previous period continued during this phase, though with a greater variety in the tool-kit - harpoons, needles with or without an eye, awls and arrow heads - made of bone, and chisels, hoes and adzes, amongst others, of stone. The inhabitants of the site continued to live in pits. Though steps were provided in the deeper pits, these did not always reach to the bottom. Three principal pottery fabrics were in use during this phase, all of them hand-made: thick coarse grey ware, fine grey ware, and gritty dull red ware. Of these, the most common shapes are the globular jars and basins, both of which have disc bases often with mat impressions. These impressions suggest a high level of development in mat making.

Period IC - this phase - the last in the sequence - marks a distinct change. The underground dwelling-pits and chambers are no longer used; most of them were filled in and covered with mud-plastered floors, which were covered with a thin coating of red ochre. Huts were now constructed above ground, being built of mud or mud-brick. The subsistence pattern apparently underwent continuing change, and this period saw a further diversification in material equipment - perhaps brought about through contact with regional or extra-regional cultures.

At this time, not only are tools with a better finish and in larger numbers recorded (indicating craft specialisation), but also new types were added to the repertoire - the small bone point, double-edged pick, spindle whorl and harvester knife (a rectangular or semi-lunate knife with holes along one side). This last item was made in both stone and bone. Similar tools have been recorded from the early farming cultures of China, particularly from the Yangshao culture of the Huang He valley (Chang 1977).

In the ceramic assemblage, a further fabric - the burnished grey ware - was added to the already existing range. Principal shapes in this ware are the high-necked globular jars, bowls and basins, amongst others. Noteworthy among the pottery finds at Burzahom, however (from the lower levels of this period), is a wheel-turned vessel of orange-slipped ware. It is decorated in black paint with a horned figure in a panel between the neck and the shoulder bands of the pot. Both in shape and in painted design, the pot resembles the pre-Harappan Kot Diji ware, and must, presumably, have been an import from the nearest site of that type - a site such as Sarai Khola situated on the Potwar plateau. From the upper levels of this period (again at Burzahom) was found a wheel-made vessel of red ware, which contained as many as 950 beads of agate and carnelian. This again seems to be out of context with the existing assemblage, and probably represents an imported item. Metallurgy does not seem to have been practised by the early farming communities of the Kashmir valley, but a few copper arrow heads, a ring, bangles and a pin were found in the deposits of Period IC. Their occurrence, however, seems to be intrusive, just as does the wheel-made painted pot, and the agate beads. As such they do not appear to have altered the basic neolithic subsistence economy and technology of the period.

Other important finds from Period IC are the two engraved stone slabs which were found fixed into a rectangular structure. One of these decorated slabs depicts a hunting scene, while the other shows an incomplete pattern, identified as tectiform (Pande 1971, 1972). Evidence for the burial practices of this period is provided by six human interments exposed at Burzahom (Sharma 1967), which indicate that primary and secondary burial was practised. Further, examples of wild dogs and two antlers of barasingha, are also attested (Sharma 1968).

Belan valley and Vindhya plateau

Discoveries at the sites of Chopani-mando, Koldihawa and Mahagara indicate a continuous sequence from the stage of intensified food gathering and selective hunting (epi-palaeolithic), through incipient food production (advanced mesolithic or proto-neolithic), to settled village farming (neolithic). This evidence, the first of its kind in India, further dispels the notion of the diffusion of neolithic culture from either west Asia or southeast Asia, and establishes the primacy of the neolithic culture of the Belan valley - especially in the light of the proposed chronology (seventh-fifth millennium BC) for the neolithic phases.

Chopani-mando is located within a former meander of the Belan river, 77 km east-southeast of Allahabad. The excavation revealed a three-fold sequence, extending from the epi-palaeolithic through the early mesolithic to the advanced mesolithic (or proto-neolithic). The first two periods were characterised by the occurrence of specific tool types as blades, the presence of geometric and non-geometric microliths, the gradual reduction in size of tools, and a change in the raw material for producing tools. In the proto-neolithic period significant additions to the tool repertory, and to other cultural equipment included:

i. tranchet tools;

ii. ground stone tools, such as hammer-stones, anvils, querns, mullers and ring-stones;

iii. the use of hand-made pottery (red ware, and khaki or brownish-grey ware) - sometimes decorated with impressed designs.

Of special importance at the site was the discovery of hut foundations and hearths. These appear from the early mesolithic period onwards. Thirteen such huts from the proto-neolithic period were exposed. They were either round or oval in plan, with an average diameter ranging from 3.5m to 5.7m. The floors of these huts were littered with a large number of microliths, anvils, hammerstones, sling balls, mullers, querns, etc, as well as fragments of burnt clay, animal bones and potsherds. These huts were all located close together. The economy of the settlement seems to have been based on gathering and hunting; there is no evidence for the domestication of animals or plants. However, from the presence of querns and mullers one can infer the practice of some sort of incipient plant cultivation; perhaps we can see here a population on the very threshold of effective food production. The excavation yielded remains of wild rice - carbonised and embedded in lumps of burnt clay - and the bones of wild cattle and ovicaprids. The mesolithic period at Chopani-mando is ascribed to c. ninth/eighth millennium BC.

The other notable sites in the region are Koldihawa and Mahagara, situated on opposite sides of the Belan river; the latter being only 3km from Chopani-mando and thus about 85km from Allahabad. The excavations at Koldihawa revealed a threefold cultural sequence from the neolithic through the chalcolithic to the Iron Age. The neolithic settlement was distinguished by the occurrence of ground stone tools including celts, microliths and hand-made pottery - amongst which were cord-impressed, rusticated and burnished wares. Palaeobotanical analysis of rice-husks used in the pottery fabric showed that the rice belonged to a domesticated variety. On the basis of the C-14 dates obtained for this neolithic deposit, a date of seventh-fifth millennium BC can be suggested for this use of domesticated rice - the earliest evidence so far known for the use of this plant crop (Sharma et al. 1982).

Mahagara is a single-culture site dating to the neolithic period. Here a 2.60m occupation deposit has provided evidence of six different phases. As many as twenty huts, represented by floors and postholes, were excavated. Of these the vast majority (eighteen) belonged to the last structural phase - VI. The sides of these huts were perhaps retained by wattle and daub screens, as suggested by the presence of burnt fragments of daub bearing impressions of reed or bamboo. On these hut floors blades and microliths, pottery querns, mullers, sling shot, celts, bone arrow-heads, terracotta beads and animal bones were found. An interesting feature of the excavation was the discovery of a feature identified as a cattle-pen. In plan it was an irregular rectangle, measuring 12.5 x 7.5m, with the longer axis running north-south. This pen seems to have been fenced by twenty postholes, with wide spaces left for openings in three places - two on the eastern and one on the western side. Within this fenced area no pottery or other finds were excavated. However, a large number of cattle hoof impressions representing cattle of different age groups were recorded; many of these were concentrated in clusters. From the number of hoof marks it is estimated that this cattle-pen could accommodate between 40 and 60 individuals. Outside the pen and close to the hut clusters the hoof marks of sheep and goats were recorded. Neolithic ceramics are represented by four wares - the cord-impressed, rusticated, burnished red, and burnished black. All of them were hand-made and poorly fired. The cord-impressed wares are undoubtedly the most distinctive.

The economy of Mahagara was based on hunting and farming. This is attested by the presence of the bones of wild cattle, and also those of domesticated cattle, sheep, goat and horse; domesticated rice is also recorded from the site. The existence of bones of wild and domesticated cattle is perhaps indicative of the process of transition from a hunting to an agricultural economy.

Copper belt of Rajasthan

The third site of importance is Ganeshwar, in Sikar District, Rajasthan. Here the chance discovery of sixty copper celts in November 1977 led to a systematic excavation and exploration of the surrounding area (Agrawal 1978, and Agrawal and Kumar 1982). This fieldwork revealed that Ganeshwar was located in the close vicinity of rich copper mines - Dariba, Ahirwala, Chiplata, Behar and Baleshwar - all in the Sikar-Jhunjhunu area of the Khetri copper belt. Further, this area contains a number of natural springs - both hot and cold ones - and these may have been important features in the location of where the tools were manufactured. The area is drained by the rivers Kantli, Dohan, Kasaunti and Sota. Of these, the Kantli (on which Ganeshwar is situated) seems, in the distant past, to have joined with the Drishadvati (or Chautang) river. It would thus have served as a link between the Indus sites on the Ghaggar-Hakra system, and the copper belt; Kalibangan is only 250km northwest of Ganeshwar. The Sota is a tributary of the Sabi, which in its turn runs into the Yamuna.

The cultural equipment from the site includes a large number of copper objects, which are associated with microliths and a type of pottery which the excavators identify as Ochre Coloured Pottery. A noteworthy find was a round terracotta cake, apparently simulating the well-known Indus type. The copper objects included arrow-heads, spear-heads, fish-hooks, spiral-headed pins, celts, bangles, chisels, etc. Some of the shapes of these objects are paralleled at various Indus sites. The associated pottery is quite distinctive. However, notwithstanding its present name, Ochre Coloured Pottery, it is a red-slipped ware often painted in black and decorated with incised linear designs. Most forms are vases of some type. This class of ceramic is found littered over many sites in the area, and was also reported from Jodhpura on the Sabi river (District Jaipur), where it was found stratified below the deposits containing the plain black-and-red ware. Radiocarbon dating of samples from the upper levels which yielded the so-called OCP ware have indicated a time-bracket of 2500-2000 BC. The excavator has speculatively added another couple of centuries to suggest a date for the earlier levels. By extension, the deposits at Ganeshwar could fall within this range - 2800/2700-2000 BC.

Discussion

We can now examine the problems which the evidence from these new discoveries presents. In Kashmir, we note the identification at both Gufkral and Burzahom of the existence of an aceramic neolithic. This is entirely in keeping with findings from Asia as far west even as Turkey.

However, the transition from the final phases of the hunter-forager stage to the farming economy, and the adaptation to post-pleistocene environmental changes has not yet been recognised in the Kashmir area. Current investigation into this complex problem has, however, revealed at Sombur a lithic industry based on jasper, silicious limestone and trap. Tool types recorded include burin points and borers (Pant et al. 1982). This industry, the first of its kind recorded from the valley, may perhaps indicate a particular stage in the extended process of transformation from an exploitative to a productive economy. De Terra and Paterson also found thin indeterminate flakes near Sombur in the lowest Jhelum terrace. They explained that this represented a late palaeolithic culture (De Terra and Paterson 1939). Thus an understanding of the origins and early spread of farming in the Kashmir valley is still insecure and fragmentary.

Turning to the inter- and extra-regional relationships of the Kashmir valley, it seems that this neolithic culture shares certain traits with the cultures of Sarai Khola on the Potwar plateau, Ghaligai and Leobanr in Swat, and Yangshao in the Huang He valley in China (Chang 1977). A closer analysis of the material culture in these three different regions indicates that the similarities between the Kashmir valley and the first two regions are limited to the ceramic technique of mat-impressed bases and the use of celts and bone objects. However, the distinctive elements of the Kashmir neolithic - the range of ceramics, the variety of bone and stone tools and the conspicuous absence of microliths - remains without parallel. As regards contact with China, there are certainly two examples of items of the material equipment of the Yangshao culture - harvester blades and jade beads - which are included in the inventory of the neolithic cultures of both the Kashmir valley (c.2300-1500 BC) and Swat (c.1500-1200 BC). The date given for the Yangshao culture in the Zhougyuan region is 6000-3000 BC, and in Gansu 3000-1800 BC (Chang 1977). In both these regions the Yangshao culture presents a different cultural style compared to Kashmir, as can be seen in the range and form of ceramics (especially tripods with solid legs), including the painted wares, terracotta human figurines, and house models. There is also the cultural habit of locating the cemeteries separately from the areas of habitation (Chang 1977). Meanwhile, a further addition to our knowledge on this subject has been made by recent discoveries in the north of Sikkim, in the Djangu area, where typical harvester blades have been found in association with neolithic tools such as celts (some with single and some with double perforations), adzes, etc (Sharma 1981a). Of interest here is that single perforated celts have also been reported from the neolithic assemblages of Honan province, in northern China. Such close affinity in artefacts in these areas could suggest a southward penetration from northern China sometime in the early part of the third millennium, or even a little later, during the period of the Lungshan cultures, some of which were characterised by the use of burnished grey-black pottery (Dikshit 1982). A possible route for this penetration into Kashmir and the Indus valley is through the series of passes which link the Gilgit valley with Wakhan and Chinese Turkestan. More fieldwork is clearly needed to improve understanding of the distribution of cultural traits.

Meanwhile, on the basis of the available evidence, one can argue that the Kashmir neolithic had its own special and distinct characteristics, while still borrowing certain elements from other regions. This northern contact seems to have taken place in the later stage; the antecedent stages still require elucidation.

In the Belan valley current fieldwork has provided evidence of the transition from wild species of cattle, sheep/goat and horse, to domesticated ones. Similar evidence is also available with respect to rice. This region, therefore, is the only one which shows the transformation from a foraging to a farming economy. Significantly, no aceramic neolithic has been recorded. Instead pottery makes its first appearance in the proto-neolithic or the advanced mesolithic period, when both animals - in the form of cattle and sheep/goats - and plants - in the form of rice - were undomesticated, thus indicating the primacy here of the manufacture of pottery over the domestication of animals and plants. Considering the date suggested for this phase (c. ninth-eighth millennium BC), it can be argued that this is the earliest recorded evidence of the use of pottery. It is well-known that in West Asia (at Jarmo, Jericho, Çatal Hüyük, Hacilar, Cayonu and Tepe Guran) and also in East Asia (the Jomon culture, and evidence from the site of Non Nok Tha), the manufacture of pottery started later than the eighth millennium BC. Consistent with this date for the advanced mesolithic period in the Belan Valley is the proposed date for the neolithic period, seventh-fifth millennium BC. This indicates a considerably earlier time range than that of neolithic cultures in other regions of India (Thapar 1978), but discounts the recent conjectural dates for the northeastern neolithic culture, put at c. 5000-2000 BC. (Sharma, T C 1981). This information on the early beginnings of agriculture in the Belan valley needs to be confirmed by further fieldwork, as well as by further closely-observed sampling for radio carbon dating. Meanwhile, the importance for data - especially that which relates to the gradual transition from a food-gathering economy to an agricultural one - should be made more widely known.

In the Ganeshwar region, exploration and excavation have provided information on the following:

i. the concentration of copper-using communities in the vicinity of rich copper mines;

ii. the occurrence in large numbers of copper artefacts, some of which are paralleled on Harappan sites;

iii. the association of the Ochre Coloured Pottery with this assemblage - and dated in this region to 2800-2000 BC (Agrawal and Kumar 1982);

iv. the use of microliths.

It is now apparent that the copper requirements of Harappan sites in Punjab, Haryana, Rajasthan, and perhaps even further west, were met by the Sikar-Jhunjhunu area of the Khetri belt. Communication was probably via Kantli, Sota and Sabi. The present evidence suggests that the Ganeshwar region supplied mainly copper objects to the Harappan sites. With the exception of a single round terracotta cake, no distinctive Harappan objects such as seals, chert weights, chert flakes, terracotta and faience bangles, terracotta carts, painted or plain pottery, etc, have been found from sites in the Ganeshwar region.

The explanation for this is perhaps to be found in the different economies of the two areas. The economy of the Harappan sites was centred, for the most part, on river-based agriculture, using the flood-plains for raising crops; there was also an urban element. On the other hand, the economy of the Ganeshwar region seems to have been only partly agricultural with settlements and was at least as importantly based on hunting, as the microliths and barbed arrowheads of copper, and the fish-hooks, suggest. There are no alluvial plains in the Ganeshwar region which could be exploited as in the areas where the Harappan sites flourished.

Of particular interest is the definition of the characteristics of the Ochre Coloured Pottery from the Ganeshwar region, as well as its spatial and temporal horizons. Until these points are clarified, it is perhaps unwise to use this term in connection with Ganeshwar, where the wares seem rather to be the product of an indigenous ceramic industry. Its relationship with the Ochre Coloured Pottery associated with the 'Copper Hoards' still remains to be ascertained.

References

Agrawal, D P 1981. Multidisciplinary Investigations in Kashmir 1979-80. A Report. Man and Environment, V, 87-90. Pune

Agrawal, R C 1978. Archaeological Discoveries at Ganeshwar, Rajasthan. Avagahana, 2, no. 1, 28-30

Agrawal, R C 1979. Three Copper Objects from Ganeshwar, Rajasthan. Journal of the Oriental Institute, XXVIII, nos. 3-4, 139-60. Baroda

Agrawal, R C and Kumar, V 1982. Ganeshwar - Jodhpura Culture: New Traits in Indian Archaeology. In Harappan Civilization, Gregory Possehl (ed.). Delhi

Chang, Kwang Chi 1977. The Archaeology of Ancient China, 3rd ed. New Haven

De Terra, H and Paterson, T T 1939. Studies in the Ice Age in India and Associated Human Cultures. Washington DC

Dikshit, K N 1982. The Neolithic Cultural Frontiers of Kashmir. Man and Environment, VI, 30-36. Pune

Khazanchi, T N 1976. Pit-dwellers of Burzahom. The Illustrated Weekly of India, Sept. 5. Bombay

Khazanchi, T N 1977. North-western Neolithic Cultures of India. News letters, 7 and 8, Indian Institute of Advanced Study. Simla

Pande, B M 1971. Neolithic Hunting Scene on a stone-slab from Burzahom, District Srinagar, Kashmir. Asian Perspectives, XIV, 134-38

Pande, B M 1972. A Neolithic Tectiform from Burzahom, District Srinagar, Kashmir. Journal of the Indian Anthropological Society, 7 (2), 175-77

Pant R K, Claire Gaillard, Nautiyal Vinod, Gaur, G S and Shali S L 1982. Some Neolithic and Ceramic Industries from Kashmir. Man and Environment, VI, 37-40. Pune

Sharma, A K 1967. Neolithic Human Burials from Burzahom, Kashmir. Journal of the Oriental Institute, XVI, no. 3, 239-42. Baroda

Sharma, A K 1968. Animal Burials from Burzahom. A neolithic settlement in Kashmir. Journal of the Oriental Institute, XVIII, nos. 1 and 2, 40-44. Baroda

Sharma, A K 1981(a). Prehistoric Explorations in Sikkim. Puratattva, no. 10, 82-83. New Delhi

Sharma, A K 1981(b). Excavation at Gufkral 1981. Paper read at the Annual Congress of the Indian Archaeological Society, held at Vishakhapatnam

Sharma, G R, Mishra, V D, Mandal, D and Mishra, B B 1982. Beginning of Agriculture, Allahabad

Sharma, T C 1981. The Neolithic Pattern of Northeastern India. In Madhu: Recent Researches in Indian Archaeology and Art History, M S Nagaraja Rao (ed.), 41-52. Delhi

Thapar, B K 1974. Problems of the Neolithic Cultures in India: A Retrospect. Puratattva, No. 7, 61-65. New Delhi

Thapar, B K 1978. Early Farming Communities in India. Journal of Human Evolution, 7, 11-22. London

SETTLEMENT PATTERNS IN THE THIRD, SECOND AND FIRST MILLENNIA IN INDIA, WITH SPECIAL REFERENCE TO RECENT DISCOVERIES IN PUNJAB

J P Joshi

Introduction

During the last six decades 1530 settlements of the Pre-Harappa, Harappa, Late Harappa, Grey Ware and Painted Grey Ware cultures have been discovered within the present-day bounds of India. Of these, 712 belong to the Pre-Harappa, Harappa and Late Harappa cultures, while 848 belong to the Grey Ware and the Painted Grey Ware cultures. Some of these sites have been systematically excavated and for some of them Carbon-14 and Thermoluminescence dates are also available. Generally, Pre-Harappa and Harappa settlements fall within the third millennium, the Late Harappa sites in the second millennium, and the Grey Ware and the Painted Grey Ware sites in the first millennium BC. It should be pointed out that the Grey Ware sites are placed in the same time range as the Painted Grey Ware sites, even though at some sites these ceramics are found in layers earlier than those containing Painted Grey Ware. This plain grey ware is the 'associated ware' of the Painted Grey Ware.

The area covered by the various Harappa settlements runs from southern Jammu to northern Maharashtra, and from southern Gujarat to western Madhya Pradesh - including northern Rajasthan and parts of the northwestern Madhya Pradesh. The area covered by the Grey Ware and Painted Grey Ware complex, on the other hand, includes the eastern parts of the Harappa culture area, as well as parts of northeastern Uttar Pradesh and Rajasthan.

These settlements, with many of which the author has had a close connection, throw important light on settlement patterns during three millennia, from three different but overlapping contexts. The purpose of this paper is to suggest, with the help of new data, the settlement patterns of prehistoric cultures which flourished primarily in the area of the Indo-Gangetic divide.

The area of exploration includes Jammu in eastern Jammu and Kashmir, Kurukshetra in western Haryana, Gurdaspur in western Punjab and Bhatinda in southern Punjab. Intensive fieldwork was carried out between 1976 and 1981 by a team led by the author, and with staff from the Explorations Branch of the Headquarters Office of the Archaeological Survey of India (New Delhi).

Importance of the area

This area has vast tracts of agricultural land which are annually inundated with a rich alluvial soil, covered by a network of snow-fed and monsoon rivers; these can maintain a large population. Climatically the area is highly suitable for human occupation. There are perennial rivers which are ideal for irrigation and which were also useful as trade routes. These rivers, however, were not geologically stable, as can be determined from a survey of their courses. Moreover, the proximity of these sites to the Siwalik Hills provided easy access to sources of forest wealth, such as timber for house-building.

River systems

Since the patterns of settlement in this region are largely based upon the major river systems of the Chenab, Ravi, Beas, Sutlej, Ghaggar, Sarasvati and Markanda, it is important to note that, due to frequent tectonic movement in the lower Himalayas, movement of river courses was a recurrent feature. This phenomenon has been particularly pronounced in the case of the eastern rivers, such as the Beas and the Sutlej. The same type of geological factor was also responsible for the drying up of the Ghaggar and for creating the shifting channels of the Jamuna. From a study of Landset Imagery for the Punjab and Rajasthan, one can clearly record the shifts in the courses of the rivers, which must also have been a feature of life in this region during the proto-historic period (Etel 1981; Agrawal and Pande 1977, 55-106).

Results of exploration and documentation

Initially, exploration was undertaken in the area of southwestern Jammu, the upper Punjab and in Kurukshetra; later on the lower regions of the Punjab were surveyed in detail. Located in this survey were: 21 Pre-Harappa and Harappa sites, 24 Late Harappa ones, and 20 Grey Ware and Painted Grey Ware sites. The current documentation of these settlements is, however, as follows: Pre-Harappa and Harappa 56; Late Harappa 191; Painted Grey Ware and Grey Ware 226.

Study of the data collected so far shows that:

i) between the Harappa site of Manda in Jammu District (Jammu and Kashmir) and Ropar, Ropar District (Punjab) there was no sign of a Pre-Harappa or Harappa site;

ii) approximately 100 sites of the Late Harappa period have been recorded in the area between Jammu and Kurukshetra;

iii) in the lower Punjab - in the region of Mansa Taluk, Bhatinda District, which adjoins Ganganagar District in Rajasthan - at least 25 Pre-Harappa, Harappa and Late Harappa settlements were recorded. Of these, there are eight sites with Pre-Harappa and Harappa material, one site with Pre-Harappa, Harappa and Late Harappa material, and one with Harappa and Late Harappa material. Further, eight sites have provided evidence of only Late Harappa occupation. The size of settlements varies from 200 to 1500m. In an area of about 1250 km, the settlements are situated, on average, every 3 to 7 km.

On the basis of data from the explored mounds, a threefold classification has been worked out. The sites with Pre-Harappa and Harappa material belong to Group A - covering an area of approximately 1000 to 1500m^2. Group B consists of sites with Harappa and Late Harappa occupation, and covering an area of approximately 500 to 900m^2. In Group C twelve Harappa and Late Harappa settlements fit within the range 200 to 400m^2. All these settlements are situated along the ancient Sirhind river (modern Sirhind nala), which is now a dried-up tributary of the Ghaggar, and which previously issued from the Siwalik Hills near Ropar. Geographically, this region of exploration forms a <u>doab</u> between the Ghaggar and the Sirhind;

iv) the incidence and concentration of Late Harappa settlements is much denser in the northern part of the region, where people could easily find small tributaries beside which to settle. As one move eastwards from Jammu towards Kurukshetra, there is an increased frequency of Late Harappa settlements;

v) at present, there is no substantial Harappa site known in the Bikaner-Ganganagar region. However, six Late Harappa sites are recorded in the Mansa Taluk of Bhatinda District;

vi) Painted Grey Ware settlements with associated Grey Ware and associated Red Ware do not occur west of Amritsar. Further, the incidence of such sites slowly increases as one moves eastward. No Painted Grey Ware sites are presently known in the Gurdaspur area. However, sites with Grey Ware (often found associated with Painted Grey Ware) have been located in the region. An overlap of the Grey Ware with Late Harappa pottery is known from the excavations at Manda, Bhagwanpura, Dedheri and Nagar (Indian Archaeology; Joshi and Bala 1980,1981);

vii) the concentration of Painted Grey Ware settlements is greatest in the eastern Punjab and in Haryana; it tapers off to the southwest, with fewer sites being recorded in the southern Punjab. In Ganganagar District there are very few of these sites, and along the upper Ghaggar-Kakra, in Pakistan, there are only 14 of them.

The emerging picture

The pattern which emerges from these data is of an uninterrupted Pre-Harappa/Harappa sequence, usually on the same sites - there are no specific Pre-Harappa settlements. There are, however, separate Harappa settlements, a fact which might show that the change from the Pre-Harappa to the Harappa took place locally.

The presence of twenty-one sites in an area of approximately 1250 km^2 in Mansa Taluk (Bhatinda District) indicates that this area was an important zone for the Harappa culture. The peoples of the Pre-Harappa and Harappa periods seem to have preferred the Ghaggar and its tributaries for settlement, as this was a more stable river system compared to those of the Beas, Sutlej and Ravi. These latter rivers tended to be erratic, often changing their courses. The Sirhind, a tributary of the Ghaggar, was one of the most important lines of communication between the Punjab and Rajasthan. It was vitally important for the transfer of raw materials such as timber, especially deodar, which was used in house construction. This route seems to have been especially busy in the third and second millennia BC. Studies of the settlement pattern of the area suggest that there were three basic types of settlement:

i) cities (See Appendix, Group A) about 1500 m^2, such as Dhalewan, Gurnikalan, Baglian Da Theh, Lakhmirwala and Hasanpur. These are situated 3 to 5 km from each other;

ii) between these larger settlements are six towns (Group B), ranging in area between 90 and 500 m^2, at Karampura, Dallewala I, Sahnewali, Hirke, Dallewala II, and Bare II. It is worth noting that these settlements were located on the eastern side of the river, where denudation caused by flood waters would have been much less substantial. The situation of large modern cities on the south side of the Jamuna, where flood damage is less severe, is interesting circumstantial evidence;

iii) a series of fourteen villages (Group C), each of which covers an area of between 200 and 400 m^2. These are: Alike, Danewala I, Danewala II, Chhoti Mansa, Lallianwali, Laluwala, Bhikhi, Gurni Kalan II,

Nehriwala and Naiwala I-V. These are all situated on the western side of the river which was, on occasion, subjected to floods.

This area, therefore, provides good evidence for all three types of settlement being located near each other, thus creating the ideal situation for a complete urban complex. Their commercial interaction was the prerequisite for a developing civilization. It seems as if Sirhind has an important function as an 'economic zone', into which were directed the resources of the lower Himalayas to the north. From here they were transported south to the Bahawalpur area via Kalibangan, and also to Harappa sites in Haryana and Punjab. Almost the same situation existed in Kachchh, where there are as many as 25 sites between Sind and Gujarat. It is pertinent to note that there was yet another 'economic zone' on the Ghaggar river in the Bahawalpur region, where M R Moghul has located approximately 250 sites in an area of 1000 km^2, stretching from Yazman to the Derawar Fort (Joshi 1972, 98-144; Possehl 1980, 49-77; Mughal 1973 and 1980).

To summarize, one may list the following suggestions:

i) the Ghaggar was a larger river than the Indus, with its own network of tributaries, along which were situated hundreds of sites. In this huge area, there were at least three 'economic zones': 1) a northern, along the Sirhand and the Saraswati; 2) a central, in the Bahawalpur area; and 3) southern, in Kachchh;

ii) Pre-Harappa and Harappa settlements were mostly located along the major, perennial rivers. This was, in part, due to the fact that in this urban phase of civilization the settlers had mastered techniques necessary to erect platforms and high defences to thwart seasonal and occasional floods;

iii) exploration has clearly established that due to the nature of the erratic course of the Ravi, Beas and Sutlej, the Harappa period settlers only occasionally located their settlements upon these river banks. For this reason, despite intensive exploration, no Harappa period site is known for the region between Manda and Ropar. However, it appears that during late Harappa times a preference for locating settlements on the tributaries of these major rivers gained impetus. Due to economic regression and population shrinkage, they were unable to maintain the necessary protection platforms against floodwater and therefore moved to the tributaries in higher regions to the north, where there was plenty of water, but less danger of flooding. A similar situation is recorded in western Uttar Pradesh where, in the Late Harappa period, there was extensive settlement of tributaries of the Jamuna, such as the Krishni (Saharanpur District) and the Hindon (Bulandshahar District) (Dikshit 1981). The same situation is seen in Gujarat. It may be that this Late Harappa phase began during the time that the Manda region in Bhatinda District was settled, as attested by six Late Harappa sites there. Significantly, this phase is not found in Rajasthan. Further, it has also been observed that there is a greater concentration of Late Harappa sites in the northern regions, where sources of necessary natural produce were more accessible;

iv) this study has revealed an eastward movement of Late Harappa and Painted Grey Ware cultures, attested by the increase in frequency of sites from west to east;

v) it appears that the Painted Grey Ware culture entered northern Rajasthan from eastern Punjab and Haryana, where there is a concentration of these settlements, along the Ghaggar;

vi) the present survey has also revealed that the Baran element, with its Pre-Harappa content, has a distribution consistent with Late Harappa sites in the upper Punjab and in Haryana, but is not found in the southern region. This may indicate that the Baran group had a closer cultural contact with the Late Harappa peoples during their second phase of settlement in the region of the upper Punjab;

vii) it has been observed that there is a type of incised red ware, which has varied designs of a Pre-Harappa 'ancestry', and which is found in considerable amounts at all Late Harappa settlements;

viii) although Cemetery H red ware is present in some of the Late Harappa settlements in the Punjab and in Haryana, no settlement which is exclusively of Cemetery H type has been found. In fact, the settlements of the users of Cemetery H pottery are, apparently, almost entirely confined to the Harappa and Bahawalpur area. Stray finds suggest some contact, but nothing more.

Conclusions

Within the ambit of the Indus Civilization, present information from Mansa Taluk (Bhatinda District) for the first time provides evidence for an important aspect of settlement patterning - the existence of 'economic zones' made up of closed circuits of villages, towns and cities, in compact areas. Such economic zones have a specific role to play in our understanding of the settlement pattern of the peoples of the eastern Harappa culture. This evidence also throws light on the settlement pattern of the Painted Grey Ware culture. All this new evidence, taken together, shows that the settlement patterns of protohistoric cultures in this part of India were entirely dependent upon the changing courses of the rivers. In other words, hydrological changes adversely affecting water availability in the middle and lower courses of the perennial river systems, like the Ghaggar/Saraswati system, made the Harappa peoples leave their settlements, and thus permanently break the habit of city dwelling. A result of these two phenomena was the fragmentation of cities - both demographically and qualitatively. It is therefore no surprise that Late Harappa sites outnumber earlier ones, but they are from a non-urban context and are much closer together than previously. In the Late Harappa period, settlers favoured the northern parts of the present states in Punjab, Haryana and Uttar Pradesh, because in these regions the older river systems still retained water. Further, the directional change, from west to east, in the settlement pattern during the Harappa to Late Harappa periods is matched by a change from settlement in the major river valleys, to the tributaries. However, during the Painted Grey Ware period the old major rivers were again favoured in the search for settlement sites, for the middle courses of rivers such as the Ghaggar, Sarasvati and Drishadvati became active once more, though on a limited scale. This difference was probably brought about by geological changes in the river valleys. The overall direction of movement, however, remained the same - west to east. Nevertheless, two new areas were occupied - the Palaeo-Jamuna channel in the Bharatpur region of northeastern Rajasthan and the Ganga system in northeastern Uttar Pradesh. This extension is into an area which is more or less the same as that where the Copper Hoard and/or the Ochre Coloured Pottery cultures proliferated.

Acknowledgements

The author tenders his grateful thanks to Dr (Smt.) D Mitra, Director-General of the Archaeological Survey of India, for giving permission to present this paper; and to Sri B K Thapar, who was Director-General when most of the fieldwork was undertaken. The author is also thankful for assistance, both in the field and at headquarters, to Miss Madhu Bala, Deputy Superintending Archaeologist; Sarvashri J G Mathur, Deputy Superintending Archaeologist; Jassu Ram, Draughtsman; Laxminarayan, Photographer; S P Chatterjee, Senior Artist; Manohar Lal; O N Rattan. A deep debt of gratitude is due to Col. Prabhakar Misra of the National Remote Sensing Agency, Dehra Dun, for readily supplying the author with Landsat imagery of Rajasthan and Punjab which made the work both quicker and easier. Finally, the author is deeply grateful to Dr S P Gupta, Keeper, National Museum, New Delhi, for discussing at length many points emerging from the fieldwork, and for making very helpful suggestions.

Note

Based on the up-to-date compilation of data of Pre-Harappa, Harappa, Late Harappa, Painted Grey Ware and Grey Ware Settlements, and their distributional patterns by Miss Madhu Bala, Deputy Superintending Archaeologist, Archaeological Survey of India, New Delhi.

References

Agrawal, D P and Pande, B M 1977. Ecology and Archaeology of Western India. New Delhi

Dikshit, K N 1981. Excavations at Hulas and further exploration of the upper Ganga-Yamuna. Man and Environment, **V**, 74 ff.

Etel, Y P 1981. Remote sensing of the 'lost' Saraswati river. Proceedings of the Indian Academy of Sciences, 318-331

Indian Archaeology 1975-76 A Review, pp. 16-17; Indian Archaeology 1976-77 A Review, pp. 19-20

Joshi, J P 1972. Explorations in Kutch and Excavation at Surkotada. Journal of the Oriental Institute, **XXII**, nos. 1-2, 98-144

Joshi, J P and Madhu Bala 1980. Manda, a Harappan site in Jammu and Kashmir. Paper read at the Sringar Conference on Harappan Studies

Joshi, J P and Madhu Bala 1981. Movement of Harappans in circa Third and Second Millennium BC. Man and Environment, **V**, 64-69

Mughal, M R 1973. Present state of Research on the Indus Valley civilization. International Symposium on Mohenjodaro, Karachi

Mughal, M R 1980. New Archaeological Evidence from Bahawalpur. Man and Environment, **IV**, 93-98

Possehl, G L 1980. Indus civilization in Saurashtra. New Delhi

Appendix: Settlements in Mansa Taluq, District Bhatinda, Punjab

Sl. No.	Name of the Site	Lat.	Long.	Area	Cultural assemblage	Village/Town/City	Group
(1)	(2)	(3)	(4)	(5)	(6)	(7)	(8)
1.	Alike	75°20'N	29°45'E	200x200	Late Harappan	Village	C
2.	Danewala I	75°20'N	29°49'E	200x200	Late Harappan	Village	C
3.	Danewala II	75°24'N	29°49'E	200x200	Late Harappan	Village	C
4.	Chhoti Mansa	75°05'N	30°13'E	300x300	Pre-Harappan/Harappan, Late Harappan	Village	C
5.	Lalianwali	75°20'N	29°50'E	200x200	Harappan	Village	C
6.	Laluwala	75°28'N	29°51'E	200x200	Harappan	Village	C
7.	Bhikhi	75°34'N	30°04'E	300x300	Late Harappan	Village	C
8.	Gurni Kalan II	75°30'N	30°00'E	400x400	Pre-Harappan/Harappan	Village	C
9.	Nahriwala	75°25'N	30°05'E	400x400	Late Harappan	Village	C
10.	Naiwala I	75°30'N	29°55'E	400x400	Pre-Harappan/Harappan	Village	C
11.	Naiwala II	75°30'N	29°55'E	400x400	Pre-Harappan/Harappan	Village	C
12.	Naiwala III	75°30'N	29°55'E	400x400	Pre-Harappan/Harappan	Village	C
13.	Naiwala IV	75°30'N	29°55'E	400x400	Pre-Harappan/Harappan	Village	C
14.	Naiwala V	75°30'N	29°55'E	400x400	Pre-Harappan/Harappan	Village	C

Appendix: Settlements in Mansa Taluq, District Bhatinda, Punjab

Sl No.	Name of the Site	Lat.	Long.	Area	Cultural assemblage	Village/Town/City	Group
(1)	(2)	(3)	(4)	(5)	(6)	(7)	(8)
15.	Dallewala I	75°25'N	29°49'E	500x500	Harappan	Town	B
16.	Hirke	75°23'N	29°44'E	500x500	Harappan/Late Harappan	Town	B
17.	Karampura	75°25'N	29°53'E	500x500	Harappan	Town	B
18.	Dallewala II	75°25'N	29°50'E	500x500	Harappan	Town	B
19.	Bare II	75°29'N	29°54'E	500x500	Late Harappan	Town	B
20.	Sahnewali	75°30'N	29°55'E	500x500	Late Harappan	Town	B
21.	Dhalewan	75°35'N	30°02'E	1500x1000	Pre-Harappan/Harappan	City	
22.	Gurni Kalan I	75°32'N	30°00'E	1200x1200	Pre-Harappan/Harappan	City	
23.	Hassanpur II	75°30'N	29°58'E	1000x1000	Pre-Harappan/Harappan	City	
24.	Lakhmirwala	75°25'N	29°52'E	1500x1500	Pre-Harappan/Harappan	City	
25.	Baglian Da Theh	50°28'N	29°57'E	1000x1000	Pre-Harappan/Harappan	City	

ASPECTS OF CONTINUITY IN INDIAN METALWORKING TECHNOLOGY: A STUDY OF GEOLOGICAL AND ETHNOGRAPHIC SOURCES

Dilip K Chakrabarti

Introduction

The purpose of the present paper is to discuss the basic nature of the geological and ethnographic data concerned with pre-industrial Indian traditions of mining and metallurgy. It will also be argued that this corpus of data reflects situations which were current in much earlier periods. During the nineteenth century there was a marked interest in these data, especially as geologists were often guided in their explorations for minerals by the traces of old workings, which they recorded with the occasional speculation as to their antiquity. Serious metallurgical interest in pre-industrial Indian smelting processes and their products is evident from various experimental reports (Farraday 1819) and the inclusion of this data in works such as John Percy's Metallurgy of 1864. The first systematic study of this material was carried out by Valentine Ball in 1881, and among the historians of ancient Indian metallurgy Panchanan Neogi deserves credit for using them (1914 and 1918). With, however, only a few exceptions (Allchin 1962; Chakrabarti 1976, 1979, n.d.; Nanda 1981), there has been no significant historical or archaeological interest in these sources in recent years.

It should be stated, at the very outset, that the significance of these sources is greatly increased by the severe limitations of the traditional literary and archaeological sources for the history both of mining and metallurgy in India. As far as mining is concerned, the available literary references do not mention the technical processes at all, and hardly go beyond general references to mining activities. For instance, the Arthaśāstra of Kauṭilya (fourth century BC), despite its emphasis on the importance of mineral exploration being under state control (Book II, Chapter XII), does not describe how the actual mining operation was carried out. The Ain-i-Akbari of Abul Fazl (sixteenth century AD), perhaps the most comprehensive text of its kind for the medieval period, mentions mines in various places, but omits the technical details. Consequently, it is impossible to reconstruct the technical history of mining in ancient or medieval India on the basis of the textual evidence alone. The archaeological data is similarly unsatsifactory in any reconstructions, for no ancient mine in India has been systematically cleared, studied and dated. In this field, the only important development is to be seen in the increasing number of radiocarbon dates from samples taken from ancient workings. Approximately fifteen such dates are available from the gold mines of Karnataka, and the copper mines of Gujarat and Rajasthan (Agrawal and Margabandhu 1975-76; Agrawal, Margabandhu and Sekhar 1976). These dates cover a very wide period - from 1260±100 BC (PRL-208b, copper working at Rajpura, Udaipur district, Rajasthan), to 1640±80 AD (PRL-254, copper working at Kaladgi, Hasan district, Karnataka). The sample is clearly very limited in number and scope. In contrast there are data in relative abundance which deal with the old workings, in various geological publications. In addition, several explicit descriptions exist from the 19th century of pre-industrial mining operations. In 1950 Kercross relied exclusively on geological and ethnographic data for his paper on the ancient mines and miners of India.

Reconstructing a systematic history of Indian metallurgical techniques is equally difficult, if one is using only the literary and archaeological data. As far as the experience of the author goes

(Chakrabarti 1979a,b), the literary data may usefully provide the ancient names of various metals as also those of some metallic artefacts. However, it is of only marginal value for the study of metallurgical technology. These texts never describe the actual manufacturing techniques, nor do they give specific terms for various objects used in the manufacturing process. In recent years there has also been an increasing number of metallographic analyses (Agrawal 1971; Agrawal, Krishnamurthy and Kusumgar 1978; Nautiyal, Agrawal and Krishnamurthy 1981; Ghosh and Chattopadhyay 1981). However, the quantity of available metallographic data is still very limited, and therefore, the analysis of actual manufacturing processes may still largely depend on the ethnographic documentation of various metalworking techniques. A large body of these ethnographic data has been recorded since the end of the eighteenth century.

Mining

The geological literature contains copious references to ancient mine workings from different parts of India. These references are not yet properly ordered, but the reports of old workings contained within this literature are about the only definite proof which survives of widespread mining activities in ancient and medieval India - indeed, in pre-industrial India generally. The following examples will make the nature of this literature clear:

Mosabani copper mine (Singhbhum copper belt, Bihar). The following is an excerpt from the report of J A Dunn on Mosabani, written in 1937:

'One of the stopes at the south end of no. 1 level, Mosabani mine, broke through into an ancient working, about 60 feet (vertically) from the surface. The working is about 4 feet wide across the lode but extended for only a short distance along it, as this point was, of course, the bottom of the ancient workings. After breaking through, old rotten timber was found, fragments 5 to 6 inches in diameter. Timbering was not a usual practice of the ancients, pillars being normally left to hold up the hanging wall.... Occasionally their tools and some utensils (frequently made of soapstone as well as pottery) have been found in the workings' (Dunn 1937).

Baragunda copper mine (Singhbhum copper belt, Bihar):

'We are not in possession of any information as to who the ancients were who made the numerous excavations at Baragunda of which ample evidence is still to be seen .... Along the main line the width of the excavations average from 25 to 30 yards. The miners appear to have thrown the debris behind them as they progressed, the depth to which they could go being limited; thus there are a succession of basin-like pits separated from one another by mounds of debris...' (Ball 1881, 254).

Gavulabhavi lead deposit (Cuddapah district, Andhra Pradesh). Regarding the old workings in this deposit, B B Rao and K S Rao's observations are as follows:

'The ancient workings consist of linear pits and trenches, shafts and inclines developed laterally underground in the form of drifts and stopes dipping at steep angles to the east in the eastern part and to the west in the western part. One of the surface diggings extends for about 280m along the strike. The main underground mine had been developed for a length of over 100m, the initial 30m being a partly-stoped drive, followed by two parallel drives interspersed with stopes and connected by cross-cuts at regular intervals. The deepest accessible stope in the mine is approximately 50m below the surface. Small workings in the form of trial pits and trenches are also noticed in the dolomite, mainly in the northern part' (Rao and Rao 1977, 91).

Wynad goldfields (South India). According to Ball (1881:182-183), these ancient mines indicate the varying degrees of mining technical knowledge available - quarrying on the outcrops of veins, vertical shafts, adits, vertical shafts with adits, and shafts on underlie. What he found most remarkable were vertical shafts which were sometimes 70 feet deep with smooth, straight sides, even in solid quartz.

Khetri copper mine (Rajasthan). A major paper for our enquiry here is that of J C Brooke (1864). He deals with the mines and miners of Khetri, in Rajasthan. It is interesting to add to this information, that recent archaeological discoveries have pushed back the antiquity of copper exploitation at Khetri to about the middle of the third millennium BC. Further, it has been generally established that this area was pre-eminent in the supply of copper ore and artefacts to the cities of the Harappan civilization, and also to the chalcolithic cultures of the contiguous areas. What makes Brooke's paper doubly significant is that his is the only description of the pre-industrial mining operation at Khetri. He described the mines as numerous shafts, which gave access to galleries which honeycombed the hillside in every direction. The shafts descended in a very irregular manner to a considerable depth, and their sides were notched and cut in such a manner as to enable the miners to move up and down the shaft without the need of a ladder. The width of the shaft measured between 5 x 4 feet and 4 x 3 feet. A large amount of firewood (5-7 tons) was stacked on the working face of the mine and ignited. This activity obviously led to the splitting of the rock-face. Three days afterwards, the miners descended again into the mine. Each labourer was provided with a lamp, a hammer, a mining chisel and a small wicker basket. The only means of dealing with the seepage of underground water was by passing pitchers, hand to hand, along the passages.

Mining at Buxa (western Duars, Assam). Again Ball (1881) recorded valuable information on pre-industrial mining operations. To him the mines seemed little more than magnified rabbit holes, with the passages meandering along, following the source of the ore. Tools used were a hammer, a chisel set in a split bamboo, and a pick; light was provided by burning thin strips of bamboo. The ore was carried out of the mines in small baskets, was then picked, crushed and finally pounded with a stone hammer or pounder fixed in a forked stick.

Further, important information has been recorded by more recent fieldwork. For instance, the author has visited the copper workings at Tamakum (Rainbandh Police Station, Bankura district, West Bengal) during archaeological fieldwork in February-March 1982. The most important feature is an open shaft, more than 100m long and at least 10m wide. It is situated along the slope of a hillock, from the base right up to the top. The shaft is now covered by debris which has fallen in from both sides. There are also two large pits in the immediate vicinity. Fragments of pottery were collected from the debris lying on the surface, but none of them could be dated.

The old workings, details of which have been cited above for a few examples only, contain in them the history of mining activity in India, from the prehistoric past to the latest pre-industrial period. That the sequence is likely to be continuous is amply demonstrated by the available nineteenth century descriptions of actual mining processes.

Metallurgy

Gold

A striking feature of the records detailing gold extraction in the nineteenth century is the wide mention of the use of panning for collecting gold in its pure form. Records have been assembled, from the hills of the northwest (Kashmir and Ladakh) on one hand, to as far as the extreme south on the other hand; the Indo-Gangetic valley does not, however, figure in this list. Certain parts of Assam (the Khasi hills, and Sibsagar and Lakhimpur Districts) were clearly important, while the Chhota Nagpur plateau (including parts of West Bengal, Bihar and Orissa) was one of the most important centres of all. Ball (1881, 193) wrote a detailed account of the gold-panning of the latter region. His description is for the Singhbhum area, but he points out that these techniques apply, with only local modifications, to the greater part of peninsular India. The gold-panning tribe of this region (known variously as Jhora, Dhora, Dokra, Tora, or Jhara) - was, according to Ball, a Gond tribe. Among these groups, both men and women searched for gold, but among the Ghasi (another local tribe) only men undertook this task. Further, it is said that among certain Kol or Munda tribes, to the west of Singhbhum, only the women were engaged in this activity. The methods employed by these different groups were more or less the same, but each of them had their own distinct areas of operation. The equipment consisted of a wooden dish with a roughly hollowed-out centre with a scraper, made of a flattened iron hook, set in the handle. The auriferous sand and gravel which accumulated amongst the rocks in the stream was collected with the scraper and placed in the dish. By various jerking and circular motions, even the smallest particles of foreign matter were separated, and the final result was a residue of black sand, in which the flecks of gold were readily apparent.

It is of interest that the practice of gold-panning has not yet entirely died out in the Singhbhum area and the adjacent tracts of West Bengal.

Silver

One of the most common natural occurrences of silver is in the form of a sulphide of other metals, such as lead, antimony, and copper. In its native, metallic form, silver has been reported from both Tamil Nadu and Karnataka, as well as from Rajasthan. In its alloyed form, particularly argentiferous galena, silver occurs in Rajasthan, Andhra Pradesh, Bihar and Himachal Pradesh. As far as the author can ascertain at present, there is no explicit record of the process by which the pre-industrial smelters of India separated silver from argentiferous galena; a more detailed search is clearly necessary.

Lead

Traces of old lead workings have been recorded in Andhra Pradesh, the Chhota Nagpur plateau, Rewa and Bundelkhand, Rajasthan, the Panjab Himalaya, Garhwal-Kumaon, Jammu, Kashmir and Baluchistan. The smelting method in the Ajmer mines in 1830 was as follows: the ore was first crushed from its surrounding matrix by being beaten with wooden clubs. It was then thrown down the hill where the mine was located, to free it of any further extraneous matter. It was washed by hand in wooden tubs, after which it was mixed with an equal weight of cowdung and kneaded into small lumps the size of pigeons' eggs. These lumps were dried in the sun and then placed in a clay furnace about 3 feet high with an upper internal diameter of 11 inches and a lower one of 10 inches. Three clay tuyères were fixed into the base and connected to bellows. Due to the use of cow-dung, the amount of charcoal which was required was comparatively small (Ball 1881, 299-300).

Tin

There are reports of the geological occurrence of tin in a number of areas of India, including Hazaribagh and Bastar. Indeed, in Bastar the deposits are substantial, and they are still being exploited commercially. In both of these regions there is evidence of the pre-industrial smelting of tin. In this context it is relevant to quote from the report on the Hazaribagh written by F R Mallet in 1874:

'During the time it was worked the ore being brought to the surface was broken up while still fresh (as it hardened considerably after exposure) with a common country dheki. The pounded ore was then placed in a basket and washed by hand, which means most of the lighter impurities, chiefly quartz and felspar, were removed. Subsequently, after drying it was sifted in a winnowing basket to separate the remaining sand. When a sufficient amount of ore had accumulated, it was smelted with charcoal in an ordinary Agaria furnace, the charges being the same as those used in iron smelting. The tin after being run out and cooled with water, was broken up, the clean metal laid aside preparatory to casting, and the rest, which was much mixed with charcoal, returned to the furnace. The clean tin was re-melted in a large open iron vessel and ladled out into the moulds, holding about 40lbs. of metal each' (Mallet 1874).

Copper

Details of the pre-industrial smelting of copper are available from two areas - the Singhana area of Khetri in Rajasthan, and Buxa in western Duars (Ball 1881). In the Khetri area the ore of copper pyrites was crushed by hammers on stone anvils (each hammer weighed between 16 and 20 lb each). The powdered ore was then mixed with cowdung and dried in the sun in the form of small lumps. The furnace, which was made of three or four circular rims of clay or fire clay, and had at the bottom at least two nozzles for the ordinary type of hand bellows, was about 30-40 inches high with an external diameter of about 15 inches. Ore was put in the furnace with charcoal and iron slag - the latter being used as a flux. 3 maunds of charcoal, 2½ maunds of ore and 2 maunds of iron slag were consumed in a working day of about 9-10 hours. The smelted metal which accumulated at the bottom of the furnace was re-melted and refined in an open furnace and cast into small ingots.

There is extensive evidence of pre-industrial mining and smelting of copper in India. Three copper-bearing areas are notable: the Khetri area of Rajasthan, the Nellore area of Andhra Pradesh, and Singhbhum in the Chhota Nagpur region of Bihar. However, apart from these major occurrences there are many comparatively minor ones - from Baluchistan in the far northwest to areas eastwards. The occurrence of native copper though, has not yet been reported from the subcontinent.

Iron

Iron ores suitable for pre-industrial smelting technology occur virtually everywhere on the subcontinent, with the exception of the area covered by the Indo-Gangetic alluvium. Although the modern, European interest in Indian iron dates from 1722, it only became prominent in the late eighteenth and early nineteenth centuries (Chakrabarti 1977). There is a singularly impressive range of information available, which has not yet been worked on in any depth by historians of metallurgy, or by economic historians.

Following Percy (1864), one can classify the pre-industrial Indian iron furnaces into three main types:

Type 1 - this form is 2-4 feet high and circular. It is 10-15 inches in width at the bottom, and 6-12 inches at the top. There are two openings, one for inserting the bellow tuyères, and the other for running off the slag and molten iron. The furnace is first of all lit with charcoal, and then alternate charges of charcoal and ore are applied until the operation is completed in 4-6 hours. The molten metal is taken out by removing the front part of the furnace, and it is then hammered into a bloom.

Type 2 - this furnace is in the form of a cylindrical cavity cut into a well-tempered bank of clay. It is approximately 2 feet 6 inches deep, and between 15 and 18 inches in diameter. The mode of operation is the same, but in this case the lump of fused metal is taken out through the top of the furnace by means of a pair of tongs.

Type 3 - this last type is usually placed on the side of a clay mound. It is 8-10 feet high on the outside, and 6-7 feet high on the inside. The working base is provided by a perforated plate of dried clay, which is placed at an angle of approximately 45 degrees to the back of the furnace. Percy adds the following when describing this process:

'The lump of iron frequently weighs from 150 to 200 lbs, and is too large to be hammered whole. It is, therefore, cut by means of a sharp-edged sledge, so that when cold it may be broken into four pieces. It usually consists of malleable iron and natural steel, the relative amounts of which are stated to depend more upon the nature of the ore than any modification of the process. When, however, the object is to produce steel, a large proportion of charcoal is employed and a gentle blast applied. The steely parts frequently represent the appearances on fracture of the best blister steel from Swedish iron: and they are carefully selected and prepared for use by being heated to a low red-heat in a charcoal fire and then cut into small pieces of convenient size for making edge-tools, etc. When iron is wanted instead of steel, the pieces into which the lump has been broken are raised to a welding heat and hammered into bars, by which it loses almost all appearances of steel. Sometimes small quantities of cast-iron are produced in this furnace to the great annoyance of the smelters, who have much difficulty in separating it from the rest of the iron. They consider that in this case the iron has been injured by raising the temperature of the furnace too high' (Percy 1864, 260).

Benjamin Heyne described the method of making the famous south Indian steel, or *wootz*:

'In order to convert the iron into steel each piece is cut into three parts, ... each of which is put into a crucible, together with a handful of the dried branches of tangedu (Cassia auriculata), and another of fresh leaves of vonangady (Convolvulus laurifloria). The mouth of the crucible is then closely shut with a handful of red mud, and the whole arranged in a circular order, with their bases turned toward the centre in a hole made in the ground for the purpose. The whole is then filled up with charcoal, and large bellows are kept blowing for six hours, by which time the operation is finished. The crucibles are then removed from the furnace, ranged in rows on moistened mud, and water is thrown on them whilst yet hot. The steel is found in conical pieces at the bottom of the crucibles, the form of which it has taken. The upper or broader surfaces are often striated from the centre to the circumference' (Heyne 1814, 359).

Except for a few locations in the Chhota Nagpur region, the Indian pre-industrial iron smelting tradition has now completely died out. However, heaps of iron slag which bear testimony to this tradition are very common features in many areas of Peninsular India. The author has come across heaps of iron-slag extending for more than 1 kilometre in certain areas of the Birbhum district of West Bengal.

Discussion

The use of copper, lead, silver and gold is well-attested by 2900-2800 BC, that is before the beginning of the Indus civilization. The evidence for copper is the earliest and comes from the site of Mehrgarh in Baluchistan; here it is dated to c.5000 BC. This could be native copper, but the evidence for copper metallurgy is indisputable in the context of the fourth millennium BC. Both lead and silver occur at Nal, again in Baluchistan, and thus belong in the fourth millennium BC date range. Gold first occurs in Period I at Jalilpur (Panjab province, Pakistan), which is also dated within the fourth millennium BC. Tin seems to occur for the first time during the Indus civilization. This period (known also as the Harappa period) witnessed a significant development in the metallurgy of copper, lead, silver and gold as well. The pattern of development and usage of these metals in the post-Harappan chalcolithic cultures of inner India is not uniform, but the knowledge of them was not lost, and in the case at least of copper there is evidence of its widespread and effective use. Iron first appears in the second half of the second millennium BC. This general metallurgical tradition continued right through the early historic period, a time which impresses today with the range and diversity of its metal artefacts. The first use of brass and bell-metal seems to belong to the first to second centuries AD.

To say that the metallurgical tradition of proto-historic and early historic India persisted until the nineteenth century (the period to which our data on pre-industrial mining and metallurgy largely belongs) would not be scientifically acceptable, unless positive proof of metallurgical continuity can be offered. Incontrovertible evidence of this can be based on only two forms of research:

1) the building up of a reliable chronology for the surviving pre-industrial mine workings;

2) the metallographic analysis of, and comparison between, metal artefacts of different areas and periods.

Research along these lines is still in a formative stage in India. At the same time, certain features tend to argue, however indirectly, in favour of continuity. These are:

a) that pre-industrial smelting operations were elementary both technologically and organisationally. This could imply that the processes have probably persisted virtually unchanged for many centuries;

b) that if one looks at certain surviving craft-forms, such as the lost-wax process of making copper-bronze objects, the process of making bell-metal utensils, etc, further inferential evidence is forthcoming;

c) that the pre-industrial smelting furnaces resemble in many cases the excavated furnaces of antiquity. There has not yet been a comparative study of pre-industrial furnaces and excavated furnaces in India, but regarding the primitive iron furnaces which he saw in 1963 in Jamshedpur (Bihar), Cleere thought that they closely resembled furnaces from the prehistoric and Roman periods in the British Isles and elsewhere in Europe (Cleere 1963). Some continuity can be suggested by this evidence;

d) that some specific metallurgical data argue in favour of continuity. For instance, in 1920 McWilliam made a comparison between the composition of the famous iron pillar of Delhi (4th century AD) and that of the iron produced by an iron-smelter from the village of Mirjati near Jamshedpur (Bihar), who used pre-industrial technology. The composition of the iron used in the Delhi pillar was obtained from Hadfield's analysis (Hadfield 1912), while the Mirjati iron was analysed by McWilliam and his Indian associates. The conclusion was that the iron from Mirjati and that from the Delhi pillar were very similar. When considering iron it is worth adding that the pre-industrial iron smelters invariably collected their ores locally. This dependence upon local ores seems to have been a general phenomenon in Peninsular India during the Iron Age.

There is as yet no analytical history of Indian metal-working technology which is complete in documentation and also contains a series of fixed dates. The present paper has only outlined the nature of the available geological and ethnographic records. It has tried to show how these may reflect a continuous mining and metallurgical tradition from, at the earliest, the proto-historic period, up until just before the industrial period.

References

Agrawal, D P 1971. The Copper-Bronze Age in India. Delhi, Munshiram Manoharlal

Agrawal, D P, Krishnamurthy, R V & Kunsumgar, S 1978. New data on the Copper Hoards and the Daimabad bronzes. Man & Environment, 2, 41-46

Agrawal, D P & Margabandhu, C 1975-76. Ancient gold workings: some new C-14 dates Puratattva, 7, 139-149

Agrawal, D P, Margabandhu, C & Sekhar, N C 1976. Ancient copper workings: some new C-14 dates. Indian Journal of History of Science, 11, 133-136

Allchin, F R 1962. Upon the Antiquity and Methods of Gold Mining in Ancient India. Journal of the Economic and Social History of the Orient, 5, 195-211

Ball, V 1881. A Manual of the Geology of India, Part III. The Economic Geology. Calcutta, Geological Survey of India

Brooke, J C 1864. The mines of Khetri in Rajputana. Journal of the Asiatic Society of Bengal, 33, 519-529

Chakrabarti, Dilip K 1976. The beginning of iron in India. Antiquity, 50, 114-124

Chakrabarti, Dilip K 1977. The Research on early Indian iron, 1795-1950. The Indian Historical Review, 4, 96-105

Chakrabarti, Dilip K 1979(a). The problem of tin in early India. Man & Environment, 3, 61-74

Chakrabarti, Dilip K 1979(b). Iron in early Indian literature. Journal of the Royal Asiatic Society, 22-30

Chakrabarti, Dilip K n.d. Mining in ancient and mediaeval India

Cleere, H F 1963. Primitive Indian ironmaking furnaces. The British Steelmaker, 154-158

Dunn, J A 1937. The mineral deposits of eastern Singbhum and surrounding areas. Memoir of the Geological Survey of India, Vol 69, Part 1

Farraday, M 1819. An analysis of wootz, or Indian steel. Quaternary Journal of Literature, Science and the Arts, 7, 288-290

Ghosh, A K & Chattopadhyay, P K 1981. Indentification of new trace element in ancient copper object from West Bengal. Science & Culture, 47, 261-263

Hadfield, R 1912. Sinhalese iron and steel of ancient origin. Journal of Iron and Steel Institute, 134-172

Heyne, B 1814. Tracts, Historical and Statistical on India. London, Black, Parry & Co

Kercross, D 1950. Ancient mines and miners of India. Indian Minerals, 4, 5-10

McWilliam, A 1920. Indian ironmaking at Mirjati, Chotanagpur. Journal of Iron and Steel Institute, 102, 160-167

Mallet, F R 1874. Geological notes on part of northern Hazaribagh. Records of the Geological Survey of India, 7, 23-44

Nanda, Rajni 1981. Lead and Silver in Early India. Unpublished M. Phil dissertation, Archaeology and Museum Unit, Department of History, Delhi University

Nautiyal, V, Agrawal, D P & Krishnamurthy, R V 1981. Some new analysis on the protohistoric copper artefacts. _Man & Environemnt_, 5, 48-51

Neogi, P 1914. _Iron in Ancient India_. Calcutta, Indian Association for the Cultivation of Science

Neogi, P 1918. _Copper in Ancient India_. Calcutta, Indian Association for the Cultivation of Science

Percy, J 1864. Metallurgy: _Iron and Steel_. London, John Murray

Rao, B B & Rao, K S 1977. Lead deposits in Varikunta-Zangamrajupalle belt, Cuddapah district, Andhra Pradesh. _Exploration and Development of Non-ferrous Metals in India_ Geological Survey of India Miscellaneous Publication, 27, 87-94

INAMGAON - ETHNOARCHAEOLOGY OF AN EARLY FARMING VILLAGE

M K Dhavalikar

Tradition dies hard, and nowhere more so than in India, where the antiquity of many cultural traits can be traced back to remote antiquity. This fact is well illustrated by a study of the evidence from the intensive excavations at Inamgaon, an early farming settlement in Maharashtra, which dates back to the middle of the second millennium BC (Dhavalikar *et al.* 1987, 1988). It is noteworthy that many aspects of the prehistoric culture of Inamgaon continue, in some form or other, even today in the village around the site.

Before, however, embarking upon a discussion of the archaeological evidence and of the corroborative ethnographic analogues, it is necessary to state clearly that there is no evidence at Inamgaon of what has been termed 'the Direct Historical Analogy' as is available, for instance, in North America, where the present-day tribals are the direct descendants of the earlier inhabitants; at Inamgaon the analogy is of the type known as 'the General Comparative Analogy'. It is unnecessary here to go into the merits and demerits of ethnoarchaeology, for, as is well known, there are extremes of opinion, one school totally discarding it as fallacious (Freeman 1968, 265) and the other arguing that all archaeology is ethnoarchaeology or it is nothing (Orme 1973). Suffice it to say that Lewis Binford, the leader of the 'processual school', who once observed that 'Fitting archaeological remains into ethnographically known patterns of life adds nothing to our knowledge of the past' (Binford 1968, 13), has now published a substantial work entitled *Nunamiut Ethnoarchaeology*, and has here advocated the validity of ethnoarchaeology. Ethnoarchaeology, it seems, is therefore gradually gaining recognition, not least because it has proved useful in interpreting archaeological evidence. In India, however, it has not yet received the attention it deserves from Indian archaeologists - this despite the fact that India, with its numerous tribal groups scattered throughout the country, who are often at strikingly different technological levels, has much to offer this study. However, in the area around Inamgaon, an ethnographic survey was carried out, and it was observed that many of the elements of the material culture of the first farmers of Maharashtra still survive in the villages located near the ancient site. Ethnographic analogues have, in this instance, proved to be of great help in explaining the evidence from the excavations.

Before discussing the excavated evidence, it will be useful first to describe the culture sequence found at Inamgaon. The ancient site is located 85 km east of Pune, on the right bank of the river Ghod - part of the Krishna river system (Fig. 1). It covers an area of 5 ha, and is one of the most extensive early farming settlements in the country. The eleven seasons of intensive work at the site have yielded rich evidence which throws light on the life of the pioneering colonisers in western India. The occupation can be divided into three cultural periods. Period I (c. 1600-1400 BC) is marked by a black-painted red pottery which suggests that the first settlers came from Malwa in Central India. They lived in rectangular houses and also pit-dwellings, and practised agriculture, animal husbandry, hunting, gathering and fishing. They cultivated mainly barley (*Hordeum vulgare*), lentils (*Lens esculenta Moench*), peas (*Pisum arvense Linn.*), horse gram (*Dolichos biflorus Linn.*), etc. Children were buried inside the houses, in two urns placed horizontally mouth-to-mouth in a pit especially dug for the purpose. A few pottery vessels, probably containing food and water, were also deposited inside the grave. They worshipped a mother-goddess, who may have been connected with fertility.

Period II (c. 1400-1200 BC) is characterised by the occurrence of the typical Jorwe painted pottery, represented by such forms as the carinated bowl and the spouted jar with a flaring mouth. This was the most prosperous period in the history of the settlement. The people lived in large rectangular houses with low mud walls and thatched roofs. In addition to the crops grown by their predecessors, they also grew wheat, which was possible because of the development of irrigation. Wheat is a winter crop, but western India does not receive winter rains, with the result that even today, wheat can only be grown in irrigated fields. These early farmers diverted the flood waters of the river through a stream into a deep channel (70m long, 7m wide and 3m deep) and were thus able to irrigate their fields. By this method they were able to raise two crops, by practising crop rotation. This constitutes the earliest and the clearest evidence of irrigation in India.

The Early Jorwe people buried their dead inside their houses. They apparently worshipped a mother goddess - a representation of which was found (minus its head) in the excavations - as well as a male divinity. Fire-worship may also have been practised. There were trading contacts established with coastal Maharashtra, Gujarat and Karnataka, as is evidenced from such trade goods as marine fish and conch-shell bangles. Some evidence of socio-political organisation is available in the form of a public granary and, beside it, a multi-roomed house, probably that of the ruling chief. One may speculate that this was a 'chiefdom society', with the chief being responsible for the distribution of water for the irrigation of the fields. There are also traces of fortifications around the settlement dating from this period.

The prosperity of the Early Jorwe period was not long lasting and from c. 1000 BC one can observe a gradual decline. At this same time the settlements on the Tapi and Godavari rivers were deserted by similar groups of early farmers - possibly because of a succession of droughts. However, here in the southern Deccan settlements continued, as is evident from Inamgaon and other Late Jorwe period sites discovered in the Bhima valley.

Period III (c. 1000-700 BC), known as the Late Jorwe period, is characterised by deterioration in every field of human activity. The houses were small round huts, with thatched walls and roofs, the pottery was coarse and crude, and the declining cultivation forced the population to subsist more and more on animal products. The irrigation channel of the previous period ceased functioning - probably due to a decrease in rainfall. For this reason the production of wheat was no longer possible. There was a yet further deterioration around 800 BC, when there was probably a change to sheep/goat pastoralism, judging from the sudden increase in ovicaprid bones at the site. In the closing phase of the Late Jorwe, the luxury of sedentary life no longer became possible - the houses do not conform to any plan, they are either irregularly circular, oval or rectangular, and flimsy floors suggest a semi-nomadic existence. Slightly later, towards the close of the 8th century, the settlement was finally deserted by these Late Jorwe people. Inroads into this area by megalith builders from the southern Deccan may also have been partly responsible for this uprooting of the pastoral nomads of Inamgaon. The site has remained unoccupied ever since.

The excavation at Inamgaon was intensive rather than extensive, because there was a concentration on an area measuring 100 by 80m where each structural level was carefully exposed. Each artefact was recorded in its stratigraphic and horizontal context. This enabled the excavators to identify a number of houses belonging to various craftsmen, such as a potter, goldsmith, lime-maker, lapidary and others. Also recovered were vast quantities of charred seeds of cultivated grains which have enabled reconstructions to be made of the history of agriculture in Maharashtra.

A substantial number of houses were exposed in the course of the excavations, and this provided a chance to study the micro-settlement pattern. It was observed that the houses of craftsmen such as the potter, the goldsmith, the lime-maker, etc., were situated in the western part of the principal area of habitation (INM-I), whereas the houses of more prosperous inhabitants were located in its central part. This is precisely the same today in the villages around Inamgaon where the same residence pattern is observed. In sharp contrast to this, the occupation in other localities, such as INM-II, III, IV and V was probably sparse because no well-defined house plans could be recovered in these areas. It is highly likely that the prosperous members of the community occupied the main area (INM-I), whereas poorer people probably inhabited the other areas. INM-I is certainly a very extensive area - about 200 by 100m - whereas the other localities are much smaller.

Although a number of houses of each structural phase have been exposed, it has not been possible to reconstruct them completely. In the course of the excavations patches of well-made house floors, as well as dilapidated fragments of walls standing to a height of only a few centimetres, were discovered. Sometimes there were also clay lumps bearing the impression of the thatched roof or wattle and daub walls. However, these were not adequate for the reconstruction of entire houses and many of the problems concerned with this mud architecture remain unsolved. From the quantity of lumps of clay found on the house floors it was possible to infer that the walls cannot have been very high - perhaps 50cm to 75cm. This led to an examination of the possible height of the entire structure. The same was true for the roofs as for the walls, as all that there was to go on were the clay lumps with wattle impressions upon them; from this alone, it was practically impossible to say anything definite about them. However, having now looked at the ethnographic analogies, it is considerably easier to visualize how these chalcolithic houses would have appeared.

Almost all the different house types unearthed in the course of excavation have parallels in contemporary dwellings to be seen in the villages around the ancient site. There are three main house types - i) pit-dwellings; ii) rectangular houses; iii) circular houses. The earliest settlers at the site lived in pit-dwellings and in large rectangular houses. The pit-dwellings, all of which are circular in plan, are not many in number (Fig. 2). Most of these pits really look more like sunken floors, being only c. 30 cm deep, while their average diameter is 2 m. However, there are also examples of deep pit-dwellings found. The floors of the pit-dwellings were well-made, being lined with lime. Along the margin of the floor, externally, were a number of post-holes; these doubtless supported a conical roof. The external courtyard attached to these pit-dwellings was all substantially made, and it was here that a cooking hearth was located. It was only because of modern parallels that it was possible to identify these structures as pit-dwellings (Fig. 3). It is only very poor people who live in such structures today, for they cannot afford to buy wooden posts of an adequate length for an above-ground construction. In order to obtain the necessary height for the roof, a pit is dug. Perhaps it was for the same reason that the first settlers at Inamgaon built these pit-dwellings.

The vast majority of the Malwa houses (that is, of period I) are rectangular in plan (c. 7m by 5m) with low mud walls and smooth floors composed of sand, black clay and yellow silt - all rammed down hard - and periodically repaired, perhaps every alternate year as is the case today. The roof, probably gabled, was supported by wooden posts (Fig. 4). However, the disposition of the wooden posts in many cases was enigmatic; some were found inside and some outside the walls. This made the relationship of walls with wooden posts problematic. This led the excavators to conclude that the walls did not support the roof. Again the ethnographic parallels provided a clue in the explanation of the evidence from the excavation. In the village of Wangdari, directly across the river from the ancient site, there are a number of huts which have extremely low mud walls, not over 30cm in height. These walls have nothing to do with the roof, and their only function is to prevent rainwater from getting into the hut. This clearly suggests the function of the mud walls in the chalcolithic houses. Similarly, in present-day huts the roof is supported on wooden posts, and between them are fixed reed screens, which may or may not be daubed with mud. For roofing, the typha grass (Typha latifolia) which grows along the banks of the streams around Inamgaon, and which is known for its water-resistant qualities, is used today. There is evidence to show that the first farmers of Inamgaon also used this same material for roofing.

There does seem to have been some degree of planning in the Malwa and Early Jorwe (period I and period II) settlements at Inamgaon (Fig. 5). The rectangular houses are usually built with the longer axis in an approximately southeast-northwest direction, aligned in parallel rows. The average distance between these rows is about 1m, which space could have served as a road. It is known from the archaeological record that the people of the Indus civilization were the first to plan their settlements on a grid pattern. However, after the decline of the Harappans this same type of planning was re-introduced into India by the Greeks who ruled in the northwestern part of the subcontinent from c. 250 to 40 BC. But for these two instances, planned settlement was not a characteristic feature of early Indian cities. Written legends claim that in the beginning of the early historic period (6th century BC) the architect, Mahagovinda, planned and built a number of cities in the Ganga valley. This, however, is not corroborated by archaeological evidence from such early city sites as Rajgir or Kausambi where there is no evidence of planning. In the light of this evidence, it is remarkable that these first farmers of Maharashtra should have planned their settlements with such care (Dhavalikar 1975). However, what is important from the standpoint of the present study is that a tribal group in modern Maharashtra which is technologically below the level of incipient agriculture plans its settlements with similar care (Mandavkar 1966, 77-79). This group, the Kolam, live today in parts of Vidarbha and Marathwada, bordering on Andhra Pradesh. They practise shifting agriculture, and their settlements are, consequently, not permanent. Having selected a hill slope for cultivation, they then build their huts on its periphery. These settlements are known as poda, a word derived from the Dravidian podu, which has the meaning 'shifting cultivation'. The poda are characterised by rectangular huts which are all of almost equal size. Their chieftain (naik), along with a few heads of families, visits the location and selects the right position for the settlement. Their planned settlements show remarkable continuity with those at Inamgaon which, though geographically close, are at least three thousand years earlier.

As already stated, the Late Jorwe (period III) settlement at Inamgaon is characterised by round huts in sharp contrast to the spacious rectangular houses of the earlier periods (Figs. 6 and 7). So far a number of such huts have been excavated, and the method of their construction can again be guessed at by studying similar huts, which are still built today in nearby villages (Fig. 8). Those from the excavations have rather low mud walls and well-made floors. From the impressions found on clay daub, it can be confidently suggested that they had thatched walls and roofs. The roof, probably conical, was supported by wooden posts. Ethnographic information indicates that for a round hut with a conical roof there is usually a post in the centre. Most of the houses from the excavation had a central post.

A few of the Late Jorwe huts are oval in plan. However, these were extremely flimsy structures which appeared to have no mud wall around them. Instead of a wall, the edge of the floor was raised up, obviously with a view to preventing the rain from entering the hut. It thus served the same function as that of the low mud wall previously mentioned. However, these huts have not provided any evidence of post-holes around the floor margin; instead there is a single post-hole in the centre, or two post-holes, one on either side of the hut. This was puzzling to the excavators, as a hut without posts was difficult to visualize. Again, however, an ethnographic analogy helped to clarify the situation. Such small oval huts are even at present built in the neighbourhood of Inamgaon during a particular season. First the area where the huts will be erected is cleared, and a framework of split bamboo or wooden sticks is constructed. Then the thatched walls are built sloping and are joined in a conical top. Thus there is no need to fix the posts in holes because the walls do not have to support the roof; they rather rest on the beam. Such huts, in fact, do not need a central post. Once more, therefore, it is only because of the survival of the tradition of constructing such huts that it was possible to further the study of chalcolithic architecture.

All these houses, both rectangular and round, had well-made courtyards where a hearth was usually located. Indeed, it is still the practice today for, except during the rainy season, the cooking is done out of doors. This re-emphasises the importance of the courtyard in Indian architecture; after all, a great deal of life is lived there. In the courtyard there were also pit silos cut into the ground. These are cylindrical, about 1m deep, and of equal diameter. The bases are usually plastered with lime. Sometimes these pit silos are located inside the dwellings. They appear identical to their modern counterparts. A most curious feature recorded in the excavations inside the rectangular houses, however, was a round mud platform, having a diameter of 1m or more, and about 15cm in height. It was made of rammed clay, and contained sand. Its function was only completely understood when it was noticed that such platforms still exist in the houses around Inamgaon (Fig. 9). These modern platforms are meant for supporting a storage bin made of wickerwork, and plastered with cowdung and mud. Inside the platform sand and thorny bushes are placed, thus preventing rodents from destroying the grain in the bin.

An important aspect of cultural life is that of social organisation. No attempt has so far been made to reconstruct the social organisation of prehistoric India - solely for want of adequate evidence. However, this aspect can also be studied with the help of ethnographic evidence. The rectangular house-type seems to indicate a fully settled life, whereas the more easily constructed round hut suggests a more mobile life (Flannery 1972). The evidence from the excavation at Inamgaon shows that the Malwa and Early Jorwe people (of periods I and II) lived in large rectangular houses, some of which were even multi-roomed. Their prosperity is reflected in the variety of grains which they cultivated, as also in other artefactual remains such as brightly painted pottery, beads of semi-precious stones, tools and ornaments of copper, and even gold. However, in complete contrast to the spacious houses of these earlier periods, the houses of Late Jorwe Inamgaon are small round huts.

This house type is said to be a distinguishing feature of only seasonally settled life (Flannery 1972). This suggestion is corroborated by the Inamgaon evidence for this Late Jorwe period, which is marked by a sharp decline in plant cultivation and an increase in the number of animal bones, indicating a shift in subsistence patterns. In the upper levels of the Late Jorwe (Inamgaon period III) there is a sudden increase in the number of sheep/goat bones, suggesting that the inhabitants of Inamgaon may have resorted to a form of pastoralism in the period around 900 BC.

A noteworthy feature of the Late Jorwe huts is that they are found in clusters of three, four or five - each cluster having a common courtyard (see Fig. 6). It would be easy to be misled into identifying each hut as an independent household. However, a careful examination of the artefactual remains shows that not all the huts in each cluster had a hearth or storage facilities, and that only one or two huts had cooking facilities. The only conclusion that the excavators could draw from this was that each cluster was an independent household unit and as such was occupied by a single family. This necessarily leads on to the question of determining why each family unit should require several huts. Possibly the answer lies in the supposition that this Late Jorwe society at Inamgaon was polygamous, and that whenever the head of the family acquired a new wife he built a separate hut for her. The Kohali of Vidarbha do exactly this to this day and the number of huts in each cluster in the settlement represents the number of wives in each family unit (Karve 1951, 112-13). It has interestingly been observed in an African context, that 'the separate living houses, functionally not self-contained, are merely the residences of co-wives in a polygamous family' (David 1971, 120).

It is not possible here to examine all the aspects of chalcolithic life. However, one further element - that of religious beliefs - deserves mention. Foremost among these seems to have been a belief in a mother goddess. Small female figurines of poorly fired or unbaked clay have been found in some numbers. One of these figurines was associated with pit silos, and may thus have been connected with a fertility cult. Another one was found in a clay box over which was placed yet another (though headless) goddess, along with a clay bull (Figs. 10 and 11). All these objects of unbaked clay were found carefully deposited in a small hole in the corner of an Early Jorwe (Inamgaon period II) house. The fact that the figurines and the box are unbaked may show that they were meant only for occasional use, after which they were carefully deposited in the hole where the excavators found them. This brings to mind the custom in Maharashtra villages today where even the water from the room of a parturient woman is not allowed to drain out of the room, but is collected in a pit specially dug for the purpose. Secondly, the headless female figurines call to mind the goddess Viśirā, one of the divinities who nurtured the newly born Kārttikeya. Perhaps, if the neck of a new-born child was not sufficiently strong, this goddess was invoked. Both of these ethnographic examples could lead one to suggest that the clay figurines may have been connected with childbirth.

These first farmers no doubt also worshipped a male divinity (Fig. 12), as two male figurines were noted in the courtyard of a Late Jorwe house where they were found deposited near a hearth. Again they are unbaked and hence may be said to have been used only on one specific occasion. Even today people at Inamgaon make such figurines of wheat flour, and worship them when a community meal is cooked. The god, now identified with Ganeśa, is placed by the side of the hearth, and is then immersed in the river after the community feast is over.

There is yet one further, but curious divinity, and it is still unknown whether this god is as ancient as the prehistoric settlement at

Inamgaon. To the west by c. 100m of the ancient habitation is the shrine of the deity known locally as Mhasoba (Fig. 13). Here is an aniconic representation of the god in the form of a huge, amorphous rock, which is presently worshipped, not by the people of the surrounding areas but, surprisingly, by Bhils, who come in large numbers from distant parts, such as Nagar, Nasik and Dhulia districts. They come at any time of the year - according to whenever is convenient - worship the god, and offer live chickens and wooden bulls. Year after year, the excavators have observed this phenomenon with curiosity, but despite often speaking with these worshippers, they cannot establish the antiquity of the god. Here an ethnographic analogy may throw some light on the question, for the Kolam of northeast Maharashtra are said to install an image of their god, Aiyyak, whenever they select a new area for locating a settlement. It is installed to the west of - and slightly away from - the new habitation. He is their principal god, identified as Bhimadeva, who is the same as Bhivsena of the Gonds. Could it be that the pioneering colonisers of Inamgaon installed this aniconic representation of their god when they first arrived here to establish a settlement?

The ancient inhabitants of Inamgaon probably believed in a life after death. They buried their dead inside their houses; perhaps they wanted the departed soul to remain close to them. Adults were buried in a supine position, in a pit dug into the house floor; pottery vessels probably containing food and water were also deposited. One of the vessels was invariably a spouted jar painted with the design of a boat with oars. This design reminds one of the Hindu belief that the soul of the dead person has to cross a river by ferryboat. More interesting, however, is the custom of chopping off the feet of the dead. This seems to have been the rule, except in very rare instances, such as that of a chief. This may have been done with a view to preventing the dead person from running away and becoming a ghost. This is precisely the reason given in Goa to this day for chopping off the legs of a woman who has died immediately following childbirth.

Children were buried in two jars, placed horizontally, mouth to mouth (Fig. 14). Of these, one was smaller than the other. They may represent, as the Vedic evidence suggests, father and mother respectively. The idea behind this is probably that, after death, the child returns to the mother's womb. Indeed, Śaṅkarācārya has said

> <u>Punar api janma punar api maraṇam</u>
<u>Punar api jananījaṭhare śayanam</u>
[A man] is born and then he dies
only to return to the mother's womb.

This evidence from the excavations at Inamgaon and the ethnographic parallels which still survive in some form or other, amply show how one can substantiate the archaeological explanations given for the customs and traditions of the prehistoric period. Indeed, a great anthropologist has observed, 'It is a phenomenon peculiar to India, that throughout time, the great civilizations have risen without obliterating or absorbing all that has gone before: the elder, more static cultures gave way not by disintegrating, but by seeking refuge in remote areas uncongenial to civilization based on an advanced agricultural economy. There can be no doubt that the so-called aboriginals inhabiting such refuge areas represent comparatively old and primitive culture types' (Haimendorf 1948).

Bibliography

Binford, L R 1968. Archaeological Perspectives. In Binford, L R and S R (eds), New Perspectives in Archaeology, Chicago, 5-32

Binford, L 1978. Nunamiut Ethnoarchaeology. New York

David, N 1971. The Fulani compound and the archaeologist. World Archaeology, 3, 111-31

Dhavalikar, M K 1975. Settlement Archaeology of Inamgaon. Puratattva, 8, 44-54

Dhavalikar, M K, Sankalia, H D and Ansari, Z D 1987, 1988. Excavations at Inamgaon, vol I, parts i and ii. Pune, Deccan College

Flannery, K V 1972. The origin of the village as a settlement type in Meso-america and the Near East. In Ucko, P, Tringham, R and Dimbley, C W (eds), Man, Settlement and Urbanism. London, 25-54

Freeman, L G Jr 1968. A theoretical framework for interpreting archaeological materials. In Lee, R B and De Vore, I (eds), Man the Hunter. Chicago, 268-73.

Haimendorf, C von Führer 1948. Culture Strata in the Deccan. Man, 48, art. 99, 87-90

Karve, I 1951. Marathi Lokanchi Samskriti. Poona (in Marathi)

Mandavkar, B 1966. Kolam, Amaravati (in Marathi)

Orme, B 1973. Archaeology and Ethnography. In Renfrew, C (ed.) The Explanation of Culture Change - Models in Prehistory. London, 481-92

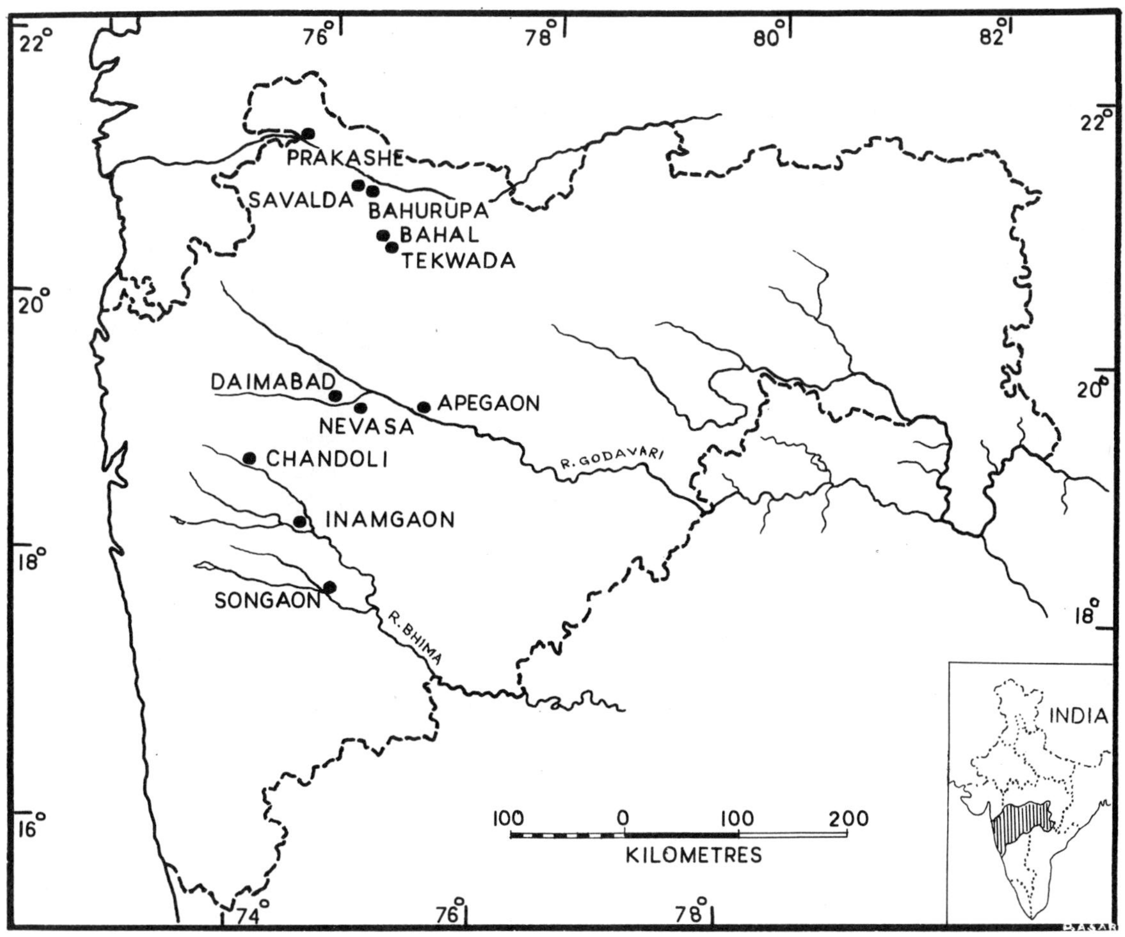

Fig. 1 Excavated chalcolithic settlements in Maharashtra.

Fig. 2 Inamgaon, pit dwelling, period I (c.1600-1400 BC).

Fig. 3 Contemporary pit-dwelling at Inamgaon.

Fig. 4 Inamgaon, house, period I (c.1600-1400 BC).

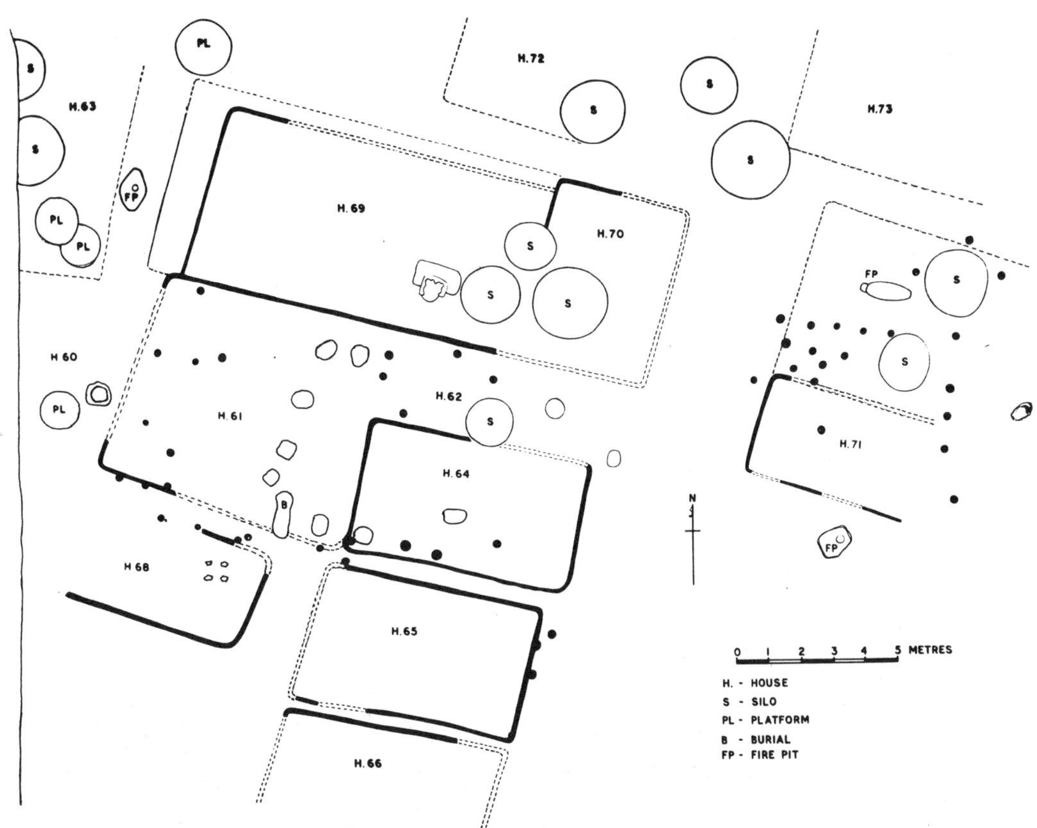

Fig. 5 Inamgaon, plan of settlement, period II (c.1400-1200 BC).

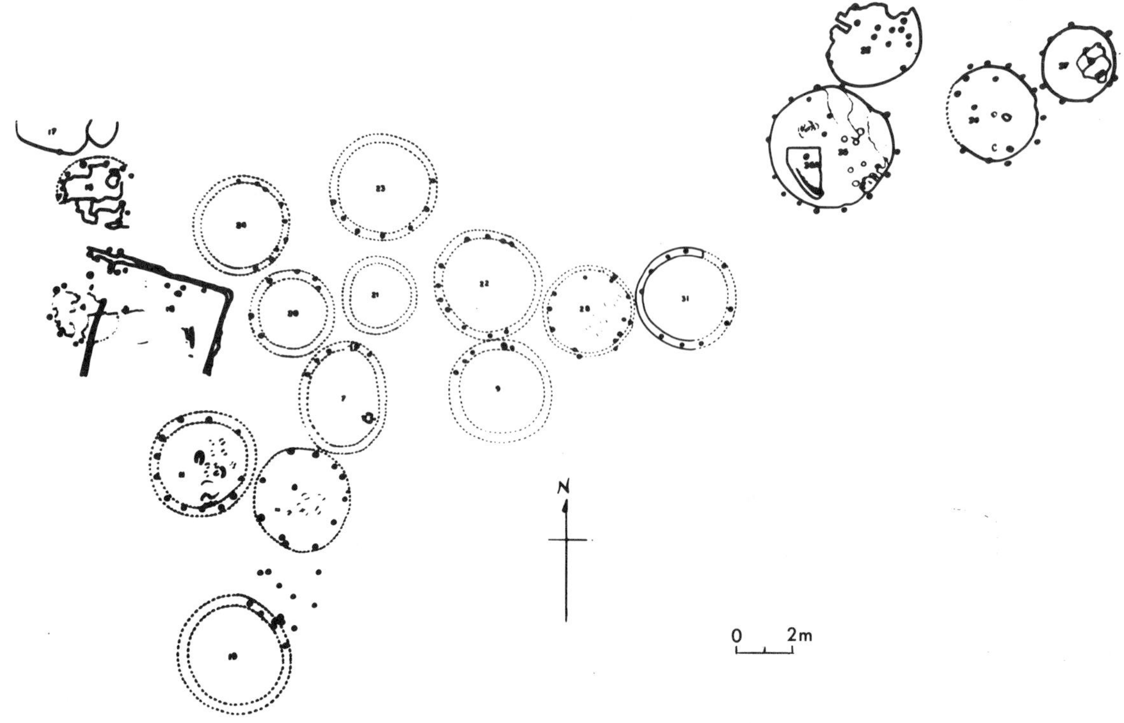

Fig. 6 Inamgaon, plan of settlement, period III (c.1000-700 BC).

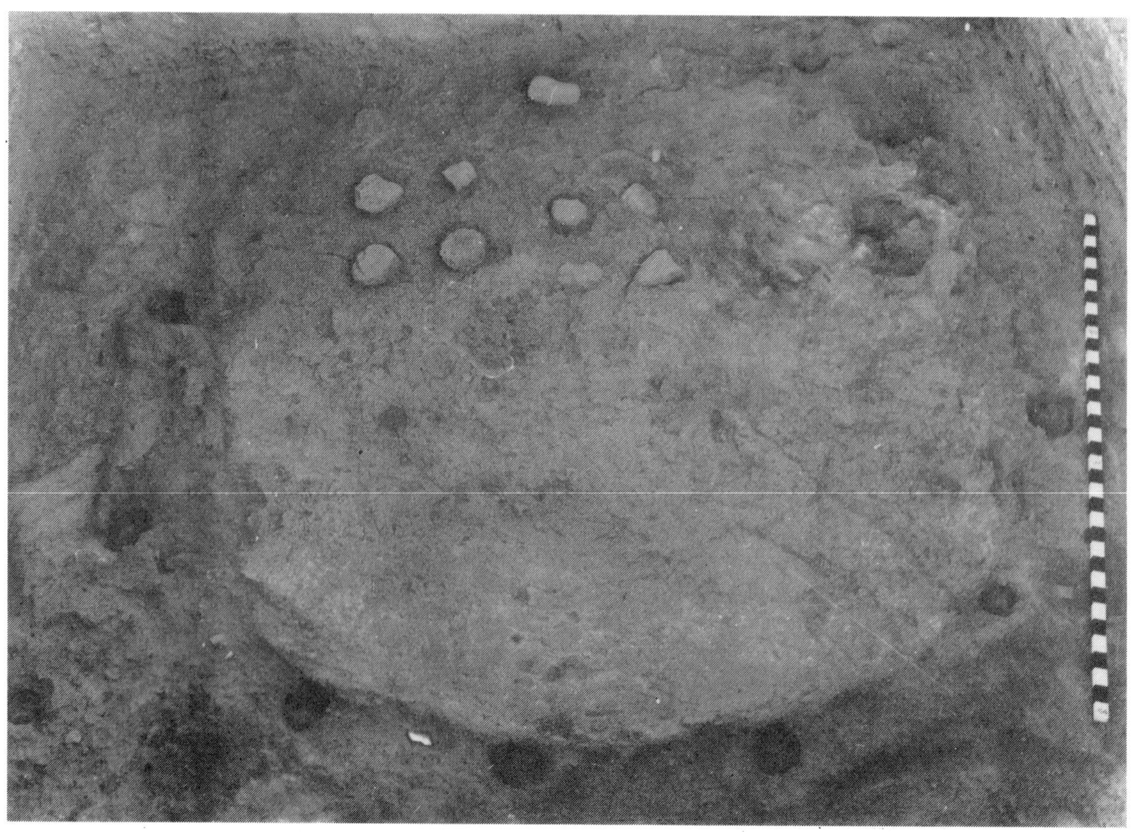

Fig. 7 Inamgaon, round hut, period III (c.1000-700 BC).

Fig. 8 Contemporary round hut in Wangdari Village.

Fig. 9 Mud platform for storage bin, Wangdari Village.

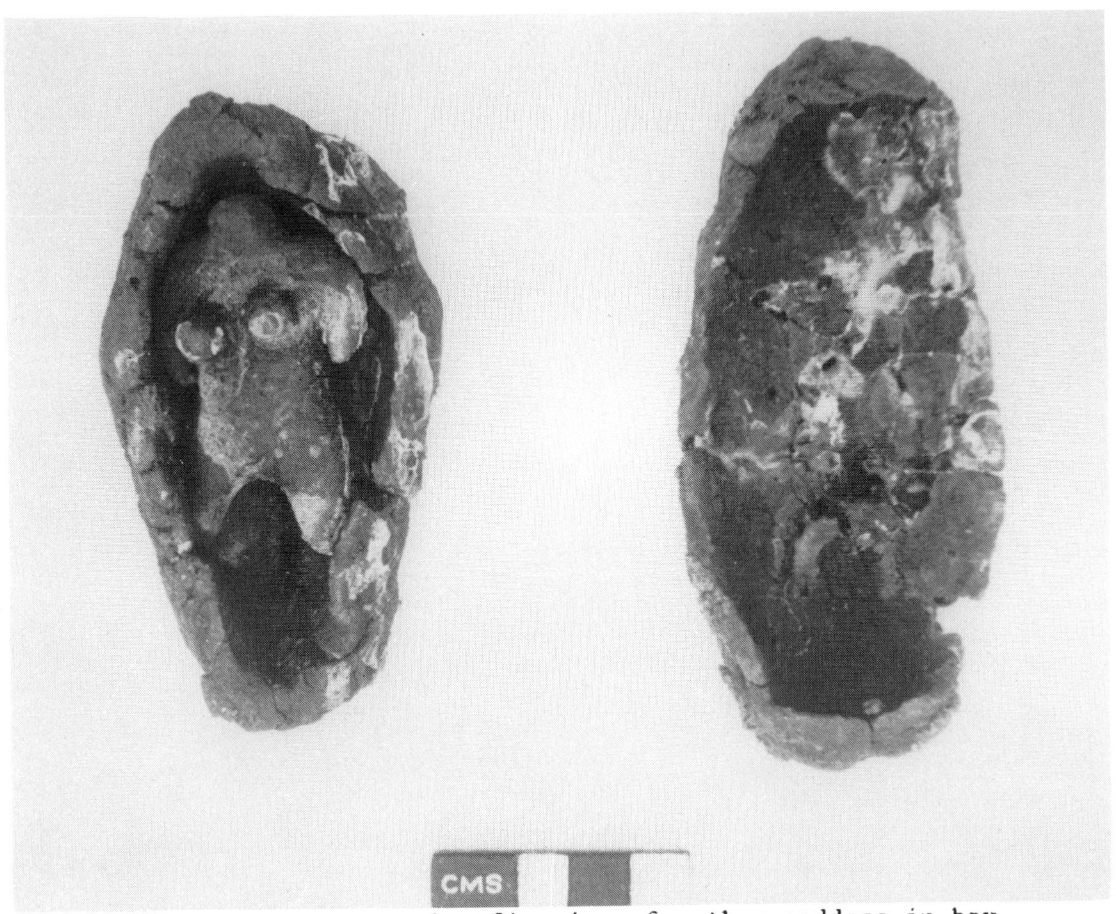

Fig. 10 Inamgaon, clay figurine of mother goddess in box, period II (c.1400-1000 BC).

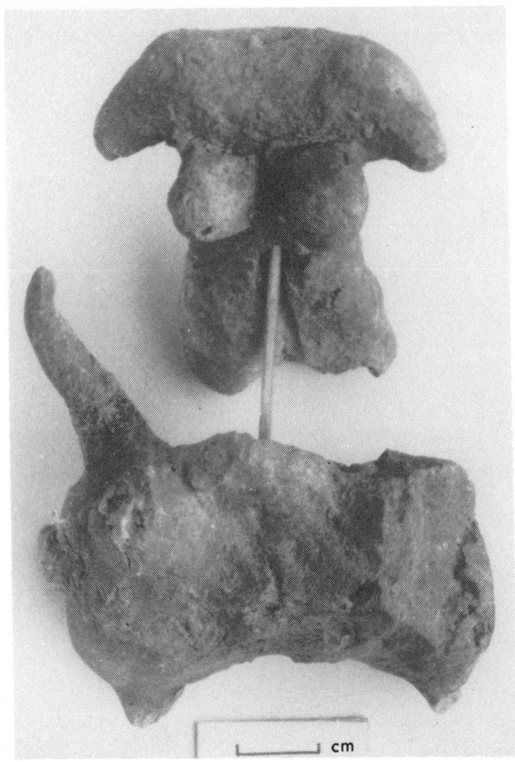

Fig. 11 Inamgaon, clay figurine of mother goddess with bull, period II (c.1400-1000 BC)

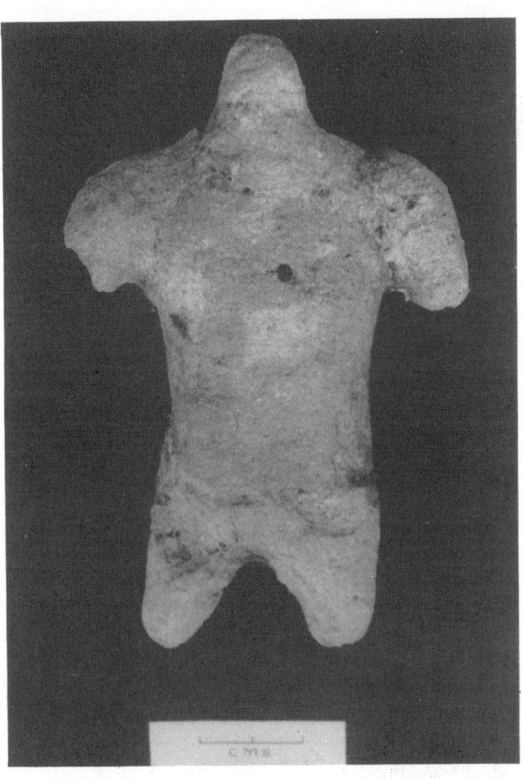

Fig. 12 Inamgaon, clay figurine of a god, period III (c.1000-700 BC)

Fig. 13 Inamgaon, the shrine of Mhasoba.

Fig. 14 Inamgaon, twin urn burial, period II (c.1400-1000 BC).

INDIAN HOSPITALITY: SOME CULTURAL VALUES AND SOCIAL DYNAMICS

R S Khare

I

Hospitality in India enjoys a distinct sociocultural position. Its conception is holistic and it is a definite part of everyday sociocultural life. It may have old and new versions, and inside and outside appraisals, but it pervades the life of the household as well as communities as a whole. Hospitality is normally held to be a part of 'civilized' behaviour between any two persons or groups. Sociologically, to question hospitality is to question the place of sharing, faithfulness, and gratitude in social relationships. Hospitality builds upon social sharing (and not only receiving and giving), and the latter on the generosity of personal conduct. Whether carried on with or without ulterior purpose, hospitality normally occurs under conditions that yield or maintain amity between hosts and guests. However, it also quickly reflects social tensions, revealing issues of change and conflict within a society. It thus offers a sensitive litmus test of prevailing social conditions.

Though a systematic comparative study of hospitality in social anthropology is still rare (e.g. Pitt-Rivers 1968), the topic has received repeated attention from earlier times, usually embedded within larger social contexts. Among earlier studies, we may mention Fustel de Coulanges (1864), Robertson Smith (1889, 1903), Morgan (1881), Boas (1909, 1921), and Mauss (1925). Simmel (1950) also sociologically considered valuative aspects relevant to hospitality. More recently, such an attempt as that of Walens (1981) on the Kwakiutl is useful for raising a general discussion of moral responsibility in food sharing. For hospitality is most of all about a moral paradigm of social sharing. Its ideological and moral customs, however, need not brush aside complementary institutional and practical uses. Hospitality is easily affected by larger issues of social cohesion and conflict; it also comments upon, and becomes an intimate commentary on, a people's interests and intentions.

The overall position of Indian hospitality has also been seldom examined in systematic terms. Sociologically, it has remained embedded within accounts of caste, kinship, and locality. The implied message of such an approach is that Indian hospitality could hardly be anything more than that controlled by the normative rules of caste and kinship institutions. Notions of sharing, faithfulness, and gratitude are also, by sociological implication, assumed to be confined to the same domains of social relationships.

The above view is necessary and useful as far as it goes, but it is blinkered and incomplete. Caste studies have helped sociology find its feet in India but they may not be capable of yielding a critical Indian sociology. For the latter to emerge, comparative sociological explanations must freely criticize one another on merit, without letting any view become an orthodoxy. A comprehensive approach does not equate Indian caste and kinship to all that society in India is, and it cannot bypass patterns of heterogeneous Indian cognition and values without deriving appropriate sociological implications. The emphasis in this view is on the whole system and not on a selected segment, however dominant. We need to study hospitality also as a comprehensive social phenomenon, examining it under different cultural premises and each cultural premise under different social conditions. It will then reflect a sociocultural complexity commensurate with the complexity of contemporary Indian society. It will begin to show affinities with a whole range of ideals, instituted rules, schisms, and individual initiatives, whether they are moral or expedient. Practical constraints are now indispensable to explication in order to show its significance to Indian social reality. The models, functions, and meanings of hospitality are changing within Indian society (as perhaps they have never done in the past), with important sociological consequences. I shall discuss some of these properties in the following pages.

Once hospitality in India is handled as a topic by itself, its proper cultural position begins to emerge. Its primary value structure surfaces, where ideas of sharing, sacrifice, reciprocation, and amity weave a paradigmatic pattern. The prevalence and persistence of hospitality in Indian social relations, within as well as outside the household, offer clues about its social character. If it is sociologically fragile and narrow in range under traditional criteria (i.e. of caste and kinship), its social practice and purpose remain much wider and its moral underpinning much deeper and holistic. Its position is systemic in so far as it neutralizes or controls social separation, identifies and confines hostility, and creates and reinforces cohesion.

Hospitality, as a quality of Indian social relationships, displays different degrees of institutionalization (i.e. from ritualized, obligatory hospitality to that ordinarily expressed during a normal social encounter) and extends to cover casual, spontaneous, and non-sacred conditions. In India, too, for example, despite communal, caste and kinship rules, people (i.e. Hindus, Muslims, Christians, Sikhs, etc.) 'entertain' each other quite regularly in rural and urban contexts for various reasons. This is so despite the fact that Indian hospitality repeatedly fails in establishing inter-communal amity. It may fail in its long-term goals yet succeeds in securing conditional social cooperation. Functional explanations of Indian hospitality, therefore, remain relevant but incomplete in the same way (and for the same reason) as functional classifications of hospitality. If hospitality concerns issues of social cohesion and conflict, it is seldom adequately defined by them. Though the social uses of hospitality are diverse and subject to sociocultural change, it may most basically be considered as a moral imperative which people normally express towards each other as humans. People are hospitable not only because it often serves practical social ends but also since it means much on its own moral basis to the people who practice it. It is both a means-end relationship and an end in itself.

Hospitality among gods, men, and demons within Indian cosmology released myriad moral and social messages for participants. It tried to secure order through social coherence, and coherence through the positive moral value which Indian cultural ideologies accord it. Hospitality is made a moral duty, an obligation that applies to all even in the face of the separation which status inequality must engender. Simultaneously, though its inspiration may be basically religious (and hence also 'social' in the Durkheimian sense), emphasizing _altruisme_ over _egoisme_ (again in Durkheim's sense), its expressions and uses need not be confined to the sacred domain.

Thus, Indian hospitality as a moral obligation translates into sacred forms on the one hand, and into customary social duties and secular civility, etiquettes and courtesy, on the other. In this way hospitality becomes a tacit social rule (in the widest sense of the term) even in a hierarchical society that must make intricate rules about who can be a guest of whom, with or without being a host in return (Marriott 1968). The same Indian system, we must remember, also insists upon 'the divinity of the guest' (Hocart 1969, 78-86), employing 'guest' as a non-restrictive as well as a restrictive category. In India gods appear as stranger-guests to test the faith, charity, and altruisme of their devotees.

We will pursue further the above general characteristics of hospitality in the Indian system by discussing four interrelated but culturally discrete models - classical, customary, the Muslim and the British-Western. I should note at this point that these models, though a specific product of Indian cultural history, will be approached as the four mutually-informing value configurations of Indian hospitality, all at present a part of Indian social reality. Together, the four models will represent a wider range of concerns which Indian hospitality now handles under different social contexts, from domestic to extra-domestic, and institutional to spontaneous.

II

Two basic cultural models

As a general social fact, hospitality in India betrays several cultural models that have, over time, kept changing their position, form, function, and meaning in relation to each other. The four paradigms of hospitality that we find necessary to identify are: ideal Indic cultural models (a multi-stranded domain), local and regional customary models (i.e. hospitality deemed proper among particular kin, caste and communal groups), and two accretionary models for their influences on the two basic models (e.g. of the Muslim model on the Hindu's, and of Western hospitality over the Hindu and the Muslim schemes).

The Indic ideology

The ideal and customary cultural schemes are variously offered by Indian texts (e.g. see Manu III, 70-115; IV, 179, 181-4; Prakash 1961, on aspects of evolving hospitality in ancient Indian texts), constituting the early cultural core of the Indian system; the two non-Indic schemes are culturally accretional but are an integral part of that composite notion of hospitality which we now call 'Indian'. These four cultural strands influence each other and blend together as they configurate within a complex social system. The practical culture of India routinely makes use of this multi-stranded configuration of hospitality.

The Indic (i.e. mainly Hindu, Sikh, Jain, and Buddhist) model underscores hospitality (atithi-satkāra) for its moral formulation, pursuit, and consequence. It applies to self as a moral duty and to society as a 'law' of the Creator; the consequences of this hospitality are truly cosmological and holistic. The guest, the receiver of hospitality, is accorded most attention, a point repeatedly made by Manu, where the guest is made to rule 'over the world of Indra' (IV, 182). To quarrel with one's guest is a sin; to insult him is to invite enmity. Indic hospitality is a part of the systemic sacrificial offerings to (and austerities of) brahmans, manes, gods, bhūtas, and man; it is mostly associated with the householder (though even an ascetic is obliged to honour his guest with 'water, roots, and fruit'). A householder's 'proper life' rests on fulfilling five sacrifices (i.e. yajñas of huta, prahuta, brāhmyahuta, prāśita, and tarpaṇa; see Manu III, 70-80), and hospitality is one of them. He who does not so sacrifice 'lives not, though he breathes'. These sacrifices uphold the cosmological order as they expiate the sins of the five 'slaughter-houses' (i.e. the hearth, the grind-stone, the broom, the pestle and mortar, and the water vessel) within the household. Such sacrifices support 'both the movable and the immovable creation' (Manu III, 68, 75). They also represent the triadic values cardinal to the householder's life-compassion (daya), gifting (dāna), and moral law (dharma). This multiple cultural coding of the sacrificial scheme points out how the integration of hospitality occurs within the larger Indic scheme.

The Indic model of hospitality must, however, tackle the same value structure that socially separates, ranks, and excludes. Ideally, this situation is not paradoxical for the system as long as the Ultimate Whole can engulf and unconditionally surpass criteria of social separation, rank, and exclusion. Society is only a moral instrument of the Hindu ideal, and thus, among other ways, the moral must generate as well as control the social tendency to separate and exclude. If Manu must ask that the hospitality be varṇa-ordered and that heretics, rogues, and those who live like cats, herons, etc. (i.e. those who are against the sacred law and lead indiscriminate lives) should not even be greeted (the most rudimentary step of hospitality; see IV, 30); he must also enjoin that all beings - even the lowliest - 'be honoured' (i.e. that they be offered food gently and with compassion; see III, 92-94). One is asked to regulate all giving and receiving 'with a full knowledge of the rules, prescribed by the sacred law ...' (Manu IV, 187). These rules enjoin the practice of values that matter most to the entire Indic cosmic and moral order (e.g. duty, charity, generosity and compassion; see Khare 1983).

The ideal model of hospitality (atithisatkāra, atithiparayanta, atithisevā), however, reaches a social climax with food sharing. The host must offer proper food with appropriate etiquette, the guest must accept and eat it, and the host must eat with the guest, especially when the guest asks. A crisis precipitates whenever this complete feeding-eating sequence is disrupted, interfered with or denied, especially among one's own kin and jāti members. With unequals, the higher-ranked host must feed the lowly guest with honour; he should do so though he will not eat with him (and nor will the guest so request). Ideally, all guests, including beggars, deserve such an honour. The point is also made another way through what Hocart (1969, 81) observed: 'In India the stranger or guest is not merely, as in Greece, a man accompanied by a god, but is himself a god, or rather gods, for he is "compounded of all the gods".' He adduces evidence from the Taittirīya Upaniṣad and even the earlier Atharvaveda to support his point.

Indian mythology further amplifies upon this property of the guest, making him sometimes a divinity testing the devotion of a lowly host (e.g. consider the cases of the low status Śabarī and Vidura), sometimes a masked trickster (e.g. the god Vāmana as the guest of the king Mahābali in Bhāgavatapurāṇa), and often a temperamental sage (e.g. Durvāsas before Ambarīṣa, Durvāsas before Draupadī and Kṛṣṇa, and Vasiṣṭha before Nimi).

The mythological and legendary cases of hospitality (drawn from the Rāmāyaṇa, the Mahābhārata, and Śrīmadbhāgavata) underscore several important cultural characteristics: (A) The Nimi-Vasiṣṭha case emphasizes, for example, the importance of proper invitation to one's ascetic guru; an exchange of curses between the guest and the host (exemplifying the power equation between a temperamental Brahman ascetic and a spiritually powerful king); and an eventual recovery by both from the curses emanating from misjudged proprieties. (B) The Ambarīṣa-Durvāsas case distinctly adds politics of hospitality, since Indra, to retain his power, had openly instigated Durvāsas to deflect Ambarīṣa (a Viṣṇu devotee) from his devout austerities. The host-guest power equation again clashed here, each being strong from his own power source (Ambarīṣa from devotion to Viṣṇu and Durvāsas from his austerities). The guest was enraged because he was given the left-overs (though not the partly-eaten left-overs). The power of devotion (of a householder-king) wins over from that of austerity. (C) The Draupadī-Kṛṣṇa-Durvāsas case is essentially similar to (B), except that it adds the notion of akṣayapātra (the 'never-emptying pot' received from Sūrya) and of a clever, powerful friend who helped under crisis (i.e. Kṛṣṇa). (D) The Kṛṣṇa-Rukmiṇī-Durvāsa's case illustrates the idiosyncratic sage-guest and his excessive demands on the divine hosts. The pleased guest gave a boon to the couple that turned out to be insufficient for Kṛṣṇa (because he had neglected to smear the sage's pudding on his feet in which he was later fatally wounded by an arrow; see the Anuśāsanaparva of the Mahābhārata).

In the context of mythological materials, the temperamental sage Durvāsa is repeatedly shown having problems with hosts, and that his problems often get expressed through abnormal food handling. Such conditions illustrate a principle: emotion infects food quickly in India; temper affects food adversely (making it a medium of curse) while happiness transforms it into a nourishing (and blessing) medium. Though space limitations do not permit its full discussion, hospitality gained a generally stronger or more catholic position with the rise of devotionalism in India. Gods increasingly became guests to test or award the devotee's staunch faith; hosts became all-sacrificing 'instruments' of the divine. (For example, see Pope 1900 for legends from Śaivism in south India, and Bhaktamālā for north India.) The devotional movement made unconditional hospitality integral to the notions of faith and total 'surrender' (śraddhā and śaraṇa) before the deity. The devotional hospitality accords greater importance to devotional intention (bhava)in food; it weakens and sublimates ritual and caste distinctions.

In the mythologies hospitality thus remains an inalienable moral duty, but with risk. The greater the spiritual power of the guest, the greater is the caution required by the attending host. The power of guests usually overtakes the higher status of hosts. Brahman-King and sage-king hosts predominate, where kings normally host the powerful sages (Brahmans or not). Such hospitality serves to resolve as well as initiate conflicts. Since the powerful are also contentious and temperamental in India, sages easily tend to curse or bless according to the situation before them. Hence they are received with ever greater care. The divine, human, and demoniac conflicts increase these risks and hospitality becomes a mine-field. This notion even now translates into the general concern which the contemporary Indian householder exhibits when he receives an ascetic (i.e. a sādhu and sannyāsin) as a guest within his household. A Brahman priest is for him far more tamed than the ascetic. One reasoning is that the Brahman, only socially higher (and now rarely spiritually powerful), can seldom make his curses effective, while the ascetic, remote with his devotions and spiritual austerities, is still a uniquely powerful and temperamental stranger. He always ranks higher than his host for extra-social reasons.

It is such cognitive-cultural connections with the ideal or mythical model that guide the customary norms of hospitality. But since the specific norms of hospitality vary greatly in India, there is little gained in directly checking whether the code of Manu (or any such body of rules) is actually followed by a group or not. Instead, the shaping may be indirect - an image-based pursuit of major cultural values (e.g. of dharma, dāna, and dayā) of the Indic moral cosmogony. The mythologies usually offer the models. Hence, as the textual rules vary among themselves, and as texts give a definite credence to local ways (e.g. see Lingat 1962, 7-16; Kane 1973, 825-84), India follows an intuitive, approximate, and locally variable pursuit of the textual ideal.

The customary scheme

It will therefore be sociologically important to give maximum attention to the local and regional systems of customary hospitality in India. (The customary channels include food vendors, halwa shops, and traditional eating places.) People mostly depend on this domestic and extra-domestic system, incorporating in it their perception of what is culturally desirable, socially obligatory, and practically feasible. A customary model is a configuration of these three considerations, and is patterned after the ideal values of duty, gifting, sacrifice, and compassion. The earlier Indic distinction between ceremonial (or yajña-related) and social invitations (nimantraṇa and āmantraṇa) is also implicitly recognized (see Prakash 1961, 101). Obligatory hospitality appears between kin and jāti members, social hospitality among friends, and alms-giving hospitality among those dispossessed, deprived, and handicapped. The first is fully institutionalized, the second is casual and spontaneous, while the third is optional. All these domains form a local system of hospitality. The ancient concept of atithi (i.e. the guest; if it was fire in the Rgveda [Prakash 1961, 27] it was with Manu a 'Brahman' - a meritorious person - staying overnight) is liberalised but kept at the centre of the customary model; it is reinterpreted to accord hospitality to increasingly varied guests - appointed as well as unappointed.

The customary practices of hospitality work essentially to promote or test social cooperation and amity among kin and caste members; it is done according to local and regional rules. The model of this hospitality, however, must maintain 'amity' in face of diverse social ranks and their conflicting inequalities (e.g. for the jural-moral use of the concept of amity - 'ethics of generosity' - see Fortes 1969; for its extension to Indian data see Carter 1975; for a general association between rank and amity of 'intimacy' in India see Marriott 1978). The Indian conceptions of sharing and the ethics of generosity (not simply 'exchange' and 'transaction'), which is a socially prominent but sociologically underestimated domain, not only mitigate ranked social distances but also translate certain notions of 'spiritual equality' in social terms. Thus, the customary system also patterns itself after the ideal holism: people try to share generously within customary model because it renders one a meritorious soul (puṇyātman) now and in future lives by the same Karmic law that distinguishes the ranks and statuses of all creatures. Thus, if the customary model yields competitive hospitality under the ranked but non-dualistic Hindu cosmology (e.g. see Marriott 1976, Khare 1976), it also simultaneously tries to secure reciprocal generosity and mutual honour at another level. Conceptually, customary hospitality must function to restrain conflict and promote amity. The cultural logic of the customary model is: amity under social differences.

Domestic hospitality, the cornerstone of all Indic hospitality from the earliest times, is in India household-based, not household-limited. It radiates outwards to beyond kin and caste groups, once the daily and ceremonial cycles of hospitality are accounted for within the household, and once the place of domestic initiatives is recognized in circulating most of the food and material support to diverse segments of society. This informal but considerable network of economic support and food circulation remains rooted in the Indic ethos of giving under sharing. The conception needs to be systematically studied and developed to lay to rest the interactional and attributional issues still paraded within South Asian anthropological studies (for a systematic review of the recent literature and a functionalist formulation of the issue, see Vatuk 1982).

All feeding and eating among Indians is regulated by a general customary ethos: feed others generously but eat only moderately (Khare 1982). The customary contexts of feasting, alms-giving while fasting, public mess under charity and philanthropy, and jajmani payments as a part of one's domestic life, all point towards the socioeconomic infrastructure which Indian society has ideally employed to distribute food with a sense of respect (ādara), generosity (udāratā) and duty (kartavya) towards those high and low, and rich and poor. Giving food with a sense of moral duty restrains social arrogance and alienation between the giver and the receiver. Such a transfer fosters a sense of amity among those near-equals, and of faithfulness and gratitude among non-reciprocating unequals (for a sociological discussion of faithfulness and gratitude see Simmel 1950, 379-95). The giver and the receiver in the Indian system rank themselves but seldom get rid of these subtler cultural senses. The normative model of hospitality asserts such social conciliation even between those steeply ranked, usually with exchange of polite words, social visits, and flowers and certain foods. If this conciliation does not always work, it nevertheless remains socially desirable, awarding a mitigated cultural quality to Indian rank differences.

Customary domestic hospitality, whether narrow (i.e. kin and caste based) or broad range (i.e. community-wide), also cultivates this cultural sense of shared unity under differences. A normal Indian household teaches its members as much about social rank as about mediating social distance. Hospitality cultivates etiquette as well as a moral cohesiveness, sometimes consciously but often unconsciously. And this comprehensive cultural sense helps develop a capacity in the Indian to rank from up close and integrate from afar. These are subtle but critical mental processes in the Indian system, and I shall illustrate aspects of this point with a full quotation from Prakash Tandon's Punjabi Century (1961,74-5). It also exemplifies social courtesy and etiquette integral to the customary model of hospitality:

> Hospitality with us was equally a matter of pride and social obligation, and its rules were inculcated from a young age. If a person from your village or a relation was visiting your town, but was staying with someone else, you went formally to invite him and his family. Etiquette made them protest by saying that wherever they were they were eating your food, so why should you trouble. You insisted and they protested, but after the procedure had taken its conventional course they very modestly agreed. There was a fresh protest when you asked them to both meals of the day. That really was too much trouble, they would say, but you always retorted that you were Khatris, not Sonars, that you should ask them to one meal only. The Sonars were the goldsmiths, who as a caste had been dubbed mean.
>
> Formalities of the invitation settled, someone of the family, usually one of us children, had to go to fetch them even if they knew their way. Unless they were close relations, they came only just before the meal, which always began with a sweet, never with a salt dish. The meal was literally a battle between the hosts and the guests, in which the latter must, after much seemly protesting, eventually lose. Men and woman ate separately, our mother eating alone, last of all. After lunch one of us would walk back with them, and again fetch them in the evening for the second meal.

> When we boys were sometimes staying with relations, other people in the town used to invite us. When we returned home mother would ask searching questions about where we had been invited, and make sure that all those who ought to have invited us had in fact done so. From the full account we gave she also made certain that we had gone through all formalities properly. Did we protest the right number of times; did we suggest that one meal would be enough, and did we accept only after the Khatri-Sonar analogy had been given; did we pretend at the meal that we were not hungry; did we begin the meal by eating the sweet; did we put forward our hands with fingers outspread over the plate when the hostess wanted to help us to more? These and many other questions were asked to make sure that we did not behave as we would have liked to by accepting the invitation with alacrity and falling on the food like young wolves.

A conciliatory expression and management of host and guest relationships are as critical to customary hospitality as to Indian domestic life itself. The point is clearly underscored in regional vernacular traditions. For example, a popular, five-part compendium in Hindi on advice to women has noted:

> Offer honour and respect to even an ordinary woman-guest. Seat her above yourself, speak with her interest in mind, express gratitude for her visit. Until she stays, indulge in virtuous talk to win her heart. When she asks to leave, insist once or twice on her staying a little longer. When she does leave, request her to visit again, indicating simultaneously [for yourself] the overwhelming domestic chores. [However] reassure her that you will also visit her sometime. [Tell her that] you remain desirous of her company ... that she should visit you again whenever she has time, that she should not mind your not visiting her [in the circumstances]. So saying, one must accompany the guest to one's outer door, if no further. (<u>Strīsubodhanī</u>, 28th edition, 1973, 122-3; my translation.)

Though rare, such a normative account of women playing host or guest to other women is significant, first for allowing us to see the issues from the woman's side, and second for subtly but clearly downgrading the idea of lone visits among women by themselves. The inference to be drawn is that good housewives do not frequently visit other women by themselves. The overt excuse is that their domestic responsibilities are overwhelming, but actually the uncontrolled social movements of women (even within the neighbourhood) must be traditionally discouraged. (Incidentally, the author of this compendium for women is a man.)

However, the hospitality to be accorded to one's relatives (<u>pahune</u>, though the term <u>pahuna</u> is also used more generally for all guests) does not suffer from such tentativeness. It underscores a cautious and careful approach, where one bends backwards to establish and maintain amity (<u>hela-mela</u>) among one's relatives (<u>biradari</u> and <u>natedari</u>):

> The housewife must always visit all of her [affinal] relatives. Since if you will not go to their places, who will visit yours? All are equal within the <u>jāti</u>. Small issues tend to give rise to quarrels. If your <u>biradari</u> invites you even indirectly, you should leave behind all other engagements and go. Women who do so do not have any problems when they perform marriage or other ceremonies; all women join the occasion with happiness. But those who do not

visit others, nobody comes to their house even after nine invitations. It is a matter of custom - tu mere to main tere; otherwise, there is nobody subordinate within a biradari. If anybody expresses arrogance or pride within a biradari, others do so ten times more. One must behave with great care towards one's biradari (Strīsubodhanī 1973, 124-5).

Domestic hospitality, as a part of the customary model, follows several social cycles of its own, and they need to be more systematically studied than hitherto (for a useful characterization see Vatuk 1982). Briefly, the domestic events of hospitality could be ordinary (e.g. as expressed every day when meals are offered to family elders), normal (expressed under routine obligatory hosting), or ceremonial (as during rites of passage). They could be simple and short, or complex and long, or reversible or irreversible, or direct or indirect. If domestic hospitality is seldom devoid of a strong sense of social closeness, it is in practice seldom free from arguments, differing opinions, overt conflicts, social manipulations, and status politics. Amity and sharing represent a whole range of social conditions for domestic hospitality, as do conflicts and quarrels. The resilience of domestic hospitality lies in restoring the first in face of the second. Though never completely successful, it seldom gives up trying. The Indian householder not only gives (or receives) foods but more importantly shares his identity with receivers to pursue the values (i.e. kartavya, dāna, dayā, sadācāra and dharma) that matter most to the Indic social order (for an exercise on this value order, see Khare 1983).

III

Two accretionary models

With no space to describe these two models in any historical and cultural detail, I shall only characterize some of their aspects in the context of the previous two schemes. This comparative perspective will however recognize the historical fact that Indic and non-Indic models of hospitality have been interacting with each other for centuries, and it is difficult, beyond a certain point, to distinguish their influences upon each other. Further, both models are internally heterogeneous (and have been so over time), increasing the complexity of present-day Indian hospitality and its purpose. Both conceptual and popularly accepted features are significant as much in these cases as in Indic ones. The logic of these models underscores selective inclusion and gradual modification and incorporation.

The point is important for studying prevalent Indian hospitality, which has developed by adapting and blending convergent cultural strands from all three cultural models - Indic, Muslim, and Western. Sociologically, the last two paradigms have worked to expand, diversify, and alter the domain of traditional Indic hospitality. They expanded the cuisine and added to the culinary art (despite vegetarian/non-vegetarian antagonism, and clearly conflicting specification of food taboos); they also added to or altered emphasis on social courtesy and etiquette. Most basically, the intimate Indic bond between social and religious domains was gradually loosened to yield hospitality for recreational, political, and instrumental reasons. As a result, the role of competitive, commercial, and 'public' considerations - the non-sacred social - has enlarged within Indian hospitality.

However, when the Muslim model introduced its elaborate courtly and regal schemes of hospitality (with corresponding notions of honour, rank, and splendour), it also supported fasting, sharing, and giving away of food under the Islamic principles of brotherhood and piety. This dual face is important to recall. The Western scheme, in comparison, introduced work- or office-related hospitality among the educated and 'service-class' Indians, creating a place not only for 'restaurants' (and hence a new dimension of commercialized hospitality) but also for 'parties', banquets, picnics, and receptions (i.e. for formal or informal 'social entertainment'). The Indic moral ethos of moderate eating and generous food-giving was now influenced by the non-sacred social values. A practical ethos emerged for regal, sumptuous, and elaborate feasting and gluttony; it elaborated food for purely personal and social enjoyment, and for wider social influence and political ends. The contemporary form of Indian hospitality must therefore reflect this whole range of heterogeneous concerns, and their vigorous interactions with one another.

I shall illustrate aspects of the above characterization with evidence from Muslim and British accounts of hospitality. In the absence of systematic sociological studies on the topic, the accounts chosen are a part of popular cultural history, hiding often ideological properties within actual or presumed customs and practices. (However, I handle these models without any pretence of considering the ideological structures of the Islamic and Judeo-Christian hospitality.) On Muslim (or Indo-Mughal) gastronomic refinements, intricacies, and etiquettes, Sharar (b.1860, d.1926) (1975) offers some culturally reliable material. He draws upon the larger Muslim court culture, though his charge is Lucknow of the Muslim Nawabs. More relevant to us is what his particular descriptions symbolize; they represent larger connections between foods and a value system. Thus Sharar (1975, 155-9) wrote on gastronomy: 'The most important activity in human life is eating. As any community or nation progresses, its diet is the most salient guide to its refinement.' This approach to eating introduces a value distinctly different from the Indic (where one must eat well but not for pleasure alone; the larger moral purposes must always guide all eating; see Khare 1982). Sharar perceptively presents the multi-sided gastronomic ethos of the Nawabs: they were 'connoisseurs of good food', at once cultivating cooks and their inventive cuisine, appreciating delicacy, opulence, and extravagance reflected in foods, testing the culinary refinement of the guest. For example, Nawab Shuja-ud-Daula and his wife received food from six different kitchens every day (representing six different chefs in his own, his wife's, and his mother's kitchens and those of his two brothers-in-law). To do so was to recognize kin-bonds, to control palace politics, and to instigate contests for culinary refinement.

Hospitality under such circumstances also became an elaborate aesthetic affair, with contests going on between Nawabs (and their chefs) to out-smart each other by elaborating, disguising, and perfecting certain dishes (e.g. see Sharar's reference to rice preparations, conserves, bread, and lentil curries). Sharar (1975, 159) notes that these kitchens employed three types of help-scullions, cooks (<u>bavarchi</u>) and chefs (<u>rakabdar</u>) on the basis of their performance; chefs were highly paid and had direct access to the ruler. A major symbol of hospitality to a Muslim was his <u>dastar khwan</u> (a Persian word for 'table cloth' with printed verses in Urdu or Persian at the edges) spread on the floor (and later on a table; <u>khwan</u> is an octagonal wooden tray for carrying food) for 'eating together'. (For a brief description of eating at the <u>dastar khwan</u> in Gujarat see Ja'far Sharif's <u>Qaanun-i-Islam</u>.) Essentially, it represents generous sharing of food with one's kin and guests under the principle of Muslim brotherhood and its egalitarian ethos. One's dastar khwan also reflects one's prosperity, etiquette, and aestheticism; among the rich, it makes a discriminating and eloquent social settlement to guests and visitors.

Complementing the concept of dastar khwan appear the feasting foods called tora and of course the betel-leaf (pan-supari) complex (Sharar 1975, 164, 218-23). Accepting betel-leaf, noted Sharar, meant accepting social responsibility; it was also a medium for Hindu-Muslim hospitality. Together, these elements constitute a cultural complex that still characterises the hospitality of Indian Muslims. This complex is representative enough for our purposes, introducing food expressly for palate, personal enjoyment, and social graces.

The festive food and betel-leaf complex is also integral to the Hindu order on its own terms. The Muslim court and palace models of hospitality have been variously adapted and emulated within the households of rich and influential Hindus. Obviously, those closer to the centres of Muslim authority were influenced first (and most), but Muslim etiquette has slowly trickled down to the majority and has added a distinct sociocultural dimension to Indian food. It has mixed with the earlier Indic strains (but perhaps more in northern India, and especially under social hospitality). This intermingling has gone on despite some well-known conflicts and allergies which Hindu and Muslim food schemes otherwise produce. Conceptually, the Muslim courtly model substantiated food in a new way for the Indic people; it made food a focus of social domination (when looked at from the Indic viewpoint), encoding more diversified economic and political messages in food as a commodity and diet. Simultaneously, however, Muslim piety and generosity encouraged not only a liberal distribution of food to the needy but also made social hospitality relatively more open and wide-ranging (given its freedom from intricate Hindu ritual rules). The Hindu Bhakti movement and Muslim egalitarianism may have vicariously worked together on loosening the restrictions on hospitality in India.

What the Muslim accretionary model thus added to present-day Indian hospitality was still further augmented and diversified by the Western (essentially British) model. Hospitality of the Raj period had included a range of British, Anglo-Indian, and Anglicized Indian influences. Again, in the absence of systematic sociological studies of these influences on Indian hospitality, we may illustrate our case by popular accounts now becoming increasingly available. However, if such evidence will let us only surmise, not conclude, it suggests the introduction of two new sociological-class and ethnic-criteria which the British had brought to the social handling and exchange of food in India. Essentially, as they brought notions of the British class system with them, and classified both themselves and Indians on the basis of wealth, power, physical differences, and squirearchy, they also classified hospitality along a mixture of race-class-caste criteria.

Based on Charles Allen's Plain Tales from the Raj (1975, which seem sociologically more reliable and significant than tales), we may observe that the British (a) brought British norms of eating and hospitality with them and practised these activities under social exclusivity as best as Indian circumstances would allow (Allen 1975, 110-115); (b) hybridized their class distributions with those of the Raj to yield such groupings among themselves as the civilian, the military, the box-wallah, the BOR (British Other Ranks), and the Anglo-Indian (Allen 1975, 231- 242); and (c) correspondingly classified the Indians into rulers (some the 'Brindians', 'great hosts - and more than equals'), Brahmans, Babus, Marwaris, Congress-wallahs, ayahs, 'bobajee' (bawarchi - cook), and mehtar (sweeper). The British Raj hospitality developed around such cultural categories as 'bobajee' (cook) and 'bobajee-khana' (kitchen), 'burra-khana' (big dinner, celebration), double khana (dinner-party), dolley (tray of gifts), dastur (literally 'custom'; by usage bribery), phal-phul (gifts to government officials), and nazar (ceremonial presents from the host to guests during a formal visit). All of these are still socially current and ethnographically verifiable categories in various parts of India and remain relevant to the current conception of Indian hospitality.

Conceptually, the British Raj notions of hospitality introduced a range of new social concerns that would attract a sociological analysis. They pursued hospitality under the domains of the 'formal' and the 'informal', the official and the unofficial, the public and the private, and the ruler and the ruled. Since these distinctions also brought with them certain definite criteria of the Western economic, political, and legal orders, they demanded definite adjustments of the existing Indic and Muslim schemes. Most importantly, Raj hospitality, accompanied by English education, administration, and class prestige, secularized in selected aspects both the domestic and extra-domestic models of Hindu and Muslim hospitality. It established a sphere for class-based, formal, and official hospitality; its conception was contained neither in the Indic ceremonial nor the Muslim courtly models. Its purpose and consequence were culturally as foreign (again a topic for systematic historical research) as were the ways of the British dinner-party-banquet-reception complex.

IV

Hospitality under contemporary social forces

The above four models, two basic and two accretionary, comprise the current heterogeneous cultural matrix of Indian hospitality. This heterogeneity is now integral to the Indian system as a whole. Thus, while each model usually dominates by social context, explaining some events better than others (e.g. the two basic models may explain most and best traditional Hindu occasions of hospitality), each model alone is necessary but insufficient to account for Indian society today. The four models together refer to an interdigitating cultural configuration that produces a social dynamic of its own. This dynamic is pervasive and creative. But simultaneously increasing social conflicts strain the moral holism of Indic hospitality; they even weaken and confront the customary scheme. As yet, however, they are seldom able to dissolve the Indic model. Civilizationally ingrained, the Indic paradigms tend to assert themselves subliminally - almost surreptitiously - in familiar as well as remote social domains.

In practice, however, Indian hospitality is now increasingly influenced by social cleavages and practical expediency. Traditional caste and kin relationships are increasingly invaded by new schisms and resultant strains, introducing tentativeness where certainty once reigned. Improvised casual or spontaneous hospitality handles issues that range beyond traditional social concerns. Therefore, while hospitality is found to be eroding, dispersing, and declining traditional areas, its overall sociological function may actually be increasing as persons find their economic, political, and legal interests defined across caste lines by Indian democracy, and as they need to realign social differences through spontaneous hospitality. This hospitality may take the form of a courteous greeting, or a glass of water, or the currently ubiquitous 'cup of tea', or an invitation to one's home for an elaborate dinner. However done, its function is pervasive and significant; it represents a major social adjustment which Indian society is now undergoing.

Spontaneous hospitality, diverse in motivation and meaning, is increasingly pursued to manage both social distance and disharmony. Migration, occupational diversity, bureaucracy, industrialisation, and urbanisation, all demand that people constantly reckon with diverse social distances, learn to handle strangers, and generate workable confidence among those who are regionally and ethnically different. Casual or spontaneous hospitality is essential for such purposes; it helps initiate new social contacts and mends those under strain or in disuse. When it fails, it must try again.

Simultaneously, diversifying social conflicts strains traditional hospitality in new ways. Such conflicts tend to muddle the obligatory domain of traditional hospitality; its moral motive of sharing and social amity is disrupted by diverse practical and expedient goals. Traditional hospitality now often tends to be socially tense, circumscribed, and inward-directed (i.e. an affair among selected kin and jāti members). Indians still feast, give, and exchange conspicuously under ceremonial obligations, but do so with an increasingly different motive - that of exploiting customs for practical, social or monetary gain. Thus, though ceremonial hospitality looks the same, and the issues of social status and honour still characterise it, it may neither mean nor signify the same to the Indian (cf. Vatuk 1982, for a summary review of the previous studies of ceremonial hospitality; for a range of related concerns see Ortner 1978, Pettigrew 1975, Ahmed 1980, and Appadurai 1981). Customary contexts increasingly project practical goals.

Further, the present-day Indian social dynamic refines casual and spontaneous hospitality as an instrument of social encounter, persuasion, negotiation, and practical goal management. Obviously, appropriate empirical studies are required of this aspect of hospitality. These newer domains of Indian hospitality now appear as people have to convert strangers into acquaintances, and acquaintances into reliable tactical allies, whether the context is a village faction, an urban market, a factory, a government office, or a political party. (Though the contexts differ, the politics of hospitality is similar to that depicted in mythological material.)

These days a person comes across at least some strangers with each move in his education, occupation, place of residence, and political arena. An urban Indian in particular encounters several such clusters of strangers in his lifetime. Normally, he encounters them with spontaneous hospitality to find his place and to manage his practical goals. Business deals, conflict resolutions, power politics, and party alignments particularly display how hospitality may be turned into a refined instrument of persuasion, negotiation and compromise. Comprehensive in purpose, this hospitality must however draw upon the same cultural repertoire that the four cultural models have already offered.

However, contemporary Indian hospitality is also directly influenced by conditions of uneven and uncertain food supply. These conditions vary regionally within India but they have raised a popularly shared ethos of food shortages and supplies. There is a popular culture and folklore concerning food shortages, especially in cities and larger towns. Though incompletely articulated, except in occasional plays, films, and songs (e.g. the Hindi film Roti, Kapra aur Makan), this culture needs to be juxtaposed to the customary scheme to discover the gaps between popular and customary expectations. The greater the gap between them, the greater is normally the attempt to reinterpret customary expectations to fit practical constraints. Thus, popular culture must, for example, carry jokes and cynical remarks on sugar when it is conspicuously costly and scarce, affecting that 'cup of tea' which symbolizes all casual and rudimentary hospitality today.

The conditions of severe food scarcity place hospitality under further strain. It may temporarily atrophy and disrupt under the extreme conditions of a drought or famine. Though no specific study of hospitality seems to exist to corroborate this point in India, there are of course accounts of famine conditions (e.g. Greenough 1980), showing severe strains on the normal morality of food sharing. Even popular writers include remarks on it to complete their picture of modern India (e.g. Mehta 1973, 557). The point of such evidence is that popular culture and folklore in India, as perhaps in any other society, reflect faithfully the gaps between the normative and the normal, and the normal and the practically feasible, offering popularly accepted cultural interpretations and explanations of the prevailing conditions. However, popular culture does not alter the normal and the normative at every turn; its function is to help people cope in the immediate situation. Its guidance is immediate. It is indispensible. It is more contextually relevant and practical than folklore, though less cumulative. It is less instructive and entertaining than folklore but more acutely practical and rational.

V

Summary and concluding remarks

Indian hospitality is at present culturally multidimensional and socially diverse. It is culturally comprised of two basic models (offered by the Indic civilization) and two accretionary models - the Indo-Mughal and the British (Western) - which have existed in India for centuries. Each of these four models has its analytically distinct cultural characteristics. The Indic model is based on comprehensive moral holism; the customary model creates and maintains domestic, local, and regional practices within a general and flexible frame of cognitive values which the Indic model offers. The Indo-Mughal model introduces Muslim notions of piety, brotherhood, court culture, and conspicuous culinary arts; and the British Raj culture intervenes with its criteria of ethnicity, class, secular food, official formality, and colonial prerogatives. All four models selectively mesh together to offer a comprehensive configuration to contemporary Indian hospitality.

The social dynamics of Indian hospitality show how traditional spheres are now facing increasing diversification. The institutionalised, obligatory hospitality of caste, kinship, and community is increasingly complemented by casual and spontaneous forms. The latter two modes of hospitality are socially flexible and less restrictive; they are therefore adapted to wide-ranging social uses in post-Independence, democratic India. They offer ways of getting along with strangers, of creating friendships and alliances, and of managing practical ends through influence, persuasion, and negotiation. The traditional domains of hospitality are increasingly being manipulated for practical ends, as the latter are multiplying under politico-economic pressures. Customary morality is exploited and larger values are pushed into the background. However, this situation flouts but does not dissolve the positive morality of Indian hospitality. Despite all the odds, Indian hospitality continues thus far to work towards the larger goals of social tolerance, sharing, and amity in newer and more different social ways. It succeeds as well as fails - but seldom completely.

As a concluding remark, we may note that a basic idiom like hospitality helps show how the multiple layers of Indian culture interact with each other at the present time. Hospitality is as much a concern of Indian folklore as of abstruse Indic texts. It simultaneously integrates cultural normality, norms, and holistic ideals. It is neither an exclusive concern of the great tradition nor of the little; both must explicate it but each alone is culturally insufficient to specify it. Indian folklore, which itself has had its own great traditions (e.g. consider the Pañcatantra and Jātaka literature), also dwells on hospitality for its diverse social value and practical uses; its didactic tales and legends illustrate a place for practical knowledge in India. Simultaneously, since such hospitality is so basic that it cannot remain only an abstract ideal, its handling must occur, as this exercise shows, for wide-ranging social sharing.

References

Ahmed, A S 1980. Pukhutun Economy and Society: Traditional Structure and Economic Development in a Tribal Society. London, Routledge and Kegan Paul

Allen, Charles 1975. Plain Tales from the Raj. London, Futura

Appadurai, A 1981. Gastro-politics in Hindu South Asia. American Ethnologist, 8, 494-511

Boas, Franz 1909. The Kwakiutl of Vancouver Island. American Museum of Natural History, Memoirs, 8, pt.2, 301-522

Boas, Franz 1921. Ethnology of the Kwakiutl. Bureau of American Ethnology, Thirty-Fifth Annual Report, pts. 1 and 2 (1913-1914). Washington, D.C., Government Printing Office

Buhler, Georg (trans) 1964 [1886]. The Laws of Manu. The Sacred Books of the East. Vol. 25. Delhi, Motilal Banarsidass [Quoted as Manu in the text]

Carter, Anthony 1975. Caste 'Boundaries' and the Principle of Kinship Amity: a Maratha Caste Purana. Contributions to Indian Sociology, 9, 123-37

de Coulanges, Fustel 1864. The Ancient City. New York, Doubleday

Fortes, Meyer 1969. Kinship and the Social Order. Chicago, Aldine Publishing Company

Greenough, P R 1980. Indian Famines and Peasant Victims: the case of Bengal. Modern Asian Studies, 14, 205-35

Hocart, A M 1969. The Life-Giving Myth. London, Methuen

Kane, P V 1973. History of Dharmasastra, Vol. III, 2nd ed. Poona, Bhandarkar Oriental Research Institute

Khare, R S 1976. The Hindu Hearth and Home. Delhi, Vikas

Khare, R S 1982. Eating and Feeding as Categories of Culture and Nutrition in India. Mimeographed. Charlottesville, University of Virginia

Khare, R S 1983. Normative Culture and Kinship: Essays on Some Hindu Categories, Processes, and Perspectives. Delhi, Vikas

Lingat, Robert 1962. Time and the Dharma. Contributions to Indian Sociology, VI, 7-16

Manu - see Buhler

Marriott, McKim 1968. Caste Ranking and Food Transactions, a Matrix Analysis. In Structure and Change in an Indian Society, eds. Milton Singer and Bernard S Cohn. Chicago, Aldine Publishing Company

Marriott, McKim 1976. Hindu Transactions: Diversity without Dualism. In Transaction and Meaning, ed. Bruce Kapferer. Philadelphia, Institute for the Study of Human Issues

Marriott, McKim 1978. Intimacy and Rank in Food. Paper presented at Xth International Congress of Anthropological and Ethnological Sciences, New Delhi

Mauss, Marcel 1967 [1925]. The Gift: Forms and Functions of Exchange in Archaic Societies. New York, Norton

Mehta, Ved 1973. Portrait of India. New York, Penguin Books

Morgan, Lewis H 1965 [1881]. Houses and House-Life of the American Aborigines. Chicago, University Press

Ortner, S B 1978. Sherpas through their Rituals. Cambridge, University Press

Pettigrew, J 1975. Robber Noblemen. London, Routledge and Kegan Paul

Pitt-Rivers, Julian 1968. The Stranger, the Guest, and the Hostile Host: Introduction to the Study of the Laws of Hospitality. In Contributions to Mediterranean Sociology, ed. J-G Peristiany (Acts of the Mediterranean Sociological Conference, Athens, July 1963), Paris and the Hague, Mouton

Pope, G U 1900. The Tiruvaçagam or 'Sacred utterances' of the Tamil Poet, Saint, and Sage Manikka-Vaçagar... Oxford, The Clarendon Press

Prakash, Om 1961. Food and Drink in Ancient India. Delhi, Munshi Ram Manohar Lal

Richards, Audrey Isabel 1932. Hunger and Work in a Savage Tribe. London, George Routledge

Sharar, Abdul Halim 1975. Lucknow: The Last Phase of an Oriental Culture. Translated by E S Harcourt and Fakhir Hussain. London, Paul Elek

Simmel, Georg 1950. The Sociology of Georg Simmel. Translated and edited by Kurt H Wolff. London, Collier-Macmillan

Smith, W Robertson 1972 [1889]. The Religion of the Semites. New York, Schocken Books

Smith, W Robertson 1903. Kinship and Marriage in Early Arabia. Boston, Beacon Press

Strisubodhani [Hindi] 1973. Five parts. Ed. Rupa Narayan Pandey. Lucknow, Tej Kumar Press (Naval Kishore Press)

Tandon, P 1961. Punjabi Century. London, Chatto and Windus

Vatuk, S 1982. Cultural Patterns for the Sharing, Exchanging, and giving of foods in South Asia, and their Implications for the study of Domestic Economics. Mimeographed

Walens, Stanley 1981. Feasting with Cannibals: An Essay on Kwakiutl Cosmology. Princeton, University Press

DOWRY AS A PERPETUATOR OF CULTURE IN KUTCH[1]

Vickie C Elson

The brightly coloured mirrorwork, embroidery and finely crafted jewellery for which Kutch is famous is primarily made as dowry for girls who inhabit one of India's poorest and most isolated regions. Kutch is a place where poverty, flood, drought and famine prevail. Daily life is a struggle for survival that is accepted and lived out much as it was generations ago. The Kutchi people are extremely conservative and nearly all the details of everyday life as well as ritual activities are governed by tradition. The most important ritual event is the marriage ceremony, and the dowry is the tangible evidence of concern with tradition and continuity. It is through the selection, manufacture and giving of dowry that a substantial portion of the culture is perpetuated. It gives proof to the girl of her value to her family and establishes the wherewithal for the girl to live up to the expectations she has for her future as a married woman. The dowry consists of those things which she will require in the early years of her married life, and guarantees her certain possessions that she will need to settle into her new situation in her mother-in-law's household. It also establishes her identity as a married woman with a place in society and well-defined roles within her community; in this sense, dowry is an important status-marker.

The objects which comprise the dowry are regarded as gifts of love from the individuals who contribute and are intended to be for the girl's exclusive use. The girl's father commissions jewellery to be made for her and also purchases vessels, utensils, and in some cases, household items made of wood including a charpoy, butter churner, and anything else he may feel that she ought to have. Both the girl and her mother may help to decide what small household items are purchased from the bazaar. Travelling salesmen who are members of local craftsmen's families occasionally visit villages enabling the women to purchase wooden things such as thread-holders, spoons, stools, chapatti boards and rolling pins which are made in distinctive local designs. Mothers make clothing and quilts, and sisters, sisters-in-law, aunts and grandmothers give embroidered household textiles, wall decorations, garments and/or panels of embroidery which can be put away and kept for future use. The girl herself also makes some embroidered items for the dowry.

The wealth and generosity of the father are reflected in the amount of jewellery in the dowry. The determination of how much will be included, or how much money will be spent on jewellery, is made at the time that the arrangements for the marriage are made between the families of the girl and the boy, and so stated. Financial hardship due to drought or flooding often causes marriage rituals to be postponed for a year or more until a family is able to provide the promised jewellery. In good times, it is common practice for the father to provide slightly more than the amount agreed upon, as a show of love, enhancing his own reputation as a generous man, and his daughter's position of having additional financial security to rely upon when hard times come.

In some communities, the boy's family also agrees to give the girl some jewellery at the time of the marriage. Very often these include heavy silver anklets and also pieces that designate the changed status of the girl. For example, in several communities including the Rabari,[2] the girl is given heavy ivory bracelets just after the marriage rituals take place. The girl wears these bracelets as long as her husband is alive. Rabari girls also receive from the boy's family a pair of earrings of a design only worn by Rabari women of their own particular sub-caste.

The dowry jewellery is made according to traditional designs that are generally worn by the women of the community, thus perpetuating the styles of prior generations. In the larger towns of Kutch some shops sell non-traditional designs that are 'in fashion'. Such jewellery is not considered suitable for the dowry, nor is it common for villagers to acquire such ornaments at other times. The selection is made by the father and may or may not be discussed with the mother and/or the girl herself. In those cases where the women do participate in jewellery selection, those far from major towns do not have the opportunity to see or purchase non-traditional designs.

The jewellery is either purchased in the major centers of Bhuj, Anjar, or Bacchau or else commissioned from local jewellery makers in the smaller towns. Relying on commissions, the latter keep little stock in hand. Most of the designs are broadly similar all over Kutch, since most of them are worn by women in different communities widely distributed throughout the district. Some specific designs have a regional distribution, for example, the earrings worn by married Rabari women. These are only made in the areas where the sub-castes live and should a woman need to replace an earring while away from her district, she waits until she returns to her own home region.

Most of the jewellery is made of a low grade silver; however, certain pieces are customarily made of gold, particularly nose-rings, nose-pins and earrings. It is common for a design worn as a nose-ring by the girls and women of one community to be worn as earrings by those of another. Also the same design may be worn as a nose-ring by the girls and as earrings by the boys, and some necklaces are worn both by girls and boys and are included in the dowry at the time of marriage. Also certain communities have specific items which are made of gold such as the Rabari medallion which is the centrepiece of the heavy silver necklace worn by nearly every Rabari woman. The other two or six elements in the necklace are also worn by members of other communities but the medallion is worn only by Rabari. Jewellery thus plays an important role in the visual vocabulary which serves in the social communication system of Kutch.

The vessels which are included in the dowry vary from a single small water container to a grand array of brass, copper, steel and aluminum containers and utensils. Commonly, a girl is given at least two large containers for water; one for carrying water from the tank or well and the other for storing water in her house. She also receives cooking pots, lidded storage containers, and plates, cups and bowls of specific shapes that are typically used for vegetables, milk and chapatti. A girl may also receive a sieve, bucket, betel nut cutter, box for storing betel, painted metal cases for her personal belongings and a wooden jewellery box. The household items in the dowry are selected from a limited range of choices available in the bazaar. Each community has its preferred sizes and shapes and there are seldom new shapes or sizes available to challenge tradition.

All over Kutch women reported that the embroidered clothing and textiles are the most important part of the dowry. Nearly all Kutchi villagers dress in traditional costumes that clearly identify the status of the wearer. Young girls look forward to the time when they will wear the dress of a married woman. The most important of the dowry clothes are the blouses or dresses which are heavily embroidered on silk or other expensive fabric with bright coloured threads incorporating mirrors and in some cases, shells and buttons. The blouses are worn with unornamented skirts and <u>odhni</u> (veilcloths) which may or may not be embroidered. Every dowry includes one such costume, and most dowries include at least three. These costumes are meant to be worn for important occasions for many years after a girl is married. One eighty-year-old woman showed me a beautiful silk costume from her dowry that she planned to wear to her grandson's marriage celebration. The designs embellishing her dowry clothing were much the same as those being made today, although the quality of the fabric was much better. Daily dress is generally identical in cut to the heavily embellished silk garments, though they are usually made of cotton and have little or no embroidery decorating them. The marriage costume itself is often given by the boy's family and is delivered just before the marriage rituals take place. In several villages it was reported that in instances where the marriage costume is more beautiful than those which other members of the girl's family may possess, they may keep the bridal costume and send her off in something less extraordinary.

The ideal number of garments in a girl's dowry varies. In the northern frontier the girl receives twenty-one blouses or panels from which blouses can be made (including some for everyday use). The Jains of the southern areas ideally receive fifty-one saris.

The religion, occupation, marital status and the origins of the community of a woman can easily be understood from her dress and, in some communities, whether or not her husband is still alive, and if she has made the Haj. In all three sub-castes of the Ahir, both sub-castes of the Kanebi, the tiny community of Brahmin, and the Oshwar (Jains), all of whom are farmers living in close proximity to each other, unmarried girls wear embroidered blouses and skirts with waistbands and also unembellished printed cotton odhni. The designs decorating the garments have many similarities. However, the colour of the fabric and those used for the embroidery are distinctly different. There are also differences in the types of printed patterns and colours chosen for odhni. After marriage, Ahir wear tube skirts, while Oshwar and Brahmin wear skirts with waistbands, and the Kanebi wear a sari-like garment called a sadlo. Between the three sub-castes of the Ahir, the differences in colour balance are more subtle, and distinguish between those whose origins were in different regions. Amongst the Rabari and Bhardwad[3] unmarried girls wear cotton skirts, blouses and odhni similar to those worn by farmers. After marriage women of these communities dress in heavy wool skirts and odhni and cotton blouses often embroidered with black thread and mirrors on black fabric. It is possible that this tradition of heavy dark clothing derives from a time when they lived in a colder climate, before their nomadic ancestors settled in Kutch.

Embroidery on dowry textiles is often begun long before they are needed. Women spend their leisure time doing embroidery and then put it away to be made up later, thus postponing the expense of purchasing the fabric for the unembroidered parts. Women with daughters spend their leisure time over a period of several years doing needlework, including quilting for their daughters' dowries. Teenagers make things for their own dowries and also for the dowries of sisters, cousins, sisters-in-law and friends. Thus, in addition to proving a girl's value to her family and that of her future in-laws, the dowry serves to strengthen affection and social ties amongst those who contribute to it.

Decorative embroidery is the primary mode of individual expression in textile-making. Women who are able to execute the traditional motifs using small, even stitches are the most respected. Because originality is not highly respected, young girls tend to avoid developing new designs and concentrate on copying the skills of the older, more conservative women of their community, in making both garments and household textiles. While styles do not change radically from decade to decade, some changes do occur. An old Rabari woman told me that buttons were used to decorate the borders of blouses when she was a young girl, and that they had begun to come back into fashion recently.

The value placed on embroidered garments varies from community to community. The Rabari are amongst those who place the highest monetary value on their needlework, valuing finely-made marriage blouses at more than five hundred rupees, while the Mutva,[4] whose work involves finer stitches and tiny mirrors, seldom value a blouse made of similar materials at more than a hundred rupees. In both communities, the highest recognition a woman receives is for her needlework. Because the embroidery is usually done on two or more layers of fabric, it often lasts longer than the other parts of the garment it was originally made for. It is customarily reused in a second and even a third garment, while the unembroidered portions of old garments become the stuffing for quilts.

Most fabric and thread is purchased at village dry goods shops. The available colours of both fabric and thread are limited and the printed patterns change from year to year. This has been responsible for some changes in 'fashion' - in printed odhni in particular - and also for differences in the embroidery done by some communities. Until about thirty years ago a fine silk embroidery yarn favoured by the people living along the Pakistan border was readily available; it is no longer found anywhere in the shops of Kutch. Consequently the same designs that were done thirty years ago look entirely different now due to the use of cotton or rayon thread.

While printed patterns used for everyday odhni change annually, the odhni worn for marriage ceremonies and other important occasions remain traditionally of bhandhanni (tie-dyed fabric) throughout Kutch. Often a second or third odhni is also part of the marriage costume, depending on the traditions of the girl's community. The use of bhandhanni is a tradition which has been so throughly absorbed into the material culture of Kutch that the people do not have any idea of its origins. Similarly the use of mushru, a satin-faced plain-weave cotton, is available only in the larger towns, and is often given as a gift by fathers to their daughters after a trip into town.

The costumes and jewellery given to girls as dowry in Kutch form the basic vocabularly for a complicated system of communications that conveys an enormous amount of information. Through the dowry both this system of communication and the structure of society itself are perpetuated. Changes occur very slowly. Changes in material culture that result from interaction between communities are faster in some communities than in others. Typically many of the clans of the Banni district share similar styles and designs of embroidery, possibly because they see themselves as part of the greater Muslim population. On the other hand, the Mutva express a strong separate identity in their embroidery. They do not copy other clans, but are often copied, though without much success.

To conclude, the importance of the dowry is manifest in the internal and external relations of families and communities. Kutch is already experiencing the effects of an influx of outsiders, and the introduction of more economic and social reforms will undoubtedly bring about great changes in the goods and materials available. In the future we must expect even greater change and eventually the end of a long and great tradition of finely wrought jewellery and exquisitely embroidered textiles.

Notes

1. I first went to Kutch in 1973 or 1974 in search of the glittering jewellery and magnificent textiles that I had seen in the shops in Ahmedabad and Delhi. I went from village to village gathering information, examples, and friends, visiting more than 70 villages and interviewing women of at least two communities in each village, over the course of a dozen or so trips during the following four years. The collection was shown in an exhibition at UCLAS Museum of Culture History in 1979; a 127-page catalogue accompanied the exhibition. The entire collection is now in their storage available to students and scholars along with several thousand slides and photographs of the Kutch region.

2. The Rabari are a caste of Hindu pastoralists. Three sub-castes are found in Kutch. Generally the men move around with the herds in search of grazing lands while the women remain in the villages. In some cases the women accompany the men and the herds.

3. The Bhardwads are a caste of herders who are frequently assumed to be Rabaris largely due to the similarity in costume of both men and women. They are the 'milkmen' of the area around Anjar and Kotaria (Elson 1979, 104).

4. The Mutva are a Muslim clan of herders living in the Banni district, bordering Pakistan. They consider themselves to be the aristocracy of the district, and other clans look to them for leadership.

Reference

Elson, V C 1979. Dowries from Kutch: A Woman's Folk Art Tradition in India. Los Angeles (catalogue for exhibition held at the Frederick S Wright Art Gallery, UCLA)

Fig. 1 Appliquéd and pieced quilts such as this from the Harijan community of the Banni District are typical dowry gifts. Women copy designs from quilts given to them as dowry gifts and also create new designs based on quilts belonging to other families in their own and other villages.

Fig. 2 In the Banni District Muslim herders and Harijans make embroidered panels for future use as blouse fronts as part of the dowry. This 'Boria' embroidery is typical of the Haliputra clan. Many clans have their own typical embroidery styles and designs, although all the clans quite happily copy the styles and designs of nearby clans or buy blouse panels to give as dowry to daughters.

Fig. 3 Because of the importance placed on the costume as a means of communicating caste identity, the brightly embroidered dowry blouses of the Ahirs of eastern Kutch are often replaced with painted or printed blouses of similar design.

Fig. 4 When several years of drought forced an entire village of Gracia Juts (who are traditionally farmers) to turn to herding, their costume also changed. Only the woman in the centre continues to wear the dress of the farmers. The others have adopted the dress of the Dhanetah Juts, who are herders. The dowry clothes are now those of the Dhanetah Juts, though the jewellery typical of even the poorest Dhanetah Juts is notably absent.

Fig. 5 The bridal blouses of the Rabaris of central Kutch are heavily embroidered with bright colours and large mirrors, but once they wear out they are replaced with dark, dull fabrics, often devoid of mirrors. The embroidery skills developed to produce the elaborate dowry embroidery are applied to children's clothes and eventually to the dowry embroideries of the next generation.

SYMBOLIC MEANING WITHIN THE TRADITIONAL HINDU AND MUSLIM HOUSES OF GUJARAT (INDIA) AND LAMU (KENYA)[1]

Linda Wiley Donley

Indian Ocean trade, made possible by the monsoon winds, has linked parts of India and Eastern Africa for centuries. To study one area without considering the other would lead to an incomplete understanding of both. Not to place an investigation within a specific historical and social context would certainly lead to misinterpretations of data. This paper is primarily based on two years of ethnographic research in the Lamu archipelago, off the coast of Kenya, and a nine-week comparative study of traditional houses in the trade-linked port towns of Gujarat, northwestern India (Figs. 1,2). The research in India was extremely limited and much of my interpretation is based on the excellent work of two Indian scholars, Professor R S Khare and Dr V S Pramar.

The traditional houses in Gujarat and the Lamu area which were studied were built during the last half of the eighteenth century and the first half of the nineteenth century. During the period leading up to this time few Africans had immigrated to India and very few Indians lived in Africa, although the trade had started in the first century AD (Schoff 1912; Gopal 1975). Arabs had settled in both East Africa and India and many Hindus had converted to Islam by the sixteenth century. At this time the Portuguese had control of the trade between India and Africa, but, as Gregory points out, the Indians did not lose their links with Africa even during this period. They continued to work for the Portuguese just as they had done for the earlier and later Muslims who had controlled the trade and many of the settlements (Gregory 1971,16). For example, in 1593 Indian masons were employed by Portuguese for the construction of Fort Jesus at Mombasa. In the seventeenth century, after Portuguese power was diminished, contact between India and Africa increased because of the Indian market for the grains produced on the African slave plantations, and the demand for African ivory (Sheriff 1971, 42,306). The part of India most associated with the Lamu area was the major seventeenth-century port near modern Surat and the areas to the north, Saurashtra (the recently revived name for Kathiawar) and Kutch (Kaccha, Kachchh or Cutch). This whole area is the present-day state of Gujarat.

Drought and unseasonable rainfall are common in Gujarat, and men were often forced to emigrate to Africa for employment, but they returned home and/or sent their earnings back to their families in India. As late as 1870 high caste Hindu traders could not bring their wives to Africa (Sheriff 1971,354; Gregory 1971,34; Mangat 1969,13; Pearce 1920,98). Hindus were not allowed to marry outside their caste (O'Malley 1932,95). Indian Muslim traders, Khoja and Bohra, who were converted Hindus, were the first to settle in East Africa, probably not before the middle of the nineteenth century in the Lamu area. However, the number of male emigrant workers who worked outside Gujarat was considerable. There are no figures before 1862, but to give an impression of the numbers the following data were given for traders, artisans, masons, blacksmiths and weavers leaving Kutch in 1862 - 25,000; 1863 - 35,000; 1864 - 23,000; 1865 - 23,750, and so forth until in 1875 50,000 were going to Africa, Arabia or Persia for employment (Gazetteer of the Bombay Presidency: Vol.V, Kutch, 1880, 102). These skilled Indians had an impact on the material culture, the houses and their contents, of the Lamu archipelago. But how similar was the symbolic meaning of these domestic spaces and artifacts within a different social setting?

To discover the symbolic meaning contained in the features of traditional eighteenth and nineteenth-century houses, both in India and Africa, it was considered necessary to study families living in houses which they claimed were built during that period by their ancestors. Within the belief systems of Hinduism and Islam, change is slow and therefore ethnographic research was relevant to the understanding of the earlier house form. The relationships between the occupants, domestic spaces and objects during ritual and mundane activities revealed the symbolic meaning of each of the three main elements: people, places and objects. People create or attribute social meaning to spaces and objects, but once this meaning is established, within daily and ritual activities, it is capable, by association, of playing a part in the maintenance of a given symbolic system, i.e. objects and domestic spaces may give social meaning to certain people, and are therefore not merely a background for social action.

My investigation of Hindu and Muslim houses has taken cues from house studies by the following anthropologists: Bourdieu (1962, 1977), Douglas (1966, 1972, 1979), Tambiah (1969), Humphrey (1974), Ardener (1981), and, the most directly relevant, Khare (1976a, 1976b). A few house features have been selected to point out how a social system marks boundaries around itself, to set it apart from others, which may be competing social systems, and how categories of persons are maintained within a given system. For example, the social system may be Hindu or Muslim, but within either system there may be subcastes, slaves, concubines and a hierarchy between men and women and elders. Social status in both the Hindu and Afro-Arab (Swahili) context is based on a concept of religious or ritual purity (Dumont and Pocock 1959; Dumont 1980; El Zein 1974). What is 'outside' their social order is seen as threatening in that contact may be defiling and thereby cause a loss of status. The Muslims in Africa are a small minority, and therefore anxious about their social margins. The Hindu caste system, while embracing all minorities, embraces them each as a distinctive, cultural sub-unit. In any given locality, any sub-caste is likely to be a minority (Douglas 1966, 124). The Muslim and Hindu houses discussed in this paper, as in the other studies of houses by the anthropologists quoted above, are considered to be a metaphor of their bounded social systems. In both types of traditional houses there is evidence of anxiety about the margins of the house, and therefore also of the boundaries of each system. This concern is represented in the protective charms associated with doorways.

Many traditional Hindu houses were built around a shared courtyard (pol) with one main gate. A room set aside for male elders was located above the gate. This gate marked the settlement boundary and was guarded not only by the elders or religious leaders who lived above it, but also by symbols of various gods and goddesses (Fig. 3). Individual houses also have these protective markers located around the doorway (Fig. 4). The following were common to the Hindu houses studied in Gujarat: 1) the elephant god, Gaṇeśa, carved in stone or wood; 2) the lotus flower, which is the symbol of the goddess Lakṣmī; 3) a peacock, a bird with sacred associations for Hindus; 4) mango leaves, either fresh or carved on the door lintel. Some of these are specifically intended to protect the fertility or wealth of the household, features linked to the purity or status of the occupants.

Rituals establish and reinforce these boundary markers. An elaborate ceremony is performed at the time when the door is erected at a new house site. This was traditionally the first step in building a house and was done before the walls were constructed or, in fact, the foundation was laid. Some houses have lamp niches with stepped arches (like the dome of a Hindu temple) on each side of the main door where the ritual burning of ghee protects the inhabitants of the house (Fig. 3). Daily prayers (pūjā) are also performed on the threshold of Hindu houses. It is part of a ritual purification which protects the house and those within from the evil and defilement of outsiders. There are times of course when a mechanism is needed to allow 'outsiders' to cross these boundaries, for example, when a bride is brought into her husband's household. A ritual mediates and marks her passage. Women are powerful within the patrilocal Hindu society because they are the ones most directly responsible for the purity of their caste. The caste of a child is always that of its mother (Douglas 1966, 125). Women, in one sense 'outsiders' to their husbands' households, are seen as the source of inauspicious events (Cormack 1961, 164). Their passage into and out of the household must be clearly marked. If a woman dies in childbirth, a nail is placed in the threshold of the door to prevent her bad spirit from returning to the house to cause the death of future infants that might be born within the household. And if the husband intends to remarry, as he is expected to do, he may not accompany his wife's bier to the cremation ground and ties a piece of her sari to the door lintel to symbolize his interest in having a new wife.

Figurative Hindu symbols, such as the elephant god, Gaṇeśa, are never found on Muslim houses either in India or East Africa because they are believed to prevent angels from entering the house. Carved lotus flowers, mango leaves and peacocks are, however, common Hindu motifs found on Muslim doors both in Gujarat and Kenya. The craftsmen who worked stone and wood were for the most part Hindus, both in India and Africa. Slave labour certainly made the construction of the large number of grand houses built in Lamu in the late eighteenth and early nineteenth century possible, but they lacked the specialised skills that the immigrant Hindu craftsmen had to offer. The fact that the craftsmen were Hindu and that the earliest Indian Muslim settlers in Eastern Africa were Bohra (converted Hindus) explains the tendency toward Hindu symbols on doors both in India and Kenya. In Lamu the earlier stone houses owned by local Sunni Muslims have doors with only a few mango leaves and lotus flowers on the centre posts. The Lamu shopfront houses on the main street were built later for, or by, Shia (Bohra) Muslims and have more elaborate carving, not only with leaves and lotus flowers, but also the sacred peacock protecting the doorways to their businesses and homes. Muslims often ordered inscriptions from the Holy Koran to be carved on their door lintels. In Gujarat an arch, similar in style to a mihrab or prayer niche in a mosque, replaces the central figure of Gaṇeśa, most common on Hindu doors. Bohra Muslims, a large trading community in Gujarat and Lamu, have many practices that are related to the fact that their ancestors were Hindus. They often use a photograph of their religious leader as a protective charm over the doorways within the house in the same way as drawings of gods and goddesses are used in Hindu homes. Various protective symbols are used by both Muslims and Hindus as well as many other ethnic groups, to protect the entrances of their homes and compounds. When houses are seen as metaphors of their social systems it is easier to understand why the marginal area, the exterior doors, require special attention by threatened minority groups.

It is not only marginal areas of the house which are given symbolic meaning, but also internal spaces, features and objects. Their symbolic value reinforced and/or established a social hierarchy within family units. From this discussion a basic knowledge of the house plan of traditional houses in Gujarat and the Lamu area is necessary. My sample was too small in Gujarat to be able to establish characteristic types, and therefore I am grateful to Dr V S Pramar for his extensive study of

Gujarat house styles (1980). He has described three types of houses found in basically three areas of Gujarat, and my limited survey supported his findings (Fig. 5): 1) the South Gujarat (Bombay to Broach) house type has two or three parallel rooms with a passage along one side connecting a men's area in the front, and a back door near where the women, hearth and valuables are located; 2) the North Gujarat (north of Broach, the Ahmedabad, Baroda, Cambay area) house type which also has the 'deep house' plan of three parallel rooms one behind the other. However, the middle room has a chowk opening to the sky and there is no rear door, unlike the southern type. A passage runs through the centre of the dwelling. Men work or entertain guests in the front of the house and women usually cook and perform daily activities around the chowk or in the rear of the house. Wall niches are common in the thick walls of this type of house. Each room is at a slightly higher level, the back room being the highest, darkest and most private. This house form is the closest to the Swahili eighteenth and nineteenth-century traders' houses in the Lamu area; 3) the third type of Gujarat house set out by Dr Pramar was the Saurashtra and Kutch style. These houses commonly have a large walled courtyard attached to the front of the house which is used for livestock. The house has a long, usually open, verandah, with two small rooms to the rear. When men are present women are usually in the rear rooms, but when men are out of the house and courtyard the women move forward. This is the most common pattern in both Hindu and Muslim houses in Lamu and Gujarat households; men use the front areas of the house and women's areas are at the back. Seclusion of women, stressed within Islam, is a contributing factor even in the Hindu belief system because it was linked with the social status of wealthy Moghul rulers (Shibani 1979, 120), and as mentioned above, with the control of women who determined the purity of the lineage or caste. The Swahili eighteenth and nineteenth-century houses, as all the Gujarat house types, have a 'deep plan': long narrow rooms one behind the other. As in the north Gujarat plan, the houses have a passage down the centre and no rear door. Also, in common with this northern plan, wall niches are also numerous. The Swahili house does not have a chowk in the rear, but has a large open courtyard in the front, similar to the Saurashtra and Kutch floor plan. If a Hindu house has bathing and lavatory facilities they are frequently located at the gate of the pol, or they are found at the front of the house near the street. Lamu houses usually have two such areas, one in the front of the house, and one in the back. The presence and position of these pit toilets and bathing areas, and the fact that cooking is done in the rear of all Hindu houses and in the front areas of Lamu houses, marks the major differences in basic form and function. If any of the traditional houses, Hindu or Muslim in Gujarat or Lamu, had a second floor level, the pattern of use and the corresponding house plan were repeated, the upper level being more often the prized area of the house. Therefore, the upper front was generally used by men to entertain guests, if sufficiently separated from the women's area in the house.

The most important symbolic pattern within a Hindu house plan is that, as people move from the front of the house to the rear, they move from impure and public space to pure and private space. Toilets and bathing facilities should be separate, but near each other, 'for after defecation the least time and distance should be involved in reaching the area of purification; cooking and worshipping places should be as far away as possible from these, but adjacent to each other (facilitating the offering the pure food to the domestic deity with, again, the least involvement of time and distance once the cooked food - symbolizing a transitional stage - is ready); and the pure and impure spaces should neither be facing towards each other nor located on the same side, nor should they be in the same enclosure' (Khare 1976b, 30). 'A food area is always...located in an interior (and ritually pure) part of the house.' (Khare, op.cit., 26). The cooking area should be located physically distant from the waste or disposal area, separate from the sleeping, sitting and guest rooms, and near the water supply. The Hindu cooking area mirrors 'most effectively the social and cultural world surrounding it at any particular moment. It [is] literally ... a structured space *par excellence*, where widely different relationships from myth, ritual and kinship, denoting a host of different meanings, are sorted out and arranged in unambiguous relations' (Khare, op.cit., 28). 'One approximate measure for determining the ritual rank of the food area (at any particular point of time) can be obtained by finding out what [persons,] ritual objects, activities, situations and relationships can be either included in it or excluded from it' (Khare op.cit., 32). If a lower caste person is in the process of washing and replastering the cooking area, its rank is low, but once that person leaves and the area has dried, the rank is 'next' to the worshipping place. Normally the living spaces are ritually pure but become impure when used during the maternity period for forty days, or by a woman during her period of menstruation. A woman in either state is not allowed to prepare food for the family or even to enter the cooking area. Her impurity is stronger and more dangerous than that of a lower caste person or an untouchable (Cormack 1961, 70; Khare 1976b). 'A person in ordinary or neutral state accordingly becomes impure upon entering the maternity place' (Khare op.cit., 29). From these few examples the general pattern of relationships that create meaning for spaces, objects and persons within the Hindu belief system can be seen to be based on purity and the position of women. Women are important in maintaining the purity of the caste lineage, the cultural heritage, by teaching and performing the household rituals, and are related to the image of the Mother Goddess (Cormack 1961, 149, 152, 154, 161). However, they are second to men because of their basic biological impurities, and are reminded of this fact in the polluting effect they can have on the household objects and spaces. Only death within the household can cause stronger pollution. The hearth reflects the ritual condition of a house when a wedding is in progress the cooking area expands; when someone has died, no cooking takes place in the house for several days (Khare 1976b, 171). The meaning or value of a space within the house can be altered by ritual events or the ritual condition of persons entering a space, although there is a general pattern that can be seen under normal conditions.

In the Muslim houses studied, as in the Hindu houses, the area near the front of the dwelling is more associated with men, public space and impurity. Men in both societies spend little time in the house, and if they do conduct their business from their homes, an extra room is generally added to the front of the house for this purpose. In the Muslim houses, like the Hindu pattern, most interior rooms of the house are associated with ritual activities and the seclusion of women. Cooking is not, within Islam, a ritual activity as it is to Hindus, and therefore the location does not require religious purity. The kitchen may in fact be located near a latrine area, and menstruating women may prepare food for the family. There is also no Hindu shrine equivalent or especially designated area for prayers. Bathing areas and latrines are to be found in both the front and rear of the Muslim houses, and the only stated concern is that married couples who sleep together should have one near their room to use for ablutions after sexual intercourse and/or before saying their prayers or coming into contact with other people. Traditionally, married Hindu couples slept in separate rooms and sexual intercourse, considered a very polluting activity, did not take place in the house.

The spaces of the Muslim houses increase with distance from the front in their ritual value, but not necessarily in their purity, as in the Hindu houses. The innermost rooms of the Muslim houses, both in Lamu and Gujarat, were the spaces used during activities that are associated with the impurity of birth, death and sexual intercourse, and yet are restricted to the highest status freeborn members of the family. Concubines and domestic slaves were limited to the outer, and if a two-storey dwelling, lower, areas of the house. However, even the freeborn mistress of the household, who in Lamu may even own the house and will surely determine the purity of her husband's lineage, will be considered defiling to her household for forty days after childbirth. And she will not be allowed to pray during her menstrual periods because of her impurity (Donley 1982). Muslim women are as powerful as Hindu women in the daily running of the household and concerning rituals that are performed within the house, but like the Hindu women they are taught to believe that they contain a basic impurity connected to their procreative powers which makes them inferior to their husbands and to men in general. The houses may be primarily associated with women but they are not equal to the mosques or temples.

The general orientation of the house is seen as important in both Islamic and Hindu belief systems. The door of a Hindu house should ideally be facing north or east (Das 1977) and a Muslim house should be on the same axis as Mecca, which is west from India and north of Lamu. All the Shia (Bohra) Muslims, formerly from India, live in houses on an east-west axis in Lamu, while the Sunni Muslim houses are basically on the north-south axis in alignment with Mecca. The floor plan of the houses occupied by the Shia Muslims in Lamu is the north Gujarat plan with the lower front part used in all cases as a shop, which was also the most common arrangement in commercial Bohra settlements in Gujarat. It seems that the converted Bohra in India had all the Hindu and Muslim directional advantages by building on the east-west axis, east for the Hindu belief system and west for Mecca. In Lamu, the Bohra shops/houses were built on reclaimed land that ran along the harbour, excellent for commercial reasons but more suitably orientated for a Hindu than for a Muslim.

Another factor, concerned with the general nature of a Hindu house, is its ideal shape. The walls splay out, making the rear of the house less than a metre larger than the front room of the house. This is called a cow-faced house or gaumukhi; the reverse, a tiger-faced house, vaghmukhi (Fig. 5), is less auspicious. The difference required is so slight that I am unable to say what percentage of the houses studied may have reflected this characteristic.

A final general fact, also concerned with Hindu building practices, relates to the auspicious placing of niches. The lamp niches located outside a Hindu house have been mentioned, but niches are also a dominant feature within the north Gujarat and the Saurashtra/Kutch house types as set out by Pramar. Niches are related to all openings, be they other niches or doors. All must be 'balanced', and to accomplish this each door or niche must face and line up with another; if not vedha occurs, which is inauspicious.[2] The vedha, or lack of 'balance', is an unstable condition which is believed to cause the inhabitants of the house to be unable to balance their accounts, to reproduce at the desired rate, or be harmonious within their extended family; they may even die as a result. On the northern Swahili coast, coral houses started to have wall niches from the mid-fourteenth century, and the niches increased as time passed. (See house plans at Shanga: Horton, 1984. figs. 18, 20 and 23.) Shanga, the oldest northern Swahili site with standing walls, has houses with niches opposite doors. They are 'balanced'. This indicates the presence of Hindu craftsmen actively influencing the building of the houses that are now the pride of Swahili culture.

Why should niches, gokala, have such power within the Hindu context? Like other symbols, the meaning may be ambiguous, but clues to the ascribed meaning may be found within the cultural context. Meaning is often, if not always, learned or transmitted through action. And therefore we must look at all of the ways gokala are used. As noted above they can house the diva lamp which is known to be the sign of knowledge. Its shape was related to the temple, but not all niches have this form or function. Most of those inside the house are large and rectangular. Only niches near the doors are for lamps. Lamu houses also have lamp niches near doorways. Rectangular niches may be used to house a family deity. There is a large, central and elaborately decorated niche, called ariyo, in most Saurashtra houses where the family god or goddess was said to have lived in the past, but in all of the houses visited it was used as a cupboard without any obvious religious overtones. In a north Gujarat house that had many wall niches, one was noted that had been blocked, but carefully white-washed around, and thus not, as was stated, showing disrespect to the location of the niche. Later, it was learned that a broken deity had been placed in this niche. The 'life' had been removed, but a spirit of the deity, with not necessarily good powers, could haunt the area. People are also warned to check niches, because enemies place dough figures in such places to curse the household. Gokala seem to house powerful ideas of both good and bad and have therefore been areas of interest and attention in the Hindu house.

Bohra Muslims, in Gujarat and Lamu, whose ancestors were Hindu, practise many Hindu customs and perhaps their symbolic use of niches carries some of the meaning associated with the Hindu belief system. In the earliest mosques, which were built from materials taken from Hindu temples, the idols housed in niches were broken and removed but the niches remained as a part of the surface decoration. This can clearly be seen in the Friday Mosque at Broach. On the innermost wall of many Bohra houses in Gujarat (north Gujarat plan) was located a five foot square, the naukhanah, composed of nine niches made of wood but set into the wall (Figs. 6,7). The niches were usually filled with imported porcelain (Bombay Gazette 1899, 93). Swahili traditional houses have rows of plaster niches, called zidaka, in the same position within the house (Fig. 8). However, there were never as few as nine, or framed with wood, although they were also filled with imported porcelain. Zidaka or naukhanah were never a part of the Bohra houses in East Africa. During the survey of Bohra wards of Mandvi and Mandra in Kutch and Rander near Surat, it was noted that one house in each town has plaster niches very similar to the Lamu zidaka (Fig. 9). It will be remembered that this was the area from which most of the Hindu craftsmen came who worked in Africa during famine years in Gujarat. The plaster niches in Bohra houses were shaped like the mihrab of the local mosque and, most importantly, were located only in the houses of Bohra religious leaders (Figs. 9, 10). Upon further questioning it was learned that these rows of small niches were considered a religious charm with powerful protective qualities. They were constructed of a durable material, i.e. not wood, often white-washed to represent their purity, and were never to be destroyed or allowed to decay. They were also associated with the magic squares of nine, which contain the names of Allah that are often placed over doorways, and the nine wooden squares of the naukhanah. Zidaka were not found in Swahili houses after the Bohra community settled in Lamu in the late nineteenth century. Plaster niches, associated only with religious leaders in India, would have been considered a sacrilege in the average Swahili Muslim house. Once Bohra traders began to settle in Lamu, the practice of the Hindu craftsmen might have been influenced by the Bohra beliefs. Perhaps earlier, in the eighteenth century, it had only been known to the Hindu craftsmen that plaster niches were an auspicious and protective Muslim decoration. If their clients wanted Muslim, rather than Hindu, plaster decorations, as the Swahili certainly would have, this was what they were given. As has been described in some detail in an earlier paper (Donley 1982), the mihrab-shaped niches are found where defilement is strongest in the Swahili houses. They are located in the innermost room, the ndani, where birth, death and sexual intercourse take place, and over the pit toilets. These are also areas most associated with women. Even the pit toilets were required inside the house as a result of the seclusion of women. The status of the family was linked to its religious purity, and many of the house features and spaces were given symbolic meaning intended to support that goal.

The symbolic meaning contained in the traditional Hindu and Muslim houses of Gujarat and Lamu has been explored within a social and historical context. Each group has no doubt influenced the other in some respects, but the fact that Hindu women did not accompany their husbands, who were traders and craftsmen, meant that Hindus did not settle in Eastern Africa, and their practices did not give meaning to objects and spaces within the house. The symbolic meaning within the Hindu and Muslim houses studied was dependant on the position attributed to women. It was her relationship to men and other women, as well as spaces and objects in the house, which created the pattern of social order. The house cannot be a metaphor of society without a woman inside.

Acknowledgements

I am pleased to acknowledge assistance from the following sources: the L S B Leakey Foundation, the Wenner-Gren Foundation for Anthropological Research, the Sir Bartle Frere Memorial Fund, the Smuts Memorial Fund, the Peter Scott Trust, the Crowther-Beynon Fund, and King's College Cambridge. The National Museums of Kenya, the South Gujarat University in Surat, and the School of Architecture and Planning in Ahmedabad all gave assistance and support to the project. I am particularly indebted to my research assistant, Mr Dilip D Patel. Other field assistants and scholars in England, Kenya and India are too numerous to name, but that in no way diminishes my indebtedness and gratitude. I would like to thank Mrs S Leakey for typing the original manuscript and Mr J Leslie for providing the house drawings and maps.

Notes

1. Fieldwork was undertaken in Kenya during most of 1980 and 1981. There was an ethnographic study of thirty-seven Swahili houses located in Lamu, Shela and Pate towns during that period. Measured drawings of the floor plans of each house were made, notes on the location of artifacts, and when and how these were placed in relation to the floor plan was recorded. The categories of person (age, sex, position in the household) who used various spaces and objects was observed within the context of daily and ritual activities. The nine-week comparative study, of twenty-one traditional houses in trade-linked port towns of Gujarat was

conducted in early 1981. The towns included in the survey were: Bombay, Daman, Navsari, Surat, Rander, Broach, Dholka, Baroda, Cambay, Ahmedabad Bhavnagar, Mahuva, Diu, Porbandar, Jamnagar, Tuna, Anjar, Bhuj, Mandvi, Mundra, Jafrabad, Patan and Sidpur.

2. Swahili houses have large singular wall niches, called kidaka, in the outer two rooms of the house, msana wa juu and msana wa tini, which are 'balanced'. See Fig. 5 for location of niches on end walls. For additional information about Swahili and Indian houses see Donley (1984 and 1987).

References

Ardener, S (ed.) 1981. Women and Space: Ground Rules and Social Maps. London

Bombay Gazette 1899. Gujarat Population Musalmans and Parsis, IX Part II

Bourdieu, P 1962. The Algerians. Boston

Bourdieu, P 1977. Outline of a Theory of Practice. Cambridge

Cormack, M 1961. The Hindu Woman. London

Das, V 1977. Structure and Cognition: Aspects of Hindu Caste and Ritual. Delhi

Donley, L 1982. House power; Swahili space and symbolic markers. In Symbolic and Structural Archaeology, I. Hodder (ed.). Cambridge

Donley, L 1984. The Social Uses of Swahili Spaces and Objects. Ph.D. thesis, University of Cambridge

Donley, L 1987. Life in the Swahili Town House Reveals the Symbolic Meaning of Spaces and Artefact Assemblages. The African Archaeological Review, 5, 181-92

Douglas, M 1966. Purity and Danger: an Analysis of Concepts of Pollution and Taboo, London and Henley

Douglas, M 1972. Symbolic orders in the use of domestic space. In Man, Settlement and Urbanism, Ucko, P, Tringham, R and Dimbleby, G (eds.), London

Douglas, M and Isherwood, B 1979. The World of Goods. New York

Dumont, L 1966 (1980). Homo Hierarchicus: the Caste System and Its Implications. Chicago (Rev. and trans. 1980)

Dumont, L and Pocock, D 1959. Pure and impure. Contributions to Indian Sociology, 3, 9-30

Gazetteer of the Bombay Presidency 1880. Vol V. Kutch

Gopal, S 1975. Commerce and Crafts in Gujarat in the 16th and 17th Centuries: a Study in the Impact of European Expansion of Precapitalist Economy. New Delhi

Gregory, R 1971. India and East Africa: a History of Race Relations within the British Empire 1890-1939. Oxford

Horton, M A 1984. The Early Settlement of the Northern Swahili Coast. Ph.D. thesis, University of Cambridge

Humphrey, C 1974. Inside a Mongolian tent. New Society, October, 273-5

Khare, R S 1976a. Culture and Reality: Essays on the Hindu System of Managing Foods. Simla

Khare, R S 1976b. The Hindu Hearth and Home. Bombay

Mangat, J S 1969. A History of the Asians in East Africa. Oxford

O'Malley, L S 1932. Indian Caste Customs. Cambridge

Pearce, Major F B 1920. Zanzibar: the Island Metropolis of Eastern Africa. London

Pramar, V S 1980. Wooden architecture of Gujarat. Ph.D. thesis, University of Baroda

Schoff, W H 1912. The Periplus of the Erythrean Sea. London

Sheriff, A 1971. The rise of a commercial empire; an aspect of the economic history of Zanzibar 1770-1873. Ph.D. thesis, University of London

Shibani, R 1979. Status of Muslim Women in North India. Delhi

Tambiah, S J 1969. Animals are good to think and good to prohibit. Ethnology, 7, 423-59

El Zein, A H 1974. The Sacred Meadows: a Structural Analysis of Religious Symbolism in an African Town. Evanston, Illinois

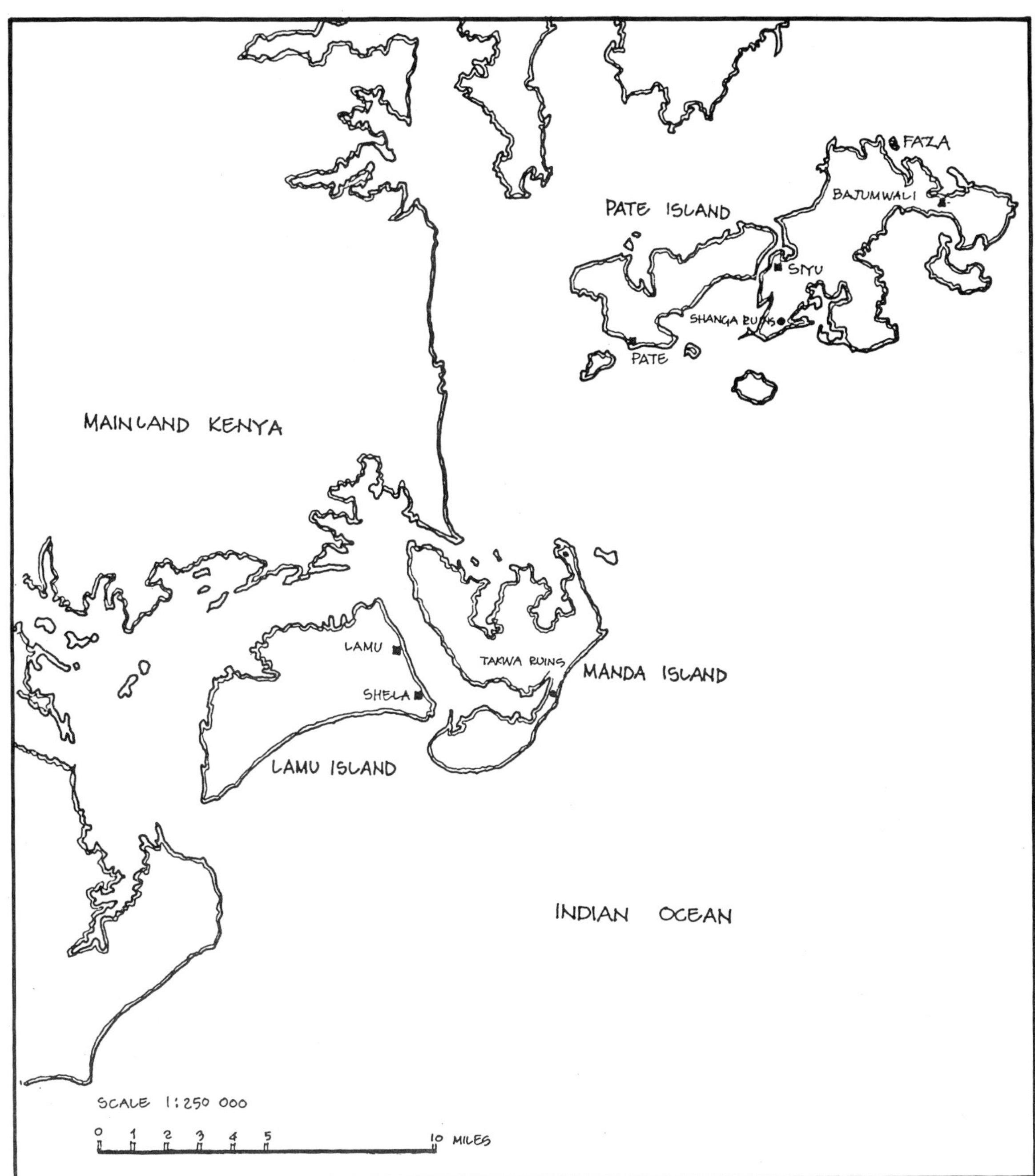

Fig. 1 The Lamu Archipelago.

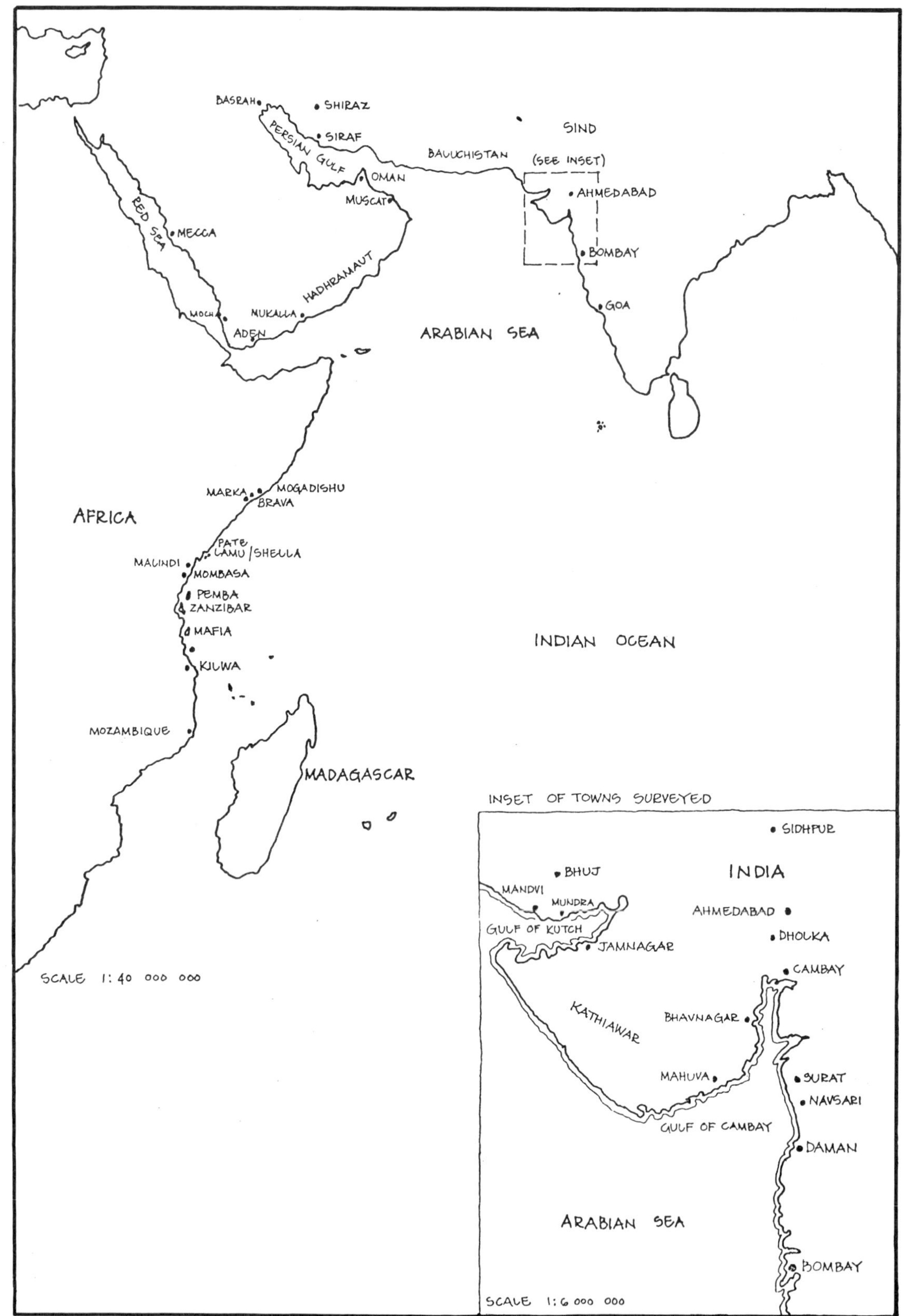

Fig. 2 The Western Indian Ocean.

Fig. 3 Pol, settlement gate.

Fig. 4 House door in Gujarat.

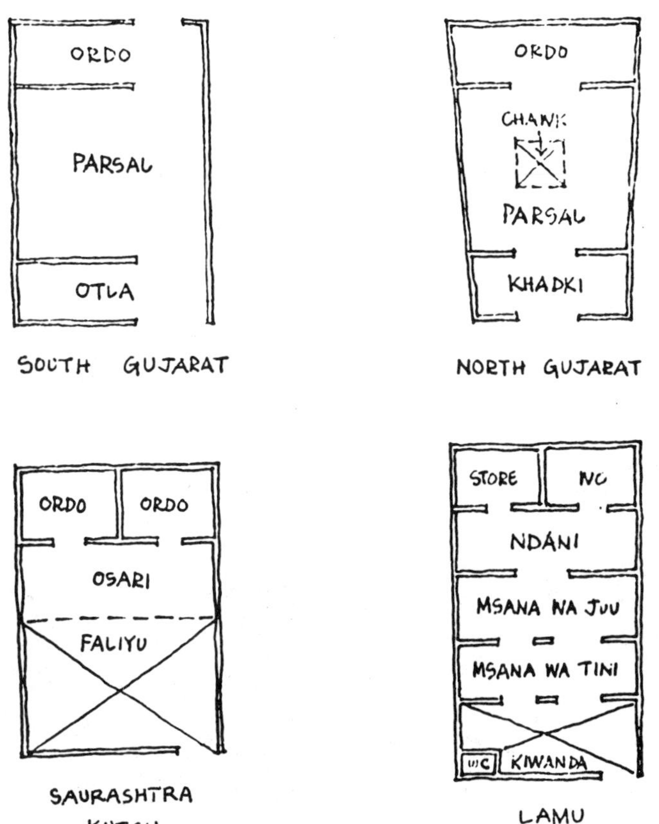

Fig. 5 House plans.

Fig. 6 Wooden niches, naukhanah, in Bohra house.

Fig. 7 Naukhanah within the inner room of a Bohra house in Dholka.

Fig. 8 Zidaka, wall niches, in a Lamu house.

Fig. 9 Niches in a Bohra religious leader's house in Kutch.

Fig. 10 Mihrab, prayer niche, within a Bohra mosque.

AN ARCHITECTURAL STUDY OF RURAL/URBAN RELATIONS IN GUJARAT

V S Pramar

Village and town are usually thought of as two disparate phenomena, the one primitive and socially backward, the other sophisticated and socially progressive. However, as this study will show, this is not the case, at least so far as Gujarat is concerned. The author's fieldwork has been concerned with architecture and its sociology, and although the data collected has relevance to the whole of Gujarat, in this paper the analysis is restricted to north Gujarat, for two reasons. North Gujarat was the region which historically, culturally and economically had a dominant position in the whole province, and it produced the models which were followed by all other regions. It also produced a novel settlement-pattern which had a clearly defined social context and which served to formulate a complete life-style for its inhabitants.

It is first necessary, however, to clarify what is meant by the terms 'village' and 'town' in the context of northern Gujarat; empirical data have here been used to arrive at characterisations.

The typical village always contained a dominant caste which owned all the land and lived mainly by agriculture. The members of this caste were related to each other by common descent from the real or imaginary founder of the village. In contrast, a minority of the inhabitants belonged to different castes which owned no land and survived by performing the supporting services required by the dominant group; they included the carpenters, potters, sweepers, etc. All these supporting castes were thought of as 'outsiders' to the village and they were permitted only on sufferance to occupy sites in the village.

This caste and occupational difference was reflected in the village settlement-pattern: the dominant group always occupied the central part of the village while the minority was forced to occupy the periphery, or perhaps only one corner of the site. This corner also contained the village pond or tank, and it was adjacent to this that any strangers to the village were expected to camp - thus emphasising the fact that they too were 'outsiders'. It was also from here that the visitors were announced to the village by the local sweepers who acted as messengers. The pond, with its minority group, thus functioned as the formal 'entrance' to the village.

Turning now to the town, we find a somewhat different situation. Instead of one dominant caste, there were several important ones, all of which retained their separate identities and lived segregated in separate wards. Generally, each of these castes was a functional caste, that is to say, each specialised in a particular occupation, other than agriculture. There would be, for example, one group manufacturing cloth, another bleaching, a third dyeing or printing, a fourth selling it, and finally a fifth which financed the various stages of the whole process. All these urban occupations were interlinked and dependent upon each other - the urban castes were <u>commercial</u> castes. Among these various castes was some kind of tacit ranking in which those who only did financial transactions were placed at the top of the system, while those who performed manual work were at the bottom. However, at the same time, this tacit ranking did not give any caste a privileged position equivalent to that of the dominant caste in a village. All urban castes had an equal right of residence in the town and none was considered an 'outsider'. The only effect of ranking was that the upper financing and trading castes always occupied the central and most important areas of the town, while the lower manufacturing castes occupied the periphery. In some cases this hierarchical urban structure was oriented to the highest group of all, namely the political authority which occupied a citadel, although in many towns only merchants occupied the best sites.

As in the village the formal entrance to the town was also located next to the lake which bordered it, as for example the Kankaria lake at Ahmedabad, or the Sursagar at Baroda. Mughal governors, and even emperors, are known to have halted in traditional fashion at the Kankaria before formally entering Ahmedabad. It is striking to find this village custom being emulated even by royalty.

From this characterisation of village and town, some important conclusions can be drawn. The village, with its single dominant caste, could never have autonomously developed into a town, for the following reasons: a) the dominant caste would never allow any other important caste to settle in the village with equal rights of residence, for by doing so it would lose its own privileged position. Without such a multiplicity of castes, however, no commercial town was viable; b) the dominant caste could, in theory, split up into sub-groups which would then take up various commercial and manufacturing occupations and thus produce the required urban diversity. In practice this was not feasible, as the dominant caste would never take up an occupation which lowered its own status, and many of the manual occupations were of low status; to engage in them would result in putting oneself outside one's caste. The only occupation which a caste of farmers could honourably take to was trade and finance, and this frequently occured when the caste migrated to a town. There are, for example, small wards in Ahmedabad inhabited by Patels from Mehsana who came to the town, settled and took to business.

However, if the village could not develop into a town, how did the town arise? (The purely administrative or garrison town is set aside, being an exception to the rule). There are two theoretical possibilities: i) that a group of traders and financiers would form a settlement and then invite the manufacturing castes to settle on the periphery. This would explain the hierarchical structure of the town; ii) that the political authority would itself establish a town to encourage commerce (for this would bring in good revenue) and allot wards hierarchically from the very beginning. There are two good examples of the second alternative. Ahmedabad and Baroda were both founded by the Muslim rulers of Gujarat and in both of them one finds the central area firmly inhabited by merchants who were Hindus or Jains. Two smaller towns founded by feudatories of the period, namely Palanpur and Radhanpur, show an identical arrangement. One known example of the first alternative is Surat where a famous Hindu trader, Malek Gopi, founded an important part of the town in the late fifteenth century. It would thus seem that both methods of foundation probably existed, and it is only by such an assumption that one can explain the hierarchical distribution of wards.

Turning now from generalisations to details, one may examine the village and town for some of their architectural qualities. The average village in Gujarat had no other significant architectural features apart from the residential areas, the occasional temple, and the pond. There was no defined place of assembly, either open or covered, no market, shop or inn; and not even a regular bazaar. The Census of India volume of 1911 on Bombay (which then included Gujarat) reported 'Thirty years ago, there were no shops to be seen in villages, and the villagers had to go to the nearest town for the purchase of such articles as cloth, sugar, salt, etc' (Census of India 1911, 14). Marketing was traditionally done at the weekly bazaar which might be held at some large neighbouring village where people from smaller villages would gather. This extreme lack of architectural differentiation was only a reflection of the introvert, uni-caste, undifferentiated existence of the villagers themselves. As long as the villager remained bound to the fixed behaviour patterns of his village, he could not change over to a new occupation such as, for instance, being a shopkeeper. The baniya caste which traditionally operated trade, shops and the bazaars was not represented in the average village at all. There was little incentive for members of this caste to settle in such a village because the turnover was too small. Instead it was this caste which organised the weekly market, and by keeping different market days for different market centres, the same group of traders could circulate among them all and increase their business enormously.

Another reason for the lack of architectural differentiation was the nature of the social organization. The village was essentially a group of related families functioning on the basis of kinship. The very strength and closeness of family ties prevented the growth of any social institution which transcended or cut across kinship. Only when such transcending institutions exist can an architecture develop to house them. The kinship group, functioning at best from the village headman's house, had no need for anything but residences and that is precisely what we find in the average village.

Lastly, there was also a commonly held view that investment in any kind of 'building' was unproductive, and that all surplus should go into acquiring more land, cattle, implements, etc. In the list of priorities which operated in the mind of the villager, architecture came last. That is why so little investment was made even in the domestic house. The idea of having, for example, a community marriage hall or a place of assembly was quite unthinkable.

The same extreme lack of architectural differentiation is also found in the town. Since the town was primarily a commercial centre, one would expect to find specific features thought essential for a commercial existence - market buildings or market squares, a town hall, a place of judgement, inns, warehouses, etc. However, these are precisely the buildings and spaces which are conspicuously absent. In no town in Gujarat are there remains of any permanent market similar to, for example, the famous suq of west Asia. The only equivalent feature was the bazaar, but this was no more than an open ground on which petty shopkeepers erected their flimsy stalls of a temporary kind. In some cases these stalls lined the main roads and were, in much later times, converted into permanent shops. The town hall never existed, because even though there were various merchant groups in existence, they were organized on caste lines and met in the residence of their chief. There was never any transcending corporate body which required an institutional building. Justice lay in the hands of the political authority, and was located in its private domain. As for inns, the only feature found in some of the towns was the sarai, but this only appeared with the advent of the Muslims and was borrowed from west Asia. There was nothing similar built by the indigenous merchants themselves. The various Hindu urban castes no doubt had their communal halls (vadi), but their function was social rather than commercial. Neither Hindu nor Jain merchants had buildings specifically intended for commercial use.

The reason for all these omissions is that commercial activity was mainly carried out as an extension of the private domain. Business was primarily 'family business' organized along caste lines, and it was transacted in the family residence. The residence was modified to provide space for clients, or sometimes an extra wing was added - but it still remained a private domain. It is this essentially private/caste character of commerce which prevented institutional organizations or institutional buildings from appearing. It was enough merely to set aside a portion of the residence to be used as a workshop by the artisan, as a shop by the trader, and as a place for negotiations by the merchant. In this private, introverted attitude to commerce there is a striking similarity to the private attitude of the villager whose world was limited to family and clan.

Nevertheless the urban juxtaposition of family and business within the same premises had social consequences which could not be ignored: it brought clients and strangers into the residence and thus partially exposed the family to them. One mitigating factor, however, was that the Hindu female in Gujarat was never socially secluded as, for example, in north India or among orthodox Muslims. A certain degree of tolerance to strangers was thus part of the life-style. Despite this, however, some controls and barriers were required and these were provided by architecture.

It has already been mentioned that each urban caste occupied a segregated ward. The Gujarati word for such a ward is _khadki_ or _pol_. A khadki (Fig. 1) is a group of houses so arranged that a cul-de-sac is formed having a single entrance guarded by a gateway. When a number of such _khadki_ all lead off from a common road which is, in turn, guarded by one or two gateways, then this is called a _pol_. In other words the _pol_ is merely a combination of individual _khadki_. The members of a _khadki_ are generally all related to each other and are therefore of one caste. The families share a number of facilities in common: the open space in front, the gateway, a well, and sometimes the privies. It will be seen that this arrangement ensures a high degree of privacy and security to the families since no stranger can enter without at once being observed. In the past, the first floor of the gateway was used as a vantage point by elderly people to keep watch on movement into the _khadki_. It was this system of internal control which permitted the residence to be used freely as a place of business. The client, upon entering a _khadki_, was clearly passing from a public area into a private one, and was subjected to different norms of behaviour. While his business might be with one single family of the enclave, yet the collective group of families were all aware of his presence and he could not enter without their tacit consent. In this way a purely commercial transaction was surrounded by private participation.

The case of the _pol_ was not very different. A _pol_, being a collection of _khadki_, would theoretically contain a great variety of castes, but in practice it was always formed by those of an upper caste. _Pol_ members shared the maintenance of the gateway along with its complement of watchmen and messengers, a public well, public privies, and sweepers to remove the night-soil. The latter were usually settled in one corner of the _pol_ and also acted as messengers. Their location and functions were similar to those of the village sweepers, again suggesting the rural origin of this urban custom.

The urban _khadki_ which provided so much commercial security was not, however, an urban invention. Every agricultural village in north Gujarat was organized according to a system of _khadki_. The village _khadki_ was a defensive arrangement designed to resist plunder and intrusion, and David Pocock (1972, 76) has described each one as a fortress whose gates were closed at night, so that the whole village was a grouping of individual fortresses. The privacy, security and system of control which we see in urban _khadki_ was identical with that exercised in the rural one. The question which naturally arises is - what was the need for such extreme security in a rural habitat? A defensive village implies that those who settled in the village were immigrants who occupied territory belonging to a hostile indigenous population. Historical references suggest that Gujarat was once ruled by indigenous _koli_ and _bhil_ (_Mirat-i-Ahmadi_ 1965, 21) and that these turbulent people kept harassing towns and villages well into the eighteenth century. Striking support for this can be seen in south Gujarat where the situation is reversed. There the indigenous koli have retained their majority, and their own villages have scattered houses without any defensive grouping whatsoever.

The khadki settlement-pattern is thus common to both town and village, and its wide distribution in the latter indicates a rural origin. It was thus that the exposed village without an armed force at hand to protect it produced the defensive khadki. Obviously the arrangement was so advantageous that it was repeated in the town, even when the physical danger was mitigated by city fortifications. The reason for this was that the life-style which developed within the rural khadki had become so firmly established as the prototype, and its family-protective functions had proved so useful, that there was no need to change it in the urban context. The town dwellers took along with them the traditional rural settlement-pattern and inevitably its accompanying life-style. The fact that urban khadki were established clearly indicates that it was never a single family which migrated and settled in a town, but always a group sufficiently large to constitute a khadki. This conclusion would fit in with what was suggested above, namely, that towns were founded by allocating wards to specific groups.

Having shown that the town dweller was merely a transplanted villager, it remains to be shown that it was rural attitudes which continued to influence two important architectural spheres - the use of urban space, and house form.

The only common urban space, apart from the bazaar already described, was the area enclosed within the residential khadki. In the village this enclosed space was used to celebrate all the many functions and festivals in which adjoining families participated. In addition, during the day when the menfolk were away in the fields, it would be used as an extension of the house by the women for many of their domestic chores, and also for socializing; in the evenings it would serve the latter purpose for the men. Precisely this same usage can be observed in a remarkable manner in towns. Many of the urban khadki have, in recent times, had their gateways and enclosing end-walls dismantled to make way for urban traffic. This drastic change in function, however, has not altered the basic attitude of the resident. They still continue to use the 'road' for all community functions, such as marriages, holi, the garba dance during Navaratri, etc. Indeed, it continues to link the families and their children socially, for they all look upon the road as an extension of the house. Through traffic always has to give way before private convenience. Nothing, perhaps, emphasises the rural origin of the town dweller more than this usage. His conception of the town is not of an abstract entity which demands a higher loyalty to support it. Rather, to an introverted rural mentality, the town is symbolized in the small enclave which the group occupies.

Let us turn now to the house form, as seen in Fig. 2, which is the plan of a typical village house common to north Gujarat. It is from Dharmaj in Kheda District (the rear door is often absent in smaller, exposed villages). Along with it, in Figs. 3 and 4 are two typical urban houses from Ahmedabad. The rear portion of the urban house, the part beyond the court, is almost identical with that of Dharmaj. The rural house has three parts - a large rear room (ordo), spanned by a beam carried on two attached columns embedded in the side walls; a shallower central room (parsal); and a front veranda with columns (otlo). The same three parts, including the beam, appear in the rear part of the urban house and they carry the same names. The comparative functions of the three parts can be judged from the following table, which shows the striking similarity between rural and urban usage:

	Rural House	Urban House
ordo	Used for cooking, storage, women's private area.	Used for storage and women's private area.
parsal	Used mainly by women for daily chores; place of lying-in; used by men in bad weather.	Used mostly by women for daily chores; place of lying-in; entry into kitchen.
otlo	Used by men generally.	Used by both men and women.

What the urban house shows as a new element in the plan is the two-part front portion beyond the court, and also some smaller rooms to one side, containing the kitchen and well. The court (chowk), is the vital barrier between the 'front' and the 'back' of the house; it served to produce an architectural discontinuity which demarcated two disparate areas. The two-part front was deliberately added to meet commercial requirements. It was here that the artisan worked, the trader had his shop, and the merchant negotiated. The client located in this area could see the women working across the courtyard (as he could do in the village khadki), but he would not cross the court because that was the barrier between domestic and commercial spheres. The name for this front portion is also khadki, for it served the same function, namely, as an entrance at which strangers were checked. Whereas the rural enclave had a single communal khadki, the urban house introduced an individual khadki to receive strangers who could not conveniently be halted at the communal khadki. It is again a rural concept transposed into an urban setting.

One important point is that the urban house is not technically a courtyard or atrium house in concept. The court arises because the new addition has to be kept at a distance; it is a secondary phenomenon. However, once it is established it is made use of by adding side rooms, especially the kitchen, the smoke from which could now escape into the open. The entrance to the kitchen, however, generally remains concealed via the parsal.

There is a further interesting comparison related to the values assigned to the various floors. In the rural house the ground floor was where the kitchen was located, and hence it formed the nucleus of family life; the parents always stayed on this floor, thus giving it status. The first floor was traditionally considered inferior and was variously used for storage, or for the use of married sons or visitors. In the urban house the same values prevailed and influenced commercial usage. While the three-part rear of the dwelling was used almost exactly as in the rural house, a new use was found for the first floor of the two-part front. In those houses where a superior kind of client was expected, the first floor was developed into an elaborate reception hall, with carved ceilings and painted walls. The name given to this hall was divankhanu, in imitation of aristocratic Mughal practice. We find here an area traditionally utilized for rural visitors (the inferior first floor) is transformed into one for clients, thus perpetuating earlier values.

Some further minor examples of rural usage in the urban house are as follows: first, the location of the stairs in the former was always in the parsal (a relic of the ladder which once went to the loft), and it was extremely narrow and steep because, not only was it modelled on the ladder, but it went to an inferior floor. In the urban house the location of the stairs and its primitive design was retained, regardless of the opulence of the family. A rope was often hung from a hook at the top to enable one to maintain balance. Second, the floor of the rural house was traditionally made of earth finished with cow dung. The urban house had paving in many of its areas, particularly where verandas were exposed to the rain. However, in its two most intimate spaces, that is, the _ordo_ and _parsal_, the cow dung surfacing was retained, even though the supporting structure might be of the finest teak wood. Whatever part or function of the urban house that one examines, one finds, underlying it, a rural prototype, be it the absence of domestic furniture, the practice of sleeping on the floors, cleaning the teeth while seated on the front veranda, bathing in the open court, etc. All this evidence suggests that the town dweller was only a very slightly modified villager, and that the very term 'town dweller' is misleading in this context.

The last aspect which remains to be examined concerns the kind of social organization which accompanied the settlement-pattern. All households which occupied a common urban _pol_ were subject to certain rules regarding their duties and obligations, such as that all households had to contribute towards the maintenance of common facilities. No house could be sold to an outsider without first being offered to the members of the _pol_. Further, from the sale price a small percentage was deducted and paid into the common _pol_ fund (Gillon 1968, 25). At weddings, funerals and other major social events all the families of the _pol_ expected to be invited. Infringement of these rules resulted in fines which went into the common fund, the management of which was in the hands of the _pol_ leaders known as _seth_. The _pol_ organization was thus nothing more than that which already existed for any well organized caste. In other words, the _pol_ organization did not represent any new kind of institution to meet any new urban needs; rather it was a caste organization transferred to a multiple-caste settlement. Yet again the origin of this organization was the village.

The typical village had a dominant caste which ran its affairs along caste lines. It decided who was to be permitted to settle in the village and to define its location; it also owned all the land. The revenue system in Gujarat known as _narwadari_ was quite different from the _ryotwari_ system of north India. Whereas in the _ryotwari_ system each individual family was recognized as tenant, and paid revenue to the government, in the _narwadari_ it was the village as a whole which paid revenue through its _patel_. The total village land was sub-divided into shares known as _narwa_, and each family was alloted a certain number of _narwa_ shares of land, according to which it paid revenue to the _patel_ who passed it on to the government. This implied a far greater degree of social organization and was doubtless the generator of the urban _pol_ system.

Some conclusions can now be drawn from the above analysis of urban/rural relations. In northern Gujarat, the town was in reality nothing more than a collection of miniature villages settled by groups which had migrated from villages and brought with them not only their rural architectural forms but also rural attitudes and life-styles. An urban culture, distinct from the rural, never came into existence. Urban commercialization remained confined within a domesticity which was little different from that of a rural artisan. In short, if one assumes a 'village tradition' to be confined only to the village, then a distinction is being made which by no means corresponds to reality. Village tradition lies firmly embedded within the urban. The reality is that there is but one unified, homogenous cultural tradition common to both village and town in Gujarat, and the difference between the two is quantitative, not qualitative.

References

Census of India 1911. Vol XVI, Baroda

Gillon, K L 1968. Ahmedabad, A Study in Indian Urban History. Berkeley, University of California Press

Mirat-i-Ahmadi 1965. Trans. M F Lokhandwala, Oriental Institute, Baroda

Pocock, D T 1972. Kanbi and Patidar, Oxford

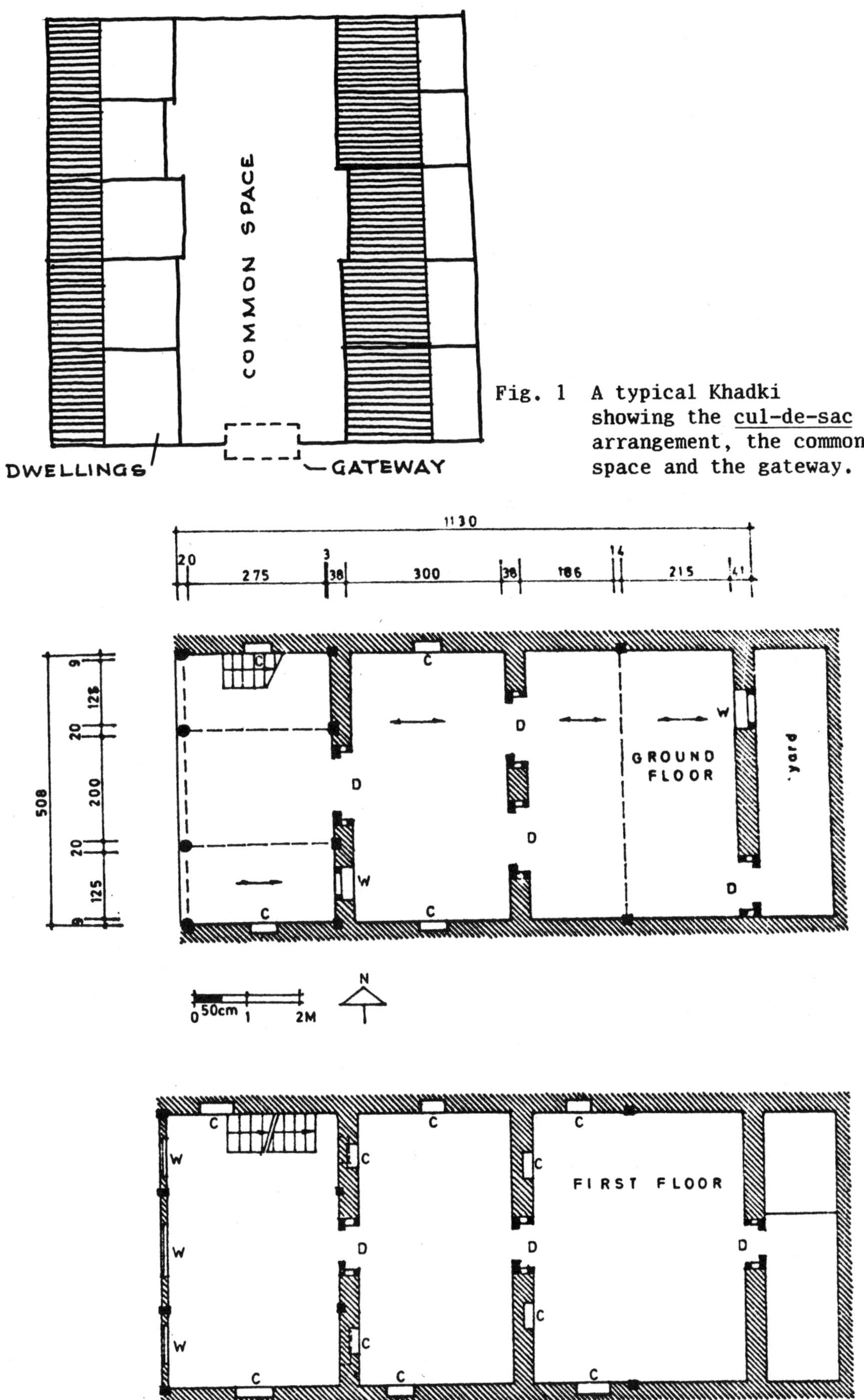

Fig. 1 A typical Khadki showing the <u>cul-de-sac</u> arrangement, the common space and the gateway.

Fig. 2 Typical rural house in Dharmaj.

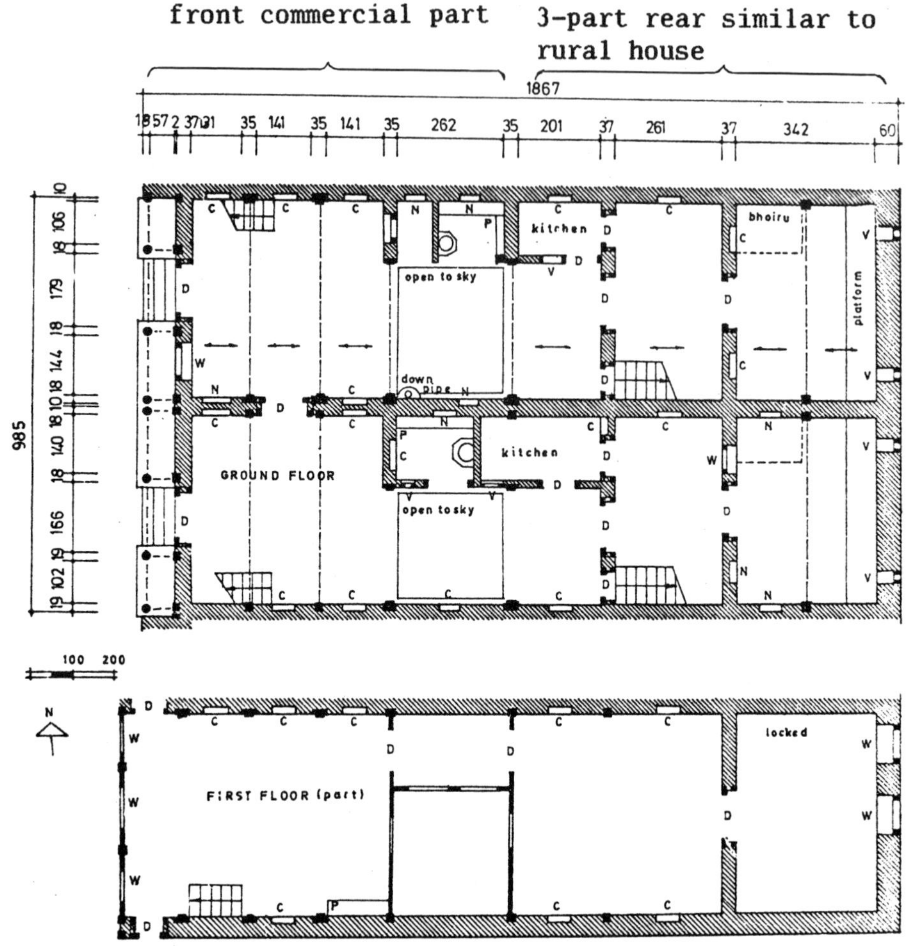

Fig. 3 Twin urban house in Ahmedabad.

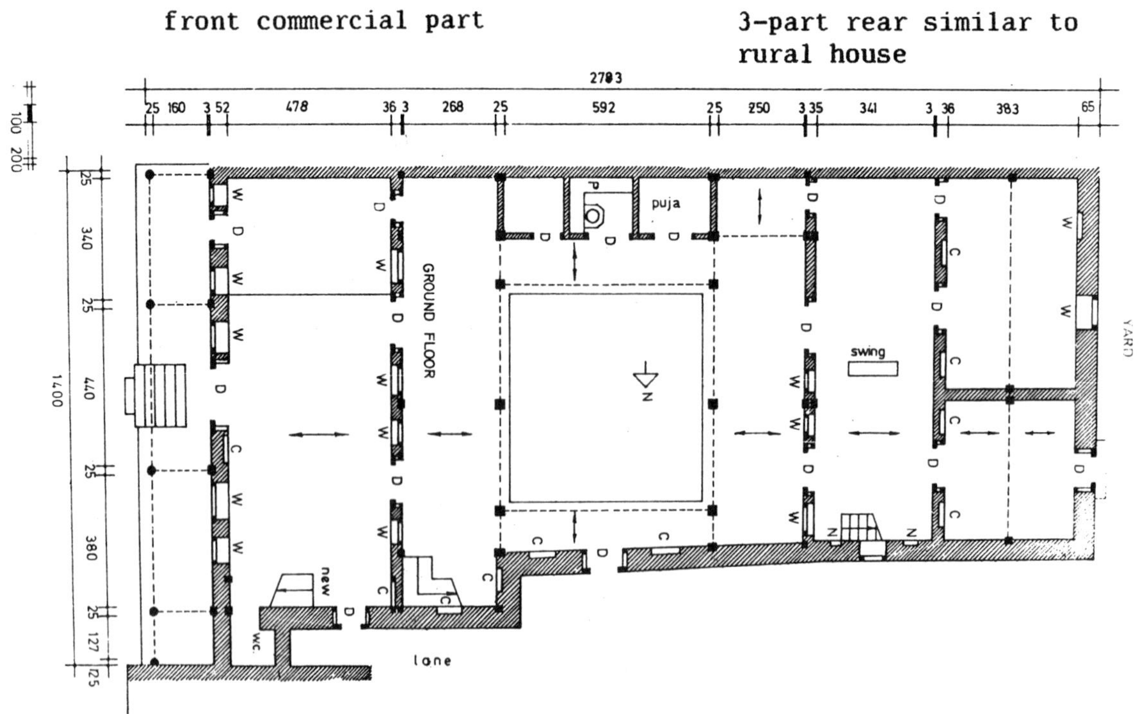

Fig. 4 Urban house in Ahmedabad.

A TEMPLE IN A TRIBAL VILLAGE

K S Singh

Vasna[1] exemplifies the cultural heritage of an Indian village, as also the process of its transformation through the development of irrigation which has encouraged its craftsmen and potters to switch over to agriculture. Indian villages are being transformed, in some cases rapidly, through the application of new agricultural technology. This process of change and development is benefitting not only the upper stratum of village society as is generally assumed, but also its poorer sections - both through its percolation effect, and also in a more direct and far more enduring manner. In the present paper, an account is given, first, of the cultural (sanskritic) heritage of a tribal village, and its adaptation to the tribal ethos, and secondly, the transformation of the village through the development process.

Diuri[2] is a tribal village sixty kilometres from Ranchi, on the national highway which connects the latter with the steel-making centre of Jamshedpur. Predominantly inhabited by the Munda tribe, it was founded by its kamal lineage, whose members form a land-owning and privileged category (khuntkattidar). Further, there are Munda belonging to the śāṇḍilya lineage, and a few artisan households. As the nomenclature of the lineages suggests, sanskritisation has been at work among the Munda for a long time. The Pancapargana region, of which Tamar (the block headquarters) is a part, has been the scene of intensive interaction between tribals and peasants at both the cultural and economic levels. This village is about three kilometres from Diuri. A fertile, low-lying region, accessible from both Bengal and Orissa, it witnessed the migration of peasant castes from these adjoining territories from as early as the late medieval period. There were conflicts between the Munda and incoming peasant castes. The Munda were also exposed to a new agricultural technology, and their acculturation to the puranic forms of the Hindu religion. The tribal region, known as the Jharkhand, of which the Pancapargana is described as the 'underbelly', emerged as a distinct historical region and was described in medieval literature as the abode of Śiva. Throughout the region a number of shrines of Śaiva and Śākta cults were constructed, and were maintained by the chiefs of the original inhabitants. As the chiefs became hinduised, they invited brahmins to settle, offered them land, and called upon them to perform ritual services at these shrines according to the sacred texts. In Tamar, particularly in the territory through which the Karkari and Kanchi rivers flow, a number of temples were built, dedicated to the Sun and the Mother Goddess. The temples represent an extension of the Bhubaneswar school of architecture. Moreover, in ritual services, puranic forms of Śakti worship co-existed with tribal religions, and were performed respectively by the Brahmin and the Munda tribal priest (pahan).

The relationship of the tribals to such temples deserves closer examination, with particular reference to the Diuri temple. According to the Munda, these temples were constructed by the Asur, indefatigable builders, according to tribal folklore. They are renowned for their uncanny habit of building at night and leaving their work incomplete at daybreak, as they have to leave the worksite by dawn. According to Munda tradition, the Asur were iron-smelters, and were akin to the present-day Lohara, the tribalised ironsmiths who are also masons and stone-cutters. Thus, in all probability, these temples were constructed by these local artisans.

The Munda ballad Sosobonga (Trigunyat 1960) describes the conflict between the Munda and the Asur, at the end of which the Supreme God of the Munda, Singbonga, emerges triumphant. The Asur are destroyed and such of their womenfolk as survived become the malevolent female spirits in the Munda pantheon (Encyclopaedia Mundarica 1900, 240-50). A part of the ballad's contemptuous reference to the Asur hastily leaving the worksite at cock-crow, and to their work remaining incomplete, could be ascribed to the contempt which the Munda felt for them.

The temple at Diuri is neither incomplete nor was it hastily constructed. It seems to have once occupied a large area, with tanks all around - a few of which survive almost intact to this day. There was also a gateway situated here, which is still remembered as the bonga dwar. This was the gateway to the temple, closer to the tank in front where the lands of the pahan are located. As the legends have it, the temple suffered damage later, at the hands of Kala Pahar the iconoclast, and of a British army officer during the Kol insurrection. Furthermore, an earthquake caused the three sides of the temple to collapse. There is little doubt that Diuri was an important seat of Śakti worship in the later medieval period. As the village name itself suggests, it was the abode of the gods - deori.

As the first wave of sanskritisation receded, however, the tribals firmly took over the management of the temple services and sought to establish their identity at the temple. The Raja of Tamar no doubt issued a land grant to a brahmin of Disipara to perform worship, but a good working arrangment seems to have been established between the brahmin and the pahan about the rituals to be conducted in the temple, in which the pahan plays a major role. The brahmin turns up every Thursday, a day of special pūjā for the Mother Goddess, and also on the Mahāṣṭhamī to conduct the pūjā as laid down in the scriptures. On other days and on the occasions of major festivals, the pahan holds sway.

The Munda insist that the village name is originally derived from the combination of the two words diuri and diri - that is, the place where lay the slab (diri - still worshipped today) belonging to the priest (diuri) who is still known by this name among the Ho, a tribe living across the hills. This was so even before the temple was constructed. Following the construction of the temple, and the taking over of its management by the tribals, the sixteen-armed mother goddess (Salabhujie) in the temple was identified with the bonga, the benevolent spirit, particularly with that of the village, the sarna, which is close by. Thus, as the pahan explains, the mother goddess as a bonga has been worshipped from time immemorial by the Munda, who flock to this temple to offer prayers. On one of my visits I saw a Munda girl sitting in the sanctum sanctorum, apparently in great distress, and offering the following prayer:

O devī mother,
You are our mother, our father.
I am an ignorant child who knows nothing.
I have come to you,
Reveal yourself to me,
Tell me the way,
Show me the light,
Save me from this misery.

It was a moving experience to see this Munda girl trying to establish a rapport with the deity.

While the brahminical rituals are complex, expensive and time-consuming, the ritual services performed by the pahan are simple - the prayers are short and the offerings consist simply of laddu (sirni), and red flowers which are especially appreciated by the goddess. The conduct of the pūjā by the pahan is reminiscent of his conduct of the worship in the sarna, the only difference being that liquor and fowl are not offered in the temple. The prayers are either the Mundari translation from the Bengali of Sanskrit prayers of the Durgā Saptaśatī, or an adaption of traditional Mundari prayers to the Singbonga, such as:

O Mother devī,
You are mother and father,
You rise like milk,
You set like curd,
This earth is yours, this creation is yours,
We stand under your protecting umbrella.
This person has come to you,
You know what he is suffering from,
Point out the way to end suffering,
Take away his sorrow and suffering.

The temple is also linked with many other aspects of tribal religion. The slab kept on the platform is worshipped when the tribals offer homage to the ancestral spirits every year. The village deity, gram deota, is worshipped in the temple precincts, among other places. Other tribal religious ceremonies are performed in houses and in the sarna. We were assured that the temple is not associated with the underworld of black magic, with the practice of sabar mantra, or with the witches' dance, najom susun. The pahan also dresses differently from other tribals and looks more like a Śākta devotee than a tribal priest.

The most remarkable aspect of the village is that it looks like a shrine - a cluster of houses with thatched roofs, tucked away in groves. According to tradition, no house in this temple village can be built of baked bricks; houses are made of either stone slabs or earth. A well-educated and well-placed Munda who has constructed an impressive-looking house has plans to build a second storey, with a thatched roof like most other houses. Non-Munda outsiders wanted to construct houses of brick but they discovered, to their horror, that the brick kilns were severely damaged by a hailstorm - as villagers recall. The mother goddess in the temple does not like baked bricks and has a preference for thatched roofs. Maṇḍapa, made of a kind of straw and with a thatched roof, were preferred for Śakti worship. It is indeed remarkable that a whole tribal village should convert itself into a cluster of maṇḍapa-like houses, in deference to tradition. This is probably the most impressive testimony to a living tradition in what undoubtedly was a seat of Śakti worship, with an āśrama organized around it.

This discussion raises an important question as to whether the Munda religion has accepted the concept of a female deity or that of a mother goddess. The Singbonga, as the Sosobonga tells us, is a male god, an avatāra, who came down to destroy the Asur. He is the Supreme Spirit, invisible and distant, known only through symbols and signs (van Exem 1979 and 1980 and see also van Exem 1978; Encyclopaedia Mundarica 1900, 3973- 88). He is without a female companion. However, there are female spirits in the Munda pantheon. Apart from the jah-era there are the candi-bonga (Encyclopaedia Mundarica 1900, 737-41) presiding over various activities. There is also the concept of the mother earth, dharti enga. Furthermore, the Sosobonga contains a beautiful invocation to a virgin goddess:

O Singbonga,
O Virgin Goddess (devī kumārī).
This is your land, this is your country,
This land which is spread in all directions,
East, west, north, south
Is your creation;
The tanks filled with lotus, the reservoirs
filled with flowers of various kinds,
Trees and plants, cows, birds and all grazing animals -
Are all your creation, your handiwork
(Trigunyat, op. cit.)

In other prayers, the Singbonga is mentioned as the lord of heaven and the devī as the goddess of earth. If the partial tribalisation of a sanskritic heritage is a pointer, the Singbonga is now likely to acquire a female companion, a wife.

Ever since the national highway linked this sleepy little village with the outside world in the early sixties, its temple has become widely recognised as an ancient seat of Śakti worship. Tourists, visitors and devotees flock from far and near. The name of the village itself has been changed from Diuri to Deori, as the signpost shows. A whole bazaar complex has developed as outsiders, including traders and liquor vendors, have moved in. Mela, or fairs, are regularly held. The Vaiṣṇava form of Śakti worship on the Rāmanavamī day had been added to the Dusserah. There is more income for the temple and its priests. The tribal pahan, however, had maintained his position. The tribals of the village have adjusted themselves to the new challenges, and have retained their identity, language and literary tradition, which are linked with a growing tribal awareness in Chhotanagpur.

This account of the cultural heritage of Diuri is not complete without a reference to its impact on the development process, no matter how remote and ephemeral it might appear to be. In the early 1960s a canal was taken off the Kanchi river. As almost the entire village came within the area which it could irrigate, many expectations were raised. However, there were initial problems - the supply of water from irrigation was inadequate, and water management was inefficient. This moved a budding Munda poet to compose a satire.

O my raja
How is this canal of yours?
There is little water though the canal is long;
It irrigates only a fringe;
The rest of the land remains barren.

This was only a passing phase. The irrigation system did stabilise agricultural production, as paddy was almost totally insured against the vagaries of drought. However, improved varieties of paddy did not appeal to the village Munda who generally kept to the traditional varieties. The new strain was vulnerable to pests and required fertilisers (which cost money), and as a dwarf variety they did not yield straw of sufficient length and thickness for making thatched roofs in the village. Here was an example of a cultural tradition acting as a constraint on economic development in the village. However, increased production increased prosperity, raised land prices and strengthened the economic power of small tribal peasant groups. Alienation of land from tribals to non-tribals is now insignificant. A few, including an artisan, have even bought back some land. Outmigration had stopped. The seasonal hunger period has shortened. Cultivation of wheat as a second crop has been expanded from the mid-1970s onwards. These are signs of change, seen against the backdrop of growing pressure of population on the land, increasing poverty, and reckless destruction of natural resources - including the forest. The tribals still nostalgically recall the days when their womenfolk went out to market bedecked with silver jewellery - and they had brass untensils in the house. In the hard days that followed, their women lost their jewels and utensils, and the families lost their land. For the first time, there are now possibilities for raising their income from agriculture through the application of appropriate technology, and from other sources.

Notes

1. See Introduction.

2. I first visited Diuri on foot from Tamar in 1961 to see the temple. I was then posted as subdivisional officer of Khunti. When I came back to Ranchi as divisional commissioner in 1978, I visited Diuri a number of times to oversee the implementation of a couple of development projects we had taken up. One result of the first visit to Diuri and similar places was a published account 'Temple in Ranchi District' (Singh 1969).

References

Encyclopaedia Mundarica 1900:
'Asur Kahani' (Hoffmann _et al_.), 240-50
'Chandi Bonga', 737-41
'Singbonga', 3973-88

Singh, K S 1969. Temple in Ranchi District. In _Dr Satkari Moorkerji Felicitation Volume_. Varanasi

Trigunyat, J 1960. _Sosobonga_. Ranchi

van Exem, A 1978. Haram and Singbonga, the Concept of the Supreme Being according to the Munda Mythology. _In Munda World_, (ed) P Ponnet. Ranchi

van Exem, A 1979. The Tribe, a Link with Singbonga. _Sevartham_ (Ranchi)

van Exem, A 1980. Man and His Imperceptible Self: the Munda Philosophy of Life. _Sevartham_ (Ranchi)

ORNAMENTS OF THE 'GREAT RENOUNCERS' OF THE RAMANANDI SECT

Richard Burghart

Introduction

Anyone familiar with the cultural heritage of India will recognise the importance of iconography in Hindu religious contexts, but while the topic of temple iconography has received considerable attention from Indian and western scholars, the topic of human iconography has been inadequately researched. Very little material has been published, for example, on the costumes and ornaments of 'human gods', such as Brahmans, ascetics, and kings, and the analysis of this material has focused primarily on the use of these costumes and ornaments as insignia rather than as icons. For example, Uberoi (1967), Tambiah (1970), Das (1985), and Burghart (1983a) have examined the ornaments of various Hindu and Buddhist ascetics as a means of marking inter-sectarian and intra-sectarian boundaries, but the intrinsic purpose for which ascetics wear such ornaments remains poorly understood by persons outside these religious traditions. An investigation of this intrinsic purpose would lead one, of course, into a vast field of inquiry, for one would have to investigate not only the ornaments themselves but also the bodies (sthūla sarira and sūkṣma śarīra) which the ornaments adorn and the cosmic body (kāya) which the ascetic constructs by means of such adornment. In this brief paper I will only report some very general observations concerning my research on the religious significance of ornaments and, wherever possible, illustrate these observations with appropriate ethnographic data. My material comes from the 'Great Renouncers', an itinerant branch of the Ramanandi sect, but my comments also pertain, I believe, to other Indian sectarian traditions.

I

Of the various celibate Vaishnavite sects in South Asia which are known collectively as Bairagi, or the 'Desireless', the largest is the one founded in the name of the Hindu saint Swami Ramanand who is said to have lived at Benaras during the fourteenth century (Burghart 1978). Among the Ramanandis today a diversity of spiritual disciplines are practised. The entitlement to practice a particular spiritual discipline is bestowed upon the disciple by his doctrinal guru (sadhak guru) in the course of a secondary initiation of the sect. One such discipline practised by some Ramanandi is called the path of renunciation (tyag) and those Ramanandis who follow this path call themselves Renouncers (tyagi) or even Great Renouncers (mahatyagi). Renouncers and Great Renouncers, like all Ramanandis, worship Ram Candra as their redeeming deity but unlike other Ramanandis, they worship Ram not only in his form possessed of attributes (saguna) but also in his form devoid of attributes (nirguna). In this attributeless form Ram is likened to the Invisible Spirit (alakh purusa) who is said to dwell within all embodied souls of the universe. A Ramanandi becomes a Renouncer or Great Renouncer (hereafter I shall refer to them collectively as Great Renouncers) by undergoing a secondary initiation of the sect in which the candidate receives the sacred ashes from his doctrinal guru and thereafter smears these ashes on his body in the course of his daily purifications. Great Renouncers usually travel in itinerant mendicant monasteries, called khalsa or jamat, and build their camp-sites on the margins of cultivated land outside villages[1]. Their wandering existence serves as a representation (rup) of that universal experience which eludes Indian villagers who are tied to their homes, ancestral fields, and country (Burghart 1983b).

Great Renouncers separate themselves even further from villagers by avoiding any relationship which would signify that they are part of the complex hierarchy of interdependence which characterizes the caste system. For example, Great Renouncers worship the salagram, a stone of black ammonite which is found in the upper reaches of the Kali Gandaki river in Nepal. Because the salagram is said to embody the primal energy (adi sakti) of Visnu Narayan, Great Renouncers do not require the services of a Brahman priest to install the soul of the image which they worship. Great Renouncers bury their dead or immerse the deceased in a sacred river; by so doing they do not require the services of the Mahapatra funeral priests. Because Great Renouncers let their hair grow long, they never call on the barber. With their loincloth fashioned from the inner bark of the banana tree or from a sacred variety of grass (munja), they have no need of tailors, cloth merchants, or washermen. Great Renouncers live in itinerant monasteries and derive their livelihood from gifts in cash and kind offered to them in alms by householders. They do not ordinarily hold rights over productive resources; thus they do not require the services of agricultural labourers, domestic servants, clerks, blacksmiths, carpenters, and other craftsmen, as is the case of those sedentary Ramanandi who live in local rent-receiving monasteries. Rather than purchase a brass waterpot from a coppersmith at the bazaar, they fashion their own waterpot from a variety of bitter gourd called tumba. In sum, Great Renouncers separate themselves completely from non-spiritual relationships with villagers. The only relationship which a Great Renouncer entertains with a villager is one in which the villager appears as a devotee at the campsite of the ascetic bearing with him uncooked food and firewood in alms or seeking a blessing, a boon, or spiritual counsel.

II

As one might imagine, the arrival at a village of these itinerant monasteries of near-naked Great Renouncers is, if not a frightening experience, at least an awesome one. The purpose of the Great Renouncers' appearance, however, is not to inspire fear in householders but to please the Invisible Spirit and to augment the ascetic's powers as he follows the path of renunciation to his ultimate goal of desirelessness. Great Renouncers consider their matted hair, ashes, firetongs, waterpot, and so forth to be bhushan, or what we would call ornaments. Concerning the etymology of this word, Coomaraswamy (1939, 377) has written that in Vedic Sanskrit bhūṣaṇa meant:

> . . . the provision of whatever properties or means increase the efficacy of the thing or person with reference to which or whom they are employed: the hymns, for example, with which the deity is said to be 'adorned' are an affirmation of and therefore a confirmation and magnification of the divine power to act on the singer's behalf. Whatever is in this sense 'ornamented' is therby made the more in act, the more in being.

Although Great Renouncers are hardly aware of the Vedic meaning of the word bhushan, nevertheless they would, in spite of a lapse of several thousand years, concur with Coomaraswamy about the power of their ornaments, for prior to adorning his body with a pristine ornament, a Great Renouncer consecrates the ornament with a ritual formula, or mantra. By pronouncing the mantra which is appropriate for the ornament, the ascetic 'awakens' the ornament to its particular efficacy. The importance of consecrating the ornament is sometimes noted in the mantra itself. For example, in the bhasm gayatri, which a Great Renouncer recites prior to taking his bath of ashes, there appears the admonition that if the ascetic smears the ashes on his body without having consecrated them or without having obtained the grace of the guru then the ascetic will end his life in death:[2]

> Recite the mantra and offer the ashes;
> so Yogis obtain the supreme post.
> Offer the ashes without reciting the mantra,
> and one is destroyed beyond belief.
> The body falls and goes to the City of Death.

These words, which alert the ascetic to his eventual fate if he adorns his body with unconsecrated ornaments, do not comprise a curse because Great Renouncers believe that the world in which 'embodied souls' live is mrtyalok, meaning the 'world of death'. That is to say, it is the way of all embodied souls to suffer the death and decay of their bodies and the passage of their souls to the City of Death where the King of Death sits in judgement. The sense of the passage quoted from the bhasm gayatri, therefore, is not a curse but an admonition that unconsecrated ornaments are imperfect; they will not be effective in releasing the embodied soul from the fate which ordinarily awaits it at the City of Death. Perfect ornaments, however, augment the power of the ascetic as he follows the path of renunciation leading to the desireless state in which the embodied soul is reunited with the Invisible Spirit.

This religious preoccupation leads Great Renouncers to value ornaments for their efficacy and obliges the external observer of Hindu asceticism to hold in abeyance the aesthetic criteria by which he normally understands and evaluates ornaments. The relation between creator and created, artist and object, or individual personality and unique style - which is significant in western discourse on art - is unimportant for the Great Renouncer since he finds himself involved in a triadic, not dyadic, relationship with his ornaments. Even though the Great Renouncer fabricates his necklace, loincloth, waterpot, and other ornaments, still he sees his role primarily as an awakener, not a creator, of these ornaments. Strictly speaking, the ornaments are not created at all; rather, they are made by the ascetic in the form of a prototype which is thought to be a manifestation or representation of the Invisible Spirit. Since the Invisible Spirit is said to encompass the universe as well as to be separate from it, these prototypes of the Invisible Spirit are similarly not bound by the spatial or temporal limitations of the universe. The knowledge of the various prototypes of ornaments was given by the Invisible Spirit to various Ramanandi preceptors in the distant past. These preceptors, such as Ramanand or Ramanand's guru Raghavanand, are thought to have 'set the ornament in motion' (calana) and then transmitted this knowledge to their disciples who, in turn, transmitted it to their disciples and so on down through the course of time. These observations may be illustrated by the mantra used to consecrate the firetongs:[3]

> The far limit of Om has not been reached;
> The firetongs have come from ages upon ages ago.

Ram and Laksman set the first firetongs in motion.
The second firetongs they sent to Vaikuntha.
The third firetongs they sent to Kailasa.
When the truth-guru bestowed his grace.
The fire tongs stood to attention.

Thus the present-day Great Renouncers do not, like artists or craftsmen, see themselves as creators of unique or typical objects; rather, they make the ornament in the form of the prototype given by the Invisible Spirit and then awaken the ornament to its power as a representation or manifestation of the Invisible Spirit.

The ornaments of the Great Renouncers may be analysed both as insignia and as icons. As insignia, they communicate to other ascetics and to householders certain information concerning the Ramanandi path of renunciation (Burghart 1983a). They are also thought to communicate this information to the Invisible Spirit. That is to say, these ornaments are visible signs which were given by the Invisible Spirit[4] and which are recognizable by the Invisible Spirit. This point is mentioned in the sankadik mantra. Sankadik is a particular hairstyle associated with the four mind-born sons of Brahma - Sanak, Sanandan, Sanatan, and Sanatkumar - which is fashioned by washing the hair in water and yoghurt and then letting it dry in the sun without combing, plaiting, or matting. The overall effect is of the hair radiating outwards from the scalp in a visible expression of the ascetic's fiery energy (tejas). In the mantra which is used to consecrate this hairstyle occur the following lines:[5]

The Vedas say that there are four branches;
by yoga saints cross to the other side.
There are the king's beard, the subject's beard,
the beards of the Brahman and merchant.
There is one beard [i.e., the sankadik] in the form
of liberation which the Invisible Spirit
recognizes.

In recognizing his own likeness in the Great Renouncer, the Invisible Spirit is also thought to protect the honour of the ascetic against his mortal enemy, the agents of time (kala).

As suggested earlier, however, the ornaments of the Great Renouncers do not serve merely as insignia; many (but not all) of the ornaments are icons which figure directly in the ascetic's spiritual discipline. By icon I mean an ornament which participates in the reality which it represents. This, of course, is the reason for the ascetic's 'awakening' the ornament, for if the ornament did not participate in that reality then the ascetic would consider the ornament to be ineffective in liberating the embodied soul from the bonds of conditioned existence. The actual means by which the ornaments effect the ascetic's liberation are too various to summarize in such a brief paper, but four general points concerning this efficacy can be made. First, it must be recognized that the embodied soul is a microcosm and, as such, the Invisible Spirit is thought to dwell in various guises within the ascetic's body, one such guise being that of a swan which swims upon a pond of subtle semen (manasarovar) in the upper region of the ascetic's head. Second, in the same way that the universe is a manifestation of the Invisible Spirit so the body of the ascetic is a manifestation of the Invisible Spirit. I deliberately use the term manifestation instead of creation in order to emphasize the absence of a separation between matter and mind in this particular concept of the body. For the Great Renouncer matter is a low energy manifestation of mind which, in turn, is a manifestation of consciousness (cit) which itself is a manifestation of the Invisible Spirit. Matter, mind, and consciousness correspond to three different bodies ('gross', 'subtle', and 'casual'), each ruled by its state of selfhood ('waking consciousness', 'dream-sleep', and 'deep-sleep') and each state of selfhood dependent upon its next higher state. Liberation comes by the technique of demanifestation (laya yoga) in which the ascetic forces his vital breath (prana) into higher and higher states of selfhood until eventually it is reunited with the Invisible Spirit upon the pond of subtle semen. Third, the iconic ornaments not only adorn the body of the ascetic but are also thought to be extensions of the ascetic's body. (This notion, however, has a much wider currency in Indian society. For example, in the pre-modern art of war Hindu soldiers recited mantra in order to make their swords and shields extensions of their arms). Fourth, in the same way that the body is ontologized into gross, subtle, and casual forms, so the iconic ornaments are ontologized and are thought to exist in both a gross form and a subtle form. It is in their subtle form that ornaments comprise part of the spiritual discipline of the Great Renouncer. Unawakened ornaments, of course, lack this subtle form and it is for this reason that they are ineffective in liberating the ascetic from the bonds of transient existence.

III

The ornaments with which Great Renouncers adorn their body include the sacred ashes, loincloth, necklace, various hairstyles and forehead markings, waterpot, firetongs, rosary, sacred thread, etc. (Figs. 1, 2). The brevity of this paper precludes a discussion of all these ornaments, but a description in some detail of one particular ornament might clarify some of the general remarks of the previous section. The ornament I shall describe is the waterpot.

The waterpot (tumba) and its diminutive, the ashpot (tumbi), figure prominently in the Great Renouncer's way of life, for every day he uses water to purify his gross body (sthula sarira) and ashes to seal his subtle body (suksma sarira) from influences of the transient world. Wherever a Great Renouncer travels, therefore, he can always be seen carrying his water and ash pots. Both of these pots are made from the same species of gourd (Lageneria vulgaris) which thrives in the arid regions of western India. The gourd is bitter, inedible, and not usually cultivated, but at the local Ramanandi monasteries which are visited by Great Renouncers the vine is cultivated in order to supply wandering ascetics with their pots. The gourd is cut from the vine, dried in the sun, scoured inside with sand to remove the flesh, and then rubbed with ghee. After two or three days the gourd no longer imparts its bitter taste to the water and the Great Renouncer begins to use it either as a waterpot, or if the gourd is immature, as an ashpot. At the time of starting to use the waterpot, he 'awakens' it by reciting the following mantra:[6]

(1) Om, first there was air, from air came water;
(2) From Parbrahma the lotus was obtained.
(3) For the very reason that Brahma asked Parbrahma
for the seed;
(4) For that reason Brahma made his abode [in heaven]
and established the earth below.
(5) Brahma asked for the seed for the four Ages.
(6) Parbrahma took the seed and gave it to Brahma.
(7) On the sixth day the seed sprouted.

(8) Hundreds of thousands of tumba began to grow.
(9) Who set in motion the first waterpot?
(10) The nine nath and eighty-four siddha set it in motion.
(11) Then who set in motion the waterpot?
(12) Guru Raghavanand set it in motion.
(13) Then who set in motion the waterpot?
(14) Guru Ramanand set it in motion.
(15) Brothers, each of you guard your own waterpot
(16) And with the second repeat the name of Ram.
(17) Having begun to use the waterpot without reciting the mantra, the body falls and goes to hell.
(18) Having recited the mantra and used the waterpot, so lords of yoga depart for Vaikuntha.

The mantra may easily be divided into three sections: the first section (lines 1-8) describes the waterpot as a manifestation of Parbrahma (equivalent in this context to the Invisible Spirit); the second section (lines 9-14) recounts the pedigree of the waterpot in the course of time; and the third section (lines 15-18) admonishes the ascetic in the use and consecration of the waterpot. A few comments will help to clarify the meaning of these three sections.

The first section comprises a Vaishnavite description of the universe as a manifestation of Parbrahma which accords roughly with Vaishnavite Puranic sources. For example, according to the Bhāgavata Purāṇa (3. 8-11) prior to the dawn of time Parbrahma reposed upon his couch formed by Sesa, the serpent, who was floating upon the Sea of Milk. Within Parbrahma lay the subtle bodies of all creatures from previous aeons. Stirred by the memory impressions of the previous actions of these subtle bodies, Parbrahma desired to become manifest. From his navel grew a lotus upon which Brahma appeared. Brahma ordered this manifestation of Parbrahma to be split into three parts - heaven, earth, and hell. Then he populated these three regions with subtle bodies - heaven, earth, and hell being the three regions in which subtle bodies experience the fruits of their actions. The first section of the waterpot mantra accords in outline with this Puranic account of the dawn of time. The seed mentioned in the mantra corresponds to the subtle body of the Puranic legend, and the sprouting of this seed on the sixth day clearly identifies the tumba waterpot with the embodied soul (jivatma)[7].

The second section of the mantra is more straightforward and recounts the names of those preceptors who set the waterpot in motion. The nine spiritual lords (nath) and eighty-four perfect ascetics (siddha) are found in numerous sectarian traditions, both Buddhist and Hindu (Dasgupta 1969, 202-10; Briggs 1938, 136-7). These spiritual lords and perfect ascetics pass freely in and out of transient existence and are empowered to transform the manifested universe. Their numbers signify universality; the nine spiritual lords, for example, are identified with the eight terrestrial directions plus the zenith. Their universal presence establishes the universality of the waterpot. The second and third names of Raghavanand and Ramanand fix the use of the waterpot within the Ramanandi sect.

The third section returns to the theme of the first. The tumba stands for the individual embodied soul of the ascetic. As such the tumba is also thought to be imbued with the personal qualities of the ascetic. The waterpots of great ascetics are remembered to have been empowered to act on the ascetic's behalf;[8] and the waterpot, together with the loincloth and meditation mat (asana), are the three Great Renouncer ornaments which the individual ascetic must not share with his fellow ascetics. The mantra enjoins the Great Renouncer to guard the first tumba (meaning his own personal waterpot) and to repeat the name of Ram with the second tumba (meaning within his own embodied soul). The mantra ends with the customary admonition concerning the inefficacy of unconsecrated ornaments and the statement that spiritual lords depart for Vaikuntha, Ram's celestial kingdom.

IV

A number of points concerning the Great Renouncers' concept of ornament may now be summarized. Even though Great Renouncers personally fabricate nearly all their ornaments for their own individual use (the fire-tongs being an exception in this respect), still they do not see their own role as producers of ornaments. This is probably due to the fact that Great Renouncers do not see themselves as being the producers of anything. Instead they derive their 'livelihood from heaven' (akasavrtti) and separate themselves from 'fieldworking householders' (kheti grhastha) whose duty is to reproduce the material universe. The observation that Great Renouncers fabricate their ornaments, therefore, is a fact pertaining to their withdrawal from caste society, not a statement of their aesthetic preoccupations. Great Renouncers instead see themselves as consecrators of ornaments and as such they are involved in a triadic relationship comprising the Invisible Spirit, the ornament as object, and the 'awakener'. Each of these three poles is separate from the others yet they are also inseparable in that the prototype of the ornament is a manifestation or representation of the Invisible Spirit; the body of the ascetic is also a manifestation of the Invisible Spirit; and the consecrated ornaments are extensions of the ascetic's body. In other words, these three poles are brought together in the vision of the ascetic's body as a microcosm. This ritual construction of the universe, which is as much present in the concept of the ascetic's body as in the structure of the Hindu temple, calls to mind the presence of certain themes which are common to both human and temple inconography; or as the Great Renouncers would say, 'the body of an ascetic is a moving temple'.

Notes

1. There are at present more than twenty itinerant monasteries which roam upper India and the Nepalese Tarai. Each monastery may number between ten and two hundred ascetics. According to the sectarian genealogists the abbots of these monasteries trace their doctrinal guru-disciple succession (i.e. the secondary initiation in which the sadhak guru bestows the ashes, not the primary initiation in which the diksa guru bestows the Ram mantra) from Mangal Das who was active during the late eighteenth century. Mangal Das was the abbot of the Mahatyagi Khalsa, which was also known as the Dakor Khalsa after the campsite of its summer retreat (catur mas) at Dakor, Gujarat.

2. The bhasm gayatri is mantra 48 in the Siddhant Patal. The text is as follows: parhi mantra bhabhuti carhavai/so jogi param pad pavai/ bina mantra bhabhuti carhavai pimda pare ke jamapur javai/. A complete translation of this mantra may be found in Burghart 1980, 27-8.

3. The complete text of this mantra (no. 5) from the Siddhant Patal is as follows: omkar ka par na paya/cipiya adi jugadi sem aya/pahila cipiya ramalaksman ne calays dusra cipiya vaikumtha pathaya/tisra cipiya kailasa pathaya/jab satagurune anugrah kiya/kari damdavat cipiya liya/. The final lines of this mantra refer to the initiation of the Great Renouncer at which time the firetongs were implanted in the ground in a position of upright salutation.

4. For example, in Ramanand's Pamca Matra found in the Siddhant Patal occur the following lines: seli simgi jamga lamgota/patra pavri damdak chota/jholi jhamda camvar arani/dini alakh purusa sahadani/.

5. The passage is from mantra no. 11 of the Siddhant Patal: nigam kahat car sakha joga samt par le jai/darhi raja darhi paraja darhi brahman baniya/ek darhi mukta svarupi jo alakh purusa pahicaniya/.

6. The complete text of the tumba bija mantra (no. 57) from the Siddhant Patal is a s follows: om pratham pavan pavan te pani/ parbrahma se kamal paya/jakaran brahma bija mangaya/takaran brahma ka vasa/talai dharti thapan kiya/car jug ka mamgaya biya/bija lai brahma ko dinha/chatthe roj ugya bija/tumba lage kaika lakh pratham tumba kavan calaya/nava nath caurasi siddhom ne calaya/phera tumba kavan calaya/guru raghavanand ji ne calaya/phir tumba kavan calaya/ guru ramanand ji ne calaya/ek ek tumba rakho bhai/dujo rakhai ram duhai/vina mantra tumba calavai/ pimda pare nark maim javai/mantra parhi tumba calavai/so jogesvar vaikumtha sidhavai.

7. Further evidence of this interpretation may be found in the legends recounted by Vaishnavite bards concerning great Ramanandi ascetics. One such legend concerns Urdhva Bahu Narayan Das, who was the abbot of the Ratna Sagar monastery at Janakpur in the eastern Tarai of Nepal. In 1885 Narayan Das prepared a feast, which was supposed to have cost 850,000 rupees, to which he invited all the ascetics of India and Nepal. Among the ascetics who accepted the invitation was a Gorakhanathi Yogi. The Yogi sat down in the courtyard of the Ratna Sagar monastery and, placing his waterpot upon the ground, asked that it be filled with parched rice. The monastery storekeeper went to the granary, collected some parched rice and poured it into the waterpot. But as much as the storekeeper poured, still the waterpot did not become full. The storekeeper returned to the granary many times but still the waterpot remained unfilled. After having poured nearly six hundred kilograms into the waterpot and seeing that the pot was not yet full, the storekeeper became alarmed and called the abbot, Narayan Das. Narayan Das told the storekeeper to take only as much parched rice as can be held in the palm of one hand and to toss that into the waterpot. The storekeeper did so and immediately the waterpot filled up and the hundreds and hundreds of excess kilograms of rice overflowed the brim of the pot. The meaning of this legend becomes clear once one accepts that the waterpot is identified with the embodied soul. In brief, desires are limitless and, therefore, one can never be satisfied by being given all that one wants. Satisfaction can only be found, not in the full expression of desire, but in the limitation of desire.

8. The waterpot being invested with the power of speech may be illustrated by the following legend concerning the founding of the Samuvapur monastery in Champaron District, Bihar. One day, many

years ago, Ram Das arrived in the region of Samuvapur which at that time was almost entirely covered with jungle. Ram Das, being a Renouncer, began to chop down trees from the forest in order to make his smouldering fire (dhuni). Since he liked to warm himself both night and day beside a huge fire, in no time at all Ram Das had cleared several acres of trees from the jungle. In that clearing he lived in the company of his bull, called Bholva, who travelled with him wherever he went. One day the royal police happened to come upon the clearing and saw that Ram Das was cutting down trees without a permit. When they asked him who had given him permission to chop down trees, Ram Das remained silent and continued chopping. The policemen returned to the palace and informed the Queen who returned the following morning with a large company of policemen intent on banishing Ram Das from the kingdom. When the Queen arrived at the camp-site, there was nobody there. She asked aloud in vexation, 'Now where has that ascetic gone?' Ram Das' waterpot, which was lying beside the smouldering fire, replied, 'He's gone to bathe in the river and will be back shortly.' The Queen was astonished and realized that Ram Das was no ordinary ascetic. When Ram Das returned to the camp-site, the Queen, instead of wanting him driven from the kindgom, begged Ram Das to stay and offered to give him whatever he desired. Ram Das replied that he was a Renouncer and, therefore, did not want anything. The Queen persisted with her offer and Ram Das said, 'For myself there is nothing wanting, but maybe the bull wants something.' The Queen asked the bull whether he wanted anything and the bull nodded his head. So the queen offered the bull as much land as he wanted to graze upon. The bull then set off walking in a large circle, the circumference of which he marked by urinating as he walked. The Queen then gave to the bull all the land within that circle (about 4000 acres) and upon that land Ram Das built the Samuvapur monastery.

References

Bhāgavata Purāṇa 1971. Trans. by G L Goswami and M A Sastri. Gorakhpur, Gita Press

Briggs, G W 1938. Gorakhnath and the Kanphata Yogis. Calcutta, Y M C A Publishing House

Burghart, Richard 1978. The Founding of the Ramanandi Sect. Ethnohistory, **25**, 121-139

Burghart, Richard 1980. Secret Vocabularies of the 'Great Renouncers' of the Ramanandi Sect. In Early Hindu devotional literature in current research, W M Callewaert (ed.) (Orientalia Lovaniensia Analecta, **8**). Leuven, Departement Orientalistiek Katholieke Universiteit Leuven

Burghart, Richard 1983a. Renunciation in the Religious Traditions of South Asia. Man (N.S.) **18**, 635-53

Burghart, Richard 1983b. Wandering Ascetics of the Ramanandi Sect. History of Religion, **22**, 361-80

Coomaraswamy, A K 1939. Ornament. The Art Bulletin, **21**, 375-382

Das, Veena 1985. 'Paradigms of Body Symbolism.' In Indian Religion, R Burghart and A Cantlie (eds). London, Curzon Press, (forthcoming)

Dasgupta, Shashibhusan 1969. Obscure Religious Cults. 3rd ed. Calcutta, Firma K L Mukhopadhyay

Siddhant Patal n.d. Attributed to Ramanand by his followers. Benaras, Thakur Prasad and Sons

Tambiah, Stanley 1970. Buddhism and the spirit cults in North-East Thailand. Cambridge, CUP

Uberoi, J P S 1967. On Being Unshorn. Transactions of the Indian Institute of Advanced Study, 4, 87-100

Fig. 1 Ram Das (left) and Ram Kisor Das (right). Both have forehead markings (tilak) of bimdi type; their bodies are smeared with sandalwood and ashes respectively. Ram Das wears a Tulsi 'diamond' necklace and a loincloth made from the bark of a banana tree; he carries a pair of fire-tongs in his right hand and a carved wooden waterpot (kamandal) in his left. Ram Kisor Das stands behind the swing upon which he leans at night (he has taken a vow to remain standing for fourteen years). He wears a loincloth made of munja grass.

Fig. 2 The itinerant monastery of Bharat Das engaged in a nine-day chanting of Tulsi Das' Rāmcaritmānas. Abbot Bharat Das, who has taken a vow to remain silent for fourteen years, is seated at the left of the photograph. In the centre foreground is the waterpot (tumba).

PAINTED PANELS AND SCROLLS FROM WESTERN INDIAN VILLAGES: THEIR MYTHOLOGY AND RITUALS

Jyotindra Jain

The tradition of narrating legends with the visual aid of painted panels or scrolls has been known since ancient times in many regions of India. Many such picture-show traditions have vanished, though some have survived to the present day. Connected with these painted panels are (or were) substantial traditions of oral literature transferred from generation to generation by itinerant story-tellers.

Some of the earliest and the most interesting references to such picture-showmen go back to the early centuries of the Christian era. Abhayadeva, commenting in the eleventh century upon the word *maṅkha* as it occurs in the third century text, the Bhāgavatī Sūtra, says that it refers to a special kind of mendicant 'whose hands are occupied with a picture board' (Basham 1951, 35). Also, an eighth-century Jain text, the Kuvalayamālā (Hamsavijayaji 1965, 291-5) refers to a wandering teacher, *upādhyāya*, who showed a Jaina monk a painted mural of *saṃsāracakra*, the cycle of the universe, which contained depictions of the pains and pleasures of the human world, the heavens, and the various actions and punishments in the different hells. The use of the painted panels and scrolls pertaining to cosmography, pilgrimage, tantric practices, etc. has survived into the contemporary Jaina tradition.

Comparable to the *saṃsāracakra* panel are the *yamapaṭa* of classical Sanskrit literature. In Viśākhadatta's *Mudrārākṣasa* there is a reference to a spy who disguised himself as a *yama-paṭika* (picture-showman) and carried with him a painted scroll showing the punishments of hell. 'He habitually entered the house of his patron, where he displayed his *yama*-cloth and sang songs, presumably of a religious type' (Basham 1951, 35). Bāṇa's *Harṣacarita* also mentions *yama-paṭika* and explains that they showed pictures and gave sermons on vice and virtue, rewards and punishments (Pathak 1958, 257).

In the *Vaddaradhane*, a tenth-century Kannada prose classic, we learn how a picture-showman's gang stole rice from a stock-pile while the picture-showman distracted the merchants with his performance (Khadabadi 1979, 23-6).

Stella Kramrisch compares the vertical scrolls from West Bengal and Bihar with the 'carved panels of the corner posts of the Bharhut railing of the second century BC, which appears to be a lithic version in relief' (Kramrisch 1968, 70) of scroll painting. In fact, if one goes a step further and examines the horizontal cross-bars of the gateways of Sanchi, one can see that these were actually conceived as partially open scrolls with prominent coils of scrolling to be seen at both ends.

The picture-story tradition exists today in several parts of India. Amongst the best known of these are: the *citrakathi* tradition of Maharashtra, the *pata-citra* tradition of Andhra Pradesh, also the *citrakara* and *jadu-patua* of Bengal and Bihar; there are also the *Pabuji* and *Dev Narayan* performances of Rajasthan (Figs. 1 and 2), and those of the Garoda of Gujarat. This paper deals with the *Garoda* tradition of *tipanu* reading in Gujarat (Jain 1980). In describing this tradition, I shall use the present tense even though at least some of its features may have remained unchanged for centuries.

The singular tradition of the picture-show in Gujarat is connected with the *Garoda* caste of priests who officiate at various ceremonies of the scheduled castes of the region. *Garoda* were concerned with astrology as well as with the narrative singing connected with *tipanu*, a picture-scroll. The vertical scroll of mill-made paper, painted with water-based colours, is approximately 14in (35.5.cm) wide and 168in (426.7cm) long. It is divided into nineteen panels containing pictures of deities and scenes showing the soul's journey after death, including punishments in several different hells, as well as narrative illustrations of various puranic and local legends. A very significant point is that this tradition combines the narration of legend with the yamapaṭa tradition, thus linking the Garoda practice with the classical ones mentioned above.

Garoda travel from village to village gathering audiences, mainly women, and narrate in prose and verse the stories contained in the painted scrolls (Figs. 3 and 4). In this respect they have been the prime carriers of oral tradition and local folklore which they have created, transferred and diffused. Although Garoda are found throughout the state, those who paint the scrolls and travel most widely telling their picture-stories are from north Gujarat.

Fieldwork in north Gujarat has revealed that there are, at any given time, four or five Garoda narrators who are also painters. They supply the painted scrolls to other Garoda who do not themselves paint. Each painter or family of painters has a distinct style - so much so, indeed, that whenever an old scroll was shown to any Garoda narrator, he was able to identify the painter and his village from the style of the painting alone. Knowledge of painting was usually transmitted within a family, from father to son, though one could also become a painter merely by aptitude. A comparison of forty scrolls collected from north Gujarat has revealed that the subject matter of each of the nineteen panels, and the sequence in which these appear, remain the same in all the scrolls, but that there were distinct differences in individual styles of drawing, pigmentation, composition and even in the interpretation of legends and iconographic conventions.

In most cases, a rough division of spaces and an approximate outline drawing of figures is done first of all in pencil. After that, different pigments are used to fill in different areas. The pigmentation resembles irregular blots which only vaguely resemble the finally required shapes. Once the pigments are applied, the semi-abstract-looking painting is worked upon in bold black outline to mark the details of the hair, the features, the limbs, the costumes, and so on. Normally the pigmented areas and the final outline do not match, and therefore the whole effect is that of flowing colours in a semi-abstract landscape of considerable charm. All figure-work is done on the natural white background of the paper, which is left unworked, although the interstices between the figures are filled with scattered patches of colour - perhaps meant to represent bunches of flowers. These are purely two-dimensional paintings, without any attempt at shading. In most cases, except in the depictions of Lakṣmī, Rāvaṇa and Bhīma, the profile is preferred to the frontal view.

The natural white of the paper is skilfully utilised in drawing fish or the almond-shaped eyes of humans and animals. The area of the eyes is marked by an outline and left white until finally a black pupil is added. Similarly, the natural white of the paper is also used for showing water in a well, a river or a reservoir. Water is indicated by a highly stylized fragmented wave pattern, with the occasional depiction of a fish or some other underwater creature. A typical feature of late western Indian manuscript illustration is that when an incident takes place inside a well it is shown through the side walls, as if these were transparent. This feature is also shared by Garoda scrolls, as where, in the depiction of the Sravana story, the waterpot inside the well is seen through the stone walls. Another common feature in this tradition is the technique of continuous narration which brings out the narrative character of the paintings (Fig. 5).

Some old village scrolls were repaired by pasting old newspaper pages, or leaves from astrological calendars on to them. These repairs give some idea about dating the scrolls, as some of the pieces used for repair contain contemporary dates. For example, on the back of one scroll there was an agreement signed in 1935 stating that the ownership of the scroll was transferred from one owner to another.

The Garoda fulfill a priestly function for many of the scheduled castes of this area. Because they can read the relevant manuals, they can predict auspicious and inauspicious occasions and make astrological statements. They can also read vernacular versions of Sanskrit legends. The profession of fortune-telling through astrology has, in recent years, become much more lucrative than their old vocation, and those who still practise story-telling are regarded by the astrologers as lower in status. The astrologer Garoda make horoscope scrolls with elaborate illustrations of the planets and the signs of the zodiac; there is a certain similarity in the style of the illustrations of the picture- and horoscope-scrolls (Fig. 6).

A typical Garoda travels from village to village, usually wearing a turban, a gathered upper shirt and a dhoti. He carries with him several bags in which he puts the grain and flour which he receives in exchange for a performance. After being invited by a host to narrate a scroll, he sits down on a charpoy or squats on the floor and starts the performance. He opens only a couple of panels from the top, and while showing them to the audience begins to invoke Gaṇeśa and other deities from the scroll. After this, he rolls up the upper end and unrolls the lower, revealing one panel at a time, and narrating it in prose and verse.

The first panel of the Garoda scroll depicts the personification of a temple with two prominent eyes flanking the śikhara. The second panel shows two horse riders who, according to some, are the personification of the sun and the moon - though according to others they depict Akalang and Nikalang, two folk deities. In the third panel, Gaṇeśa is installed with his consorts (Fig. 7). The fourth has Śiva and Pārvatī on a bull - flanked, interestingly, by the images of Pārvatī as a Bhil woman and as a naṭī or street juggler performing with snakes and scorpions (Fig. 8). The fifth panel features the goddess Lakṣmi. The sixth illustrates the narrative of Dhana Bhagat, a local saint, who obtained a harvest of pearls from his field due to the grace of Viṣṇu, whose devotee he was (Fig. 9). In the seventh panel, the goddesses Bahucara and Durgā kill a demon, usually in the form of a buffalo but in some cases in the form of Bhairava. Bahucara is one of the popular local goddesses of Gujarat (Fig. 10). The eighth panel displays the scene of Kṛṣṇa quelling the serpent Kāliya (Fig. 11). The ninth shows the Rāmāyaṇa legend of Śravaṇa's pilgrimage along with his blind parents, and of Daśaratha's killing him by mistake (Figs. 12 and 13). The tenth, eleventh and twelfth panels show Rāma and Lakṣmaṇa hunting the golden deer (Fig. 14), Hanumān carrying the hill with the herbal plants (Fig. 15), and the ten-headed Rāvaṇa with attendants (Fig. 16), respectively. The next panel shows the story of king Hariścandra and his wife Tārāmatī, who even when reduced to a state of slavery did not betray the principles for which they had lived (Fig. 17). The fourteenth panel features the game of amli-pipli in which the Pāṇḍava, Bhīma, shakes the tree to punish the Kaurava. According to popular belief, Bhīma's body was half of copper and half of iron, and therefore he is depicted in two different colours (Fig. 18). The fifteenth panel represents Sagalsa and Cangavati grinding their son's head to feed a mendicant, who was none other than God himself testing the worth and extent of their devotion. The sixteenth panel depicts Ramdev Pir. The remaining three panels show the soul's journey after death, and the punishments to which it is subjected in hell. In the seventeenth we see the procession of a man being carried in a celestial palanquin, followed by his wife in the form of a black bitch; this indicates that the man performed virtuous deeds to obtain his celestial chariot, but that the uncharitable actions of the wife have caused her to be transformed into a bitch. The eighteenth panel contains a scene which illustrates the Hindu belief that a dead person has to cross the river Vaitaraṇī on the way to hear the verdict of the Lord of Death. Due to past good actions the deceased is provided with a chariot or a cow, with the help of which the river can be crossed (Fig. 19). The last panel shows the possible punishments which await those who do not worship 'god' through bhājana or chanting (Figs. 20 and 21).

Partly entertaining, but mainly ethical and didactic, the oral tradition preserved by the Garoda is certainly rooted in local mythology, beliefs and practices. Incidents from the Hindu epics and purāṇa are often parochialised and local deities, beliefs and customs are sanskritised. For example, the game of amli-pipli, where Bhīma shakes the tree to bring down all the Kaurava, is not mentioned in the Mahābhārata, but it is described, at great length, by the Garoda who have developed a special iconography for this incident.

A good example of how a folklore genre develops from the mingling of sanskritic and vernacular traditions is contained in Ratnadāsa's version of the Hariścandra story (Dhruva 1927). Here it is said that Viśvāmitra, taking the form of a wild pig, destroyed Hariścandra's garden, running away afterwards into the forest only to be followed by the aggrieved Hariścandra. The latter was then drawn into patronising a marriage, and thus losing his kingdom and wealth as a ritual gift to the bride. This incident of the wild pig has little basis in the purāṇa, but it has, nevertheless, had a formidable influence on Gujarati folklore literature and art. Similarly, the purāṇa story of the goddess Mahiṣāsuramardinī does not involve the Gujarati goddess Bahucara as found in the panels and narratives of the Garoda.

The narrator of picture-stories in a way invokes the deities when he sings of their glory. In this sense the atmosphere becomes charged with the divine presence. Listening to the divine stories in the 'presence' of the invoked deities becomes an act of merit for the audience. It is to obtain this merit that the above-described picture-shows are patronised by the devotees.

References

Basham, A L 1951. History and doctrine of the Ajivika, a Vanished Indian Religion. London

Dhruva, K H (ed) 1927. Ratnadāsa, Hariścandrākhyāna. Ahmedabad

Hamsavijayaji, (ed) 1965. Kuvalayamālā. Bombay

Jain, Jyotindra 1980. The Painted Scrolls of the Garoda Picture-showmen of Gujarat. Quarterly Journal, National Centre for the Performing Arts, vol. ix no. 3

Khadabadi, B K 1979. Vaddaradhane: a Study. Dharwad

Kramrisch, Stella 1968. Unknown India - Ritual Art in the Tribe and Village. Philadelphia

Pathak, J (ed and trans) 1958. Harṣacaritam. Benares

Fig. 1 Narrating the legend of Pabuji with a painted screen; Rajasthan.

Fig. 2 Narrating the legend of Dev Narayan with a painted scroll; Rajasthan.

Fig. 3 A Garoda narrating a picture scroll in Gujarat.

Fig. 4 A Garoda narrating the scroll while sitting on a charpoy.

Fig. 5 Garoda scroll. A demonstration of the use of continuous narration. Here the grinding of the head of Celaiyya (centre) and his return to life (left) are shown in the same panel.

Fig. 6 An example of an astrological scroll painted by the <u>Garoda</u>.

Fig. 7 Garoda scroll. Gaṇeśa with his consorts.

Fig. 8 Garoda scroll. Śiva flanked by Pārvatī, in two different forms.

Fig. 9 Garoda scroll. The story of Dhana Bhagat.

Fig. 10 Garoda scroll. Goddess killing the demon.

Fig. 11 Garoda scroll. Kṛṣṇa quelling the snake Kāliya.

Fig. 12 Garoda scroll. Śravaṇa fetching water for his old parents, and then being shot by the arrow of Daśaratha.

Fig. 13 *Garoda* scroll. Another version of the Śravaṇa story (cf. Fig. 12).

Fig. 14 *Garoda* scroll. Rāma and Lakṣmaṇa shooting the golden deer.

Fig. 15 Garoda scroll. Hanumān.

Fig. 16 Garoda scroll. Rāvaṇa.

Fig. 17 Garoda scroll. The story of king Hariścandra.

Fig. 19 Garoda scroll. Crossing the mythical river Vaitaraṇī

Fig. 18 Garoda scroll. Bhīma shaking the tree during the game of amli-pipli.

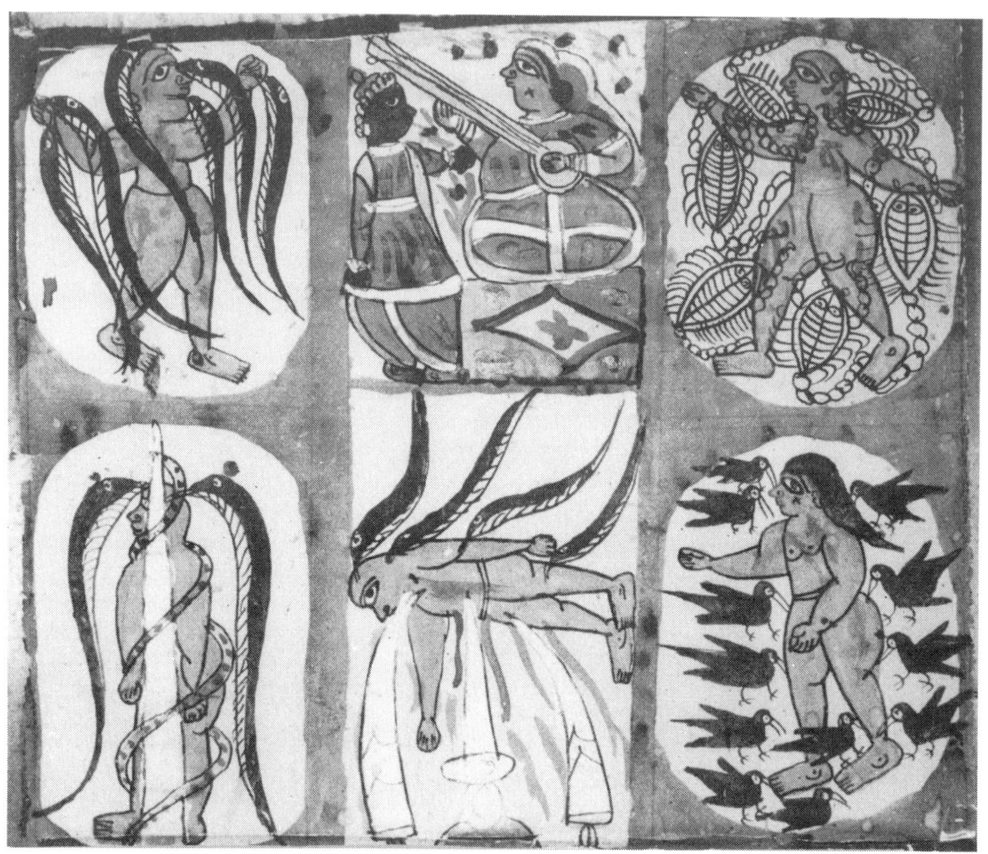

Figs. 20, 21 Garoda scroll. Sinners being punished in various hells.

VILLAGE TRADITION AND HISTORICAL SOURCES IN WEST BENGAL

J D Robinson

This paper is concerned initially with tradition in general, and then continues with an examination of the artistic tradition in the context of the Bengali village.

First, tradition implies continuity. It refers to a belief or custom that is handed down through the ages. Who hands down this custom? It is handed down through a teacher-pupil relationship that in India at least is predominantly hereditary. The tradition is maintained by the protector of the tradition, the patron, and his client. No tradition can survive without this patron-client relationship. The client, in turn, is capable of causing significant modification to the tradition and also determines whether the tradition continues or disappears due to the withdrawal of his support. Tradition is given great importance in India. The remoter its history, the greater the sense of a tradition's efficacy or importance. Many traditions are given a totally mythical origin. Their heritage is connected with a legendary figure who may or may not have existed.

Second, a tradition is either oral or recorded. The recorded tradition is usually a codified formalisation of what was originally an oral tradition. It may take a long time for such a recorded source to become available, and the original tradition may be altered in the process. Recorded tradition is subject to change at the hands of scribes. The original tradition may lose its significance and value for society, so the safety of a tradition is not necessarily guaranteed by its becoming codified in literature. As well as a living patron-client relationship, there has to be a community which understands and faithfully maintains the tradition. The tradition survives on the balance of these two factors.

The Indian artistic tradition is both recorded and oral. The recorded tradition is that of classical Indian art with its canons of iconography, rules of symmetry, proportions and aesthetic values. It is the elite art of ancient and medieval India. The canons of this art result from the accumulated experience of generations of artists. They standardise what was previously a heterogeneous oral tradition. All other forms of art which do not follow such guidelines and do not conform to a standard technique or outlook, are termed 'folk'. This term is highly misleading since it covers a variety of art forms produced by a wide range of peoples. In its broader sense it is acceptable as meaning the art of the people, or community art, but it implies a primitive, crude form of art which is not always the case.

Here I would like to distinguish between the traditional craftsman who follows an oral tradition and a layperson who also follows an oral tradition but has no technical skills and produces art for personal use. The craftsman maintains the tradition peculiar to his craft and sells his work or finds commissions. His hereditary craft is maintained within an endogamous group bearing a common guild title. The layperson, on the other hand, may also produce works of art and maintain a tradition, but the art will be for personal use only and not for a commercial market. The craftsman's art always depends on the customer's demands. The craftsman repeats standard patterns but also attempts to stretch his skills and expand his resources. He is different from the *ad hoc*-ist, the inventor or improviser who, like the 'bricoleur' of Claude Lévi-Strauss, assembles items, bric-à-brac, whatever comes to hand, for the purpose of a particular project. The craftsman reproduces his craft in a standard, repetitive way. This ensures his livelihood. The materials he uses may be cheap and readily available, but the time and skill put into his work of art may be great. Not all 'folk' art is only for temporary use.

Lastly, it should be noted that a village is a very small unit of society which is affected by local and regional idiosyncracies. Within Bengal itself, the art forms and materials that are used vary from district to district, let alone village to village. However, the village has always been an important unit of society in Bengal and it is from the village level that most Bengali art forms have emerged.

The Bengali village tradition

Bengal began to develop a regional character between the thirteenth to eighteenth centuries, the period characterised by Muslim rule. Prior to this period the various regions of eastern India which comprise modern Bengal were offshoots of the great Buddhist and Hindu dynasties of the Palas (c. 760-1142 AD) and the Senas (c. 1118-99 AD). The name Bengal is an Anglicised version of Vangala, a term used by Muslim rulers to refer to the area between the Ganges and the Brahmaputra rivers. When the British East India Company gained control of Bengal in the mid-eighteenth century, Bengal was still part of a vaguely-defined area of eastern India that included Bihar, Assam and Orissa. It was not until the first decade of the twentieth century that Bengal became distinct from its neighbours. In 1947, with Independence, Bengal was divided into West Bengal and East Pakistan, and later, in 1971, East Pakistan became the predominantly Muslim state of Bangladesh.

Bengali language developed around the thirteenth century. It was within the Muslim period that local authors composed Bengali poems called mangal kavya propagating the cults of such village deities as the snake goddess Manasā, the goddess Candi and the god of righteousness, Dharma. These deities are still popular today and the most famous mangal poems are the Caṇḍī Mangal of Mukundarama Cakravarti (otherwise known as Kavikaṅkana, the jewel among poets) composed in c. 1589, and the Manasā Mangal of Ketaka Dasa (otherwise known as Kṣemānanda) composed in the mid-seventeenth century. The Hindu Epics, the Mahābhārata and the Rāmāyaṇa, were translated into Bengali along with versions of Hindu mythology, the Purāṇas; Sanskrit, however, remained the language of learning among Hindus.

In the sixteenth century Bengal came under the influence of the Vaishnavite saint, Caitanya Mahaprobhu (1486-1533), a native of the Nadia district, who inaugurated Gaudiya Vaishnavism.

The religious art which was motivated by the growth of popular Hinduism and the devotionalism of Caitanya is what defines the art of Bengal. From the seventeenth to nineteenth centuries a new type of temple architecture developed - the bangla and cala style terracotta temples. Narrative art popularised both Puranic and village deities, whether on temple walls in terracotta friezes or in the scroll paintings of the patua painters of Bengal. Craftsmen developed their own distinct styles and wandered through the districts of Bengal, working to commission and taking their painting style with them. They worked in family groups covering several districts as far north as Assam. The Bengali style developed in this period and became dissociated from the influence of its neighbours, Bihar and Orissa. This painting could not have been easy under Muslim rule since Islam is predominantly iconoclastic, allowing only floral or calligraphic decoration.

The advent of the British in the mid-eighteenth century brought about significant changes in the village tradition. The main factor in this transformation was the development of Calcutta from three obscure villages set in marsh and jungle into a flourishing fortress town and trade centre. Urban life affected the artists who were open to greater cosmopolitan influence than they had been in the remote villages. They absorbed foreign influence but were also forced to mass-produce their art on a scale they had not been used to before, except perhaps at fairs or during festivals. In the village a few families at most would require their craft and the craftsmen would have to travel through other districts to earn a meagre living. The urban centres gave them the opportunity of tapping a constant influx of people. Instead of the artists being itinerant, they could establish guild quarters in the new urban centres.

Two important groups of artists moved into Calcutta when it first started attracting the attention of Bengali businessmen in the mid-eighteenth century. Kumar, the potters who made clay images of deities for regular and seasonal worship, moved into the northern village of Sutanuti on land owned by Govinda Candra Mitra in the latter half of the eighteenth century. Many of these came from towns such as Krishnanagar and Shantipur in the Nadia district. Simultaneously in the south, patua moved into the area around the Kali temple at Kalighat which was starting to attract pilgrims. By the time of Holwell, the potters' quarter was known as Kumartuli while the painter's quarter was called Patuapara. Kumartuli is now one of the most famous centres of clay image making, besides Krishnanagar in the Nadia district. Today many Bengalis in Europe and North America import clay images from Kumartuli for their Durga Puja celebrations during the autumn. Patuapara flourished as the centre of Kalighat art until about 1930 when it finally died out as a result of competition from modern presses.

Both these art forms, clay image making and patua painting, underwent significant transformations in their journey from the village to the urban milieu. Their art was dictated by their customers, but they themselves were influenced by foreign art forms. Under British influence the patua began to use watercolour instead of tempera; folio-sized sheets of thin Chinese paper instead of thick paper mounted on cloth; shading to represent volume instead of a flat, one-dimensional outline; and representation of the figure in three-quarter relief instead of in profile. The kumar began to use tinsel (daker saj) on their images and painted the figures in pink flesh tones in imitation of European features. They even adopted the heraldic lion of the British East India Company as the lion of Durga.

Although the art of the kumar and patua underwent transformation in Calcutta during the British period, they were protected to a certain extent by the conservatism of the wealthy Bengali families who were settled in Calcutta at the time. In the mid-eighteenth century, many landowners began to celebrate the festivals of major Hindu deities such as Durga and Kali. They tried to outdo each other in pomp and splendour, spending vast sums of money and often bankrupting themselves in the process. These lavish celebrations set a social trend among other groups of Bengalis. Townsfolk set up puja committees and were able to imitate the grandeur of their peers, subsidising the festivals by communal subscriptions. On the one hand, craftsmen who supplied the images for festivals (the kumar, patua and the mali or decorators) were employed as a team by the traditional families according to the old system of patronage whereby the artist received grants of tax-free land as payment and artist families became affiliated to them for life. On the other hand, these craftsmen had to meet the demand of the more modernistic puja committees who were also in competition with each other and wanted more and more bizarre kinds of images. Today kumar still produce the traditional images maintained by the descendants of the old Bengali families of the eighteenth century, while at the same time they make new images for the puja committees. They no longer receive land payments but are paid directly. The old system of patronage is slowly dying out with the breakdown of landownership and the collapse of the joint family system.

The transformation of the art of the kumar and patua into an urban art indicates the manner in which Bengali 'folk art' moves within a changing social environment. The art of the patua did not survive the ordeal. The modern printing press was much faster than the hand-painting methods of the Kalighat artists and prints soon replaced paintings in popularity. The kumar on the other hand thrived in the urban environment. The clay images which they produced were in constant demand. Despite their opportunism, the kumar have continued to maintain the itinerant lifestyle of village artists. Although they take up residence in Calcutta for a few months of the year during the peak season, during the off-season they return to their villages to farm land or continue their trade which still remains the production of earthenware, although the more artistically-minded take up sculpture or make other kinds of images. The traditional 'off-peak' production of clay dolls for sale at fairs in the winter months has been transformed by the kumar of Krishnanagar into a lucrative business with the production of realistic models of Bengali village characters. Many kumar also have studios in Assam and travel far afield in their work. The idea of district style remains and the artists still mark out their areas of business.

Clay images and patua paintings produced in the village are stylistically very different from those made in the city. The village style is less sophisticated, uses a narrower range of materials and is not mass-produced. It is not necessarily conservative in that the artists do not have a pedantic approach to maintaining their style, but the conventional means of production, and the repetition of patterns, ensures the survival of the village style in the modern environment.

An interesting feature of the transformation of village art, or at least its exposure to foreign influence, is the ability of the artists to make witty observations on the social situation. Many terracotta panels from the Bengali temples of the seventeenth to nineteenth centuries depict the Portuguese and British at work and at play. Likewise, the Kalighat artists responded to the anti-nationalistic attitude of Calcutta society in 1870-1900 by attacking modernisation through their drawings. The capacity to absorb and reflect on foreign influence indicates a sophistication beyond the connotation of primitive or naive that the term 'folk art' implies. It also distinguishes the art of the craftsman from that of the layperson in Bengali society, which suggests that Bengali art is also defined by the works of art produced by laypeople for their own personal use.

This branch of art is derived primarily from the religious tradition of the villagers. We may call it vrata art, since the objects produced by the layperson in this case are for the purposes of a vrata or vow. Vrata are domestic rituals practiced mainly by women and are directed to a host of popular village deities who offer protection against disease and disaster. The small clay images used in vrata ritual to represent their deities, as well as human and animal figures, are reminiscent of the terracotta finds at Harappa and Mohenjo Daro. They are crudely-formed figures without legs or hands whose facial and body details are worked out by pinching and incising the soft clay and applying small pellets of clay for decoration. They are usually fired and given a basic glaze or layer of bright paint. Many of these figures of village deities are theriomorphic; anthropomorphic representations are rare. Even in the more sophisticated vrata art produced by the village artists, the deities are usually depicted as busts attached to ceremonial waterpots. Much of this vrata art is exemplified by the terracotta animals which are placed as votive offerings in shrines or under trees. The village artists use a variety of materials and pay little attention to such details as iconography in the portrayal of deities. The materials used are generally cheap and easily available such as pith (sola) which is cut into strips and modelled, or else used as a base for painting.

The historical sources for the layperson's art and that of the craftsman making vrata art are limited. The mangal kavya composed in the Muslim period supply the researcher with valuable material on the religious practices of Bengali villagers at the time. The poets who composed these poems invariably give a brief autobiographical account at the beginning of the poem to explain why they have composed a mangal to the presiding deity. Although the explanation is not necessarily factually correct, the rest of the account is often reliable documentary. But like all forms of art, the mangal genre is guided by its own standard conventions. All worship is described in terms of puja to a ceremonial waterpot (ghata) rather than to an image or painting. The deities are not given distinctive iconographical features. Female deities, for instance, are always described as beautiful young women with dazzling features and a profusion of ornamentation. There are few references to other art forms or craftsmen. Either literary standards ruled out such social documentation or else the craftsman was considered unworthy of mention. Whatever the case may be, the mangal are a limited source of information about village artistic tradition. We are left to guess the kind of objects produced and the artists involved by referring to the present situation in the villages of Bengal.

The historical sources for the British period (eighteenth to twentieth centuries), on the other hand, are more readily available, partly due to the technology which characterised the period. The first printed Bengali books appeared in the first decade of the nineteenth century and included editions of some of the mangal kavya (from existing manuscripts dating back no earlier than the seventeenth century), as well as epics and works on the social history of the period. There was a sudden interest in discovering India's past, encouraged by the foundation of the Asiatic Society by Sir William Jones. Also, records of European travellers, missionaries and artists comprise a relatively comprehensive picture of events.

Apart from these sources there are the archaeological finds now to be found in Bengali museums. Non-classical art has been documented to some extent and many Bengali academics are becoming increasingly interested and informed about the village artifacts of the various districts of Bengal. Perhaps this will lead to a greater understanding of the artistic trends and the mode in which Bengali craftsmen have responded to changing conditions.

Reference

Robinson, J D 1983. The Worship of Clay Images in Bengal. Unpublished D. Phil thesis, University of Oxford (Bodleian Library, shelfmark C4545)

Fig. 1 Face of Viśvakarma, god of artisans. Kumartuli, Calcutta.

Fig. 2 Painting of Viśvakarma images. Kumartuli, Calcutta.

Fig. 3 Traditional Kali image. Hooghly district temple.

Fig. 4 Traditional Durga image. Calcutta.

VOTIVE TERRACOTTAS OF GUJARAT

Haku Shah

In Gujarat, terracotta figures are found in almost every village near the tribal areas and are made by the Varia and Gurjar castes who are kumbhar (potters). These terracottas vary from 2cm to 100cm in maximum dimension. The smaller ones are of solid clay, the larger ones are hollow, and yet still others are made up of a mixture of both hollow and solid parts. There is a sexual division of labour which shows regional variation. In general, men work on the potter's wheel while women usually only do hand-work. In north Gujarat the men throw the clay, while the women merely assist them, whereas in south Gujarat, where the clay is unsuitable for throwing, terracottas are usually made by women, and are made in very large numbers. The style of terracottas made by each family varies markedly every 30 to 50 km. The tribal groups, on the other hand, make only unbaked figures, or baked utensils, but never figurines. Nevertheless tribal people influence terracotta production, because their needs are taken into account by the non-tribal potters.

Tribals such as the Bhil Garasia, Dungri Garasia, Sokla Garasia, Chodhri, Gamit, Vasava, Bhil, Koli, Bariya, Dubla and others visit the potters whenever they have to make an offering of terracotta horses, or other items. The entire process - from the creation of the clay form to the offering of the terracottas to the tribal gods - forms part of a ritual which is followed with great respect and with strict adherence to tradition. Among the full-figure forms made are the following: purus (man); astri (woman); men and women figures in various postures; ghodo (horse); hathi (elephant); vagh (tiger); balad (bull); vachhadu (calf); bhens (buffalo); and khokhli (terracottas representing combined animal and human forms). Other items represent parts of the body: hath (hand); pag (feet); duti (navel); ankh (eyes); kan (ears); guntan (knee); golo (stomach); bobla (breast); pansali (lungs); goli (testicles); and muth (fist). Terracotta representations of whole limbs, or of animals like worms, are also offered to the gods concerned. The terracottas are sold at the local market, or at the potters' houses. Tribals buy those needed for a particular ritual, as advised by their priest. Prices vary from 5 paise to Rs.15.00. They are sometimes bought in large numbers of forty to fifty at a time, to be offered at different sanctuaries to different gods.

The gods to whom these terracottas are offered are many and varied, operating in different spheres of human interest. There are mountain gods and goddesses; crocodile and other animal gods; medicine gods; field gods; gods for crops; ancestral gods; and a great variety of smallpox deities, such as Cosath jogni mata, Angahi mata, Bhuri mandan mata, Goligadh mata, Kuldevi mata, Gosaimata, Dhabas mata, Tabukli mata, Khedbai mata, Pandar devi, Devli madi, Demi Dohi, Goval dev, Balia dev, Vaida dev, Baba dev, Kac humor dev, Babo akho dev, Saiyad Kaka, Ahindro, Kalakakad, Bhakher, Tubraj, Valinath maharaj, Vanjaro Bhut, etc.

Technique of production

The quality of the clay for making terracottas varies from one place to another. The clay found in south Gujarat is not suitable for throwing on the wheel, and so the terracottas made in that region are neither large, nor entirely hollow. In north Gujarat, by contrast, the clay is excellent and eminently suitable for this purpose. Through experience, the potters know the best clay sources, and also how to mix the clay required for different purposes. The process of making terracotta figures is illustrated in Figs. 1-10.

Attitude and preparation

Preparing the clay is an arduous task: potters rise at 4.00 a.m. or earlier to start their work. The preliminary task of kneading the clay takes a great deal of time, and is usually done by the women. The penlis, or lumps of clay which they prepare resemble the lingam - the phallic symbol of Śiva, the god with whom the potting craft is most closely connected. They use only a few simple tools, but it is this ritual approach to their work that helps create such fine terracotta figures.

Hollow figures are made by joining together wheel-thrown cylinders and pots of various shapes which are basically household items. The prominent ears of the clay elephant, for example, are simply traditional clay lamps fixed vertically to the side of the head.

The solid terracotta figures may consist of one or more carefully shaped lumps of clay, which are joined together after they have dried a little. The final form of the terracotta horse, for example, which may look oddly contrived to an outsider, is the result of a gradual evolution towards technical perfection. The potters have shaped it and created supports, moving the neck to balance it and to make the form of the horse firm and solid. The technique itself, therefore, plays an important part in creating the final distinctive form of the figure.

The third type of terracotta figure combines both hollow and solid parts. Such figures are all medium-sized, usually around 30 to 40cm high, and with hollow torsos. In some cases the legs and neck are also hollow.

Joining the parts

The technique of joining component parts together plays an important part in the process of terracotta production. Special clay mixtures are prepared for the joints and the potter determines how the various parts of the figures are to be related. He seeks the optimum balance between the duration of throwing, the size of the torso, the relationship of the legs to the torso, and also the relationship between solid and hollow parts. The basic problem is how to achieve a balance. The potter will also decide if a figure has to be solid or hollow or joined, or if any lumps have to be added in order to shape certain parts as desired. Potters have to devise their own methods of joining parts of their clay figures while considering two other aspects: how to shape the clay easily from within, and how to allow the air to circulate, so that the figure can be fired effectively.

It is with these considerations in mind that holes are retained in many hollow terracottas. Sometimes the legs are inserted and locked inside the torso, while others are merely joined from outside by blending in the clay.

The method of joining varies between different areas:

i) in north Gujarat the neck is inserted so that its edges lock in place, but the legs are left open from within, not using a locking method to fix them to the torso;

ii) in central Gujarat, the legs and necks of larger figures are usually sealed from inside, again without a locking system being employed;

iii) in south Gujarat, the necks or legs of figures are sealed with clay, but not locked, and sometimes these figures are hollow throughout.

The precise method followed depends on the size of the figure and on the different working methods of the individual potters (see Fig. 11).

Adding the details

In north Gujarat, and formerly elsewhere, the finishing work is minimal; round lumps of clay are simply stuck on the figure at different points, and slit crosswise to signify bells. Alternatively, such lumps may be slit diagonally to represent tridents, or to suggest a saddle. Bell-like clay lumps may also be stuck on to the belly or torso. Later, more elaborate finishing came into vogue in central Gujarat. Numerous lumps of clay are added all over the figures to create additional bells, reins and other trappings - and for further decoration potters sprinkle white colour on the red terracotta figures, which is considered a prerequisite by tribal people when purchasing such an item.

In south Gujarat finishing is so elaborate that outsiders may fail to recognize the figures as horses (or whatever animal is involved) at all. However, when one analyses the technique used, the identity of the figure can easily be determined. The women in south Gujarat add extra clay lumps bearing different designs, to create figures worthy of receiving prayers. An enormous variety of styles in terracotta figures has thereby evolved, showing great creative talent.

North Gujarat wheel-thrown terracotta figurines show a sort of royal hierarchy in the manner in which they are graded. Of limited variety, they are elegant, technically refined and finished with only a few added elements. In south Gujarat, by contrast, because of the liberty of working only with the hands, the variety of forms is enormous. These forms vary in shape from the simple to the profusely embellished. Sometimes they appear rather odd, and even crudely-worked. Yet the different forms are excellently created using a variety of round and flattened pipes. Above all, the finishing touches are often inspired. Special care is taken when depicting the nostrils, ear holes, genitals, eyes, navel, neck and so on. These are formed in many ways, ranging from the slightest touch of a finger to a prominent mark for a horse's nostril. At times a pipe-like form is created and then pressed evenly from the top, so that it looks like a chain or garland. All this is done dextrously with the fingers. Potter women create many different kinds of terracottas, but the finest and the most ornate are the horses and the human figures.

Firing

Prepared figures are fired along with ordinary domestic pots and other utensils in simple 'bonfire' kilns. These can be made in about an hour, and are always constructed in an open area, away from the living quarters. Firing begins in the mid-afternoon and is completed overnight, so that the kiln can be dismantled and the contents removed the next day. Kilns may be shared when convenient, but usually each potter makes his or her own, with assistance from family members.

From the initial preparation of the kiln to the final extraction of the products, the work process combines technical skill with ritual observances, as the following typical schedule illustrates:

10.45 a.m.: the animal figures are coloured, from the mouth and head right down to the legs, with a brick-red powder (*geru*). If the colour does not turn out well, the customers for whom the figures are intended may say that it looks inferior, bakh nathi janato, rupak nathi;

11.25: the painting of the horses is completed;

11.27: the kiln, lembhado, is cleaned and the old ash, rakh, from the previous firing is swept away. Meanwhile, a mixture of grass and donkey dung is prepared which will later form a layer, tharo, to seal the completed kiln;

11.31: a layer of wood is placed in the botton of the kiln;

11.37: a bundle of cotton twigs is arranged in a layer over the wood, and is then compacted firmly underfoot;

11.40: a second bundle of twigs is spread firmly over this first layer. The fire will only burn evenly if the layers are well-distributed, harkhu jamave etle baltan harkhu rahe. They are firmly packed and stuck together resembling a quilt, hajjad karine sotadi nakhiye, godadi na jem;

11.45: cowdung, adaya, is spread over the layers of wood and twigs. One basketful of cowdung covers about a quarter of the area; about six baskets are required to cover it generously. Broken pots will be placed only after the figurines are arranged in the kiln;

12.05: the figurines are carefully arranged on top of this bed of fuel;

12.25: gunny bags, kothla, or blankets, dhabla, are spread over the top of the pile of figures to protect them from being damaged by the outer layers to be added next;

12.30: grass, clay pot rims, kanthla, and powdered donkey dung are then arranged over the bags or blankets;

12.35: the fire is set, devata lagadya, and then the following words are chanted:

> Insects beware, the fire is coming,
> The kiln is set afire.
> Beware insects, ants and all living beings.
> May the evil caused by killing these insects
> Fall upon him who has returned evil for good
> And taken away things without appreciation.
> May the Lord strike such a one with leprosy.

Then these words are chanted before work resumes:

> O Lord Gaṇeśa, you come to those who remember you.
> You manifest yourself, and eat laddu, sweet-balls.
> If one does not invoke you, you pursue him.
> Whoever learns the art of throwing clay on the wheel,
> and shaping it
> Will give you a jar full of laddu.

As the fire burns, the mounded part of the kiln subsides, and more dry grass and crumbled donkey dung have to be added to keep it going. A potter called Jethabhai says that if the bed of cotton twigs is well laid, the burning takes place slowly and evenly throughout the entire period of firing. More material for the fire should be placed at the bottom so that the flames can reach the highest level of figurines in the kiln. In this case, Jethabhai pointed out, six baskets of cowdung were required. When firing earthenware utensils, pots, etc., only four baskets of cowdung are normally required. Clay horses are only thrown on the wheel, while waterpots are first thrown and then shaped using the paddle and anvil technique. Because of this method, the pots have thinner walls than the horses, and thus require less heat for firing.

Gujarati terracottas are generally either red or white in colour, but there are exceptions. In north Gujarat, one occasionally finds black elephant figurines, while in the south, clay animals may be painted with lime. With the latter type the tribals sing 'We go to offer the horses to our gods, and they are as white as cranes'. In central Gujarat, terracotta horses and elephants are spattered with white lime - in this area tribals will reject as unsuitable any which are not treated in this way.

Exchange and the village gods

In central Gujarat, horses are offered to *Dev* (*Guru dev* or *guru na dhani*), the supreme being of the village. The tribals buy terracottas in large numbers to offer to their gods, and the potter who supplies them receives, in exchange, rice or maize, and perhaps also money, depending on the number of horses ordered. The potter is also given a live cock, which is let loose if the potter does not wish to eat it; he also receives liquor and coconuts. The priest ties red threads around the necks of five terracotta horses. This is called *nada chhadi*. A red spot is then made on the forehead of each. The potter prepares the horses exactly as the tribal asks him to. When the tribals are ready to leave, they honour Gaṇeśa, and then sing and dance and venerate and pay respect to all the objects.

To give an idea of the scale of these activities, when a ritual pilgrimage was undertaken recently *Dev Gurudev* was offered sixty to seventy small horses, eighteen large horses, four elephants, sixty to seventy *dhabu* (small dome-shaped houses) and a hundred *kodiya* lamps, as well as *kundi* for storing milk. These items were obtained from a potter in exchange for $1\frac{1}{4}$ maund (about 100lb) of grain, a cock, a bottle of liquor, and Rs.450 in cash. Those who acquired the terracottas included the *patel* (head of the village), the *pujari* (priest), the *dholi* (drummer), the *sahanaiya* (pipe players), and people from the village who accompanied the others in ritual celebration.

The procession went first to the shrine at Ratanmahal, where ten large terracotta horses were offered; then four more were offered at nearby Jangra. At a third place, Khedbai, another four were offered, goats were sacrificed, and the meat was distributed to everyone present before they all went to the priest's house and eventually dispersed, forgetting their burdens and troubles. This type of ceremony keeps the participants' houses, livestock, fields, walls and families safe from ill fortune.

Potters occupy certain distinct parts of the larger villages, and it is here that the tribals come to buy. These areas are invariably located near the approaches to a village, and therefore on its outskirts. Potters are generally neat people, orderly and always busy with clay. It is ironic that there are two names for them, each with very different connotations - kumbhar and prajapati. The first, innocuously, signifies 'he who makes the pot' (sometimes when a child is a dullard, he is abused as 'kumbhar' - a potter). The second word means 'the lord of the people', and no marriage ceremony can proceed without prior worship of the potter's wheel. Potters sell the tribals large quantities of figures and pots. They sell cooking vessels to other communities as well, such as the Hindus and Muslims. Terracotta figurines are, however, only made for tribals. Figures and utensils are both produced and then sold together. Some figures are kept on view in the open verandahs of the potters' houses, some are placed in their front rooms, while yet others are stored in the attics.

Nathiben, a potter's wife, told of how Nathabhai (one of the potters) once went into a trance and spoke to his personal deity, the mountain god Tubraj. He said Hun Sadyo su, Maru dapu bandhi apo (I am now in a trance, fix the amount that I should charge [for my terracottas] from today). Tubraj instructed him to accept the following in exchange for his images:

¼lb of ghee for a horse with a rider, Patwi ghodo, Royal Horse;
½lb of ghee for a horse without a rider, Thathvi ghodo, Grand Horse;
¼lb of ghee for an ordinary horse Rodyo ghodo.

Denotation and function

The use of terracotta figures as votive offerings for appeasing the gods is based on a fairly obvious symbolism. You offer a clay eye to heal your own eye, a hand to set your hand right, and an entire human figure to make yourself well all over (Figs. 12, 21). The symbolism, however, is not only of form, but of substance. Clay and flesh have been linked since time immemorial (and not only in India). In fact, the word mati, clay, also means man, and this idea is one which is deeply ingrained in the minds of the tribals who offer their powerful deities a cow for a cow, a buffalo for a buffalo, and a calf for a calf.

For many reasons the horse (Figs. 13, 14) is considered next to man in importance and has become a symbol of great significance. Myths, legends and wise sayings confirm (even if they do not, strictly speaking, 'explain') the pre-eminence of the horse. According to one epic story, Jagdev Parmar once killed a five-year-old buffalo with a single stroke of his sword. This brave act pleased his god who rewarded him with a horse. From that day, the horse was considered a worthy animal, one loved by the gods, and indeed, it is often referred to in such terms:

> Jagubhai Varia, from north Gujarat, says -
>
> Ghoda jevo manas thay, the man becomes like a horse (if the man is sick he becomes as energetic as a horse); and Dev ne besva ghoro joie, ena per besi e fare, the god needs the horse to sit on, and travels around.
>
> The horse is a god of the family and offers virtue. If a vow has been made to the Mother Goddess and is not kept, she will come to you in a dream, sit on your chest, and ask 'Why did you not give me the horse that you promised me?'
>
> Bhera Natha, a Bhilgarasia tribal, from Poshina village, said -
>
> Once, all of a sudden, my brother became mad. We called the priest and took a vow, taro ghoro tane sadavi, jo haru thahe to, 'if he

recovers, a terracotta horse will be offered to you'. After two months he recovered. Devat ni anti pari gei. Ado farelo, 'the god was displeased and made my brother mad again. Tubraj bavasi be ghora sadavela', two horses were offered to Tubraj, the mountain god, and while offering the horses, we told the god - Tane maharaj ne sadava. Aj ri boli suti, 'to you god I offer; from today I am relieved of my word.'

Terracotta elephants (Fig. 9) are also offered for vows pertaining to either human or animal fertility. An elephant is offered by the tribals, especially at the birth of a son. In Kutch Muslim potters make elephants for Hindus (Fischer and Shah, unpublished manuscript). When a son is born in a household, gifts of terracotta elephants are brought to them as gifts. In return for the elephant, the potter is given grain or money - or even a live camel.

Sometimes offerings are designed to benefit several people simultaneously, as in the following case of Govind, his son Shukkar and grandson Ashok. The offerings were made by Govind's wife Rami, in the presence of only Shukkar and Ashok. Govind, her husband, stayed at home. The chart below gives details of the offerings and why they were made:

Duration	Name and Age	Cause	Offerings
Annually for 12 years	Govind 60 years	Hernia (descended testicle)	Rami offered three coconuts, three terracotta goli, one terracotta horse, three red goli, kumkum, and incense; also the lamps were lit.
This year only	Shukkar 27 years	Pain in the scrotum due to injury while riding a bicycle	
This year only	Ashok 4 years	Suddenly enlarged testicle	

Rami explained why they offered certain articles and the reasons for some of their actions. She said that Rupa no golo (a ball of lead), sagadi, bedu (an oven and pot), ful, manta ni goli (flowers and terracotta balls), marad, dhup sali (a male figure and incense), nariyel (coconuts), and ghee na diva (a butter oil lamp) had to be carried to the shrine to be offered for the vow. She added that one had to remember to say Hambharna kari levanu ... tamne jatra na divse manta muki dehu ('we are fulfilling our vow on your pilgrimage day'). Everything has to work out alright after this. She explained that twelve or thirteen years ago her husband had had this trouble, Bar ter varah uper thailu. One must repeat the offerings to avoid recurrence; Mukavu pade nahi to pachha thay was the way she put it. In other words, the hernia recurs if the ritual is not repeated each year. She also explained - Pet ma golo jevo thay to golo jevo fare, astri ne to paki astri ne golo ape .... - that if the stomach swells up like a ball, then a terracotta ball is required. If a woman is affected as well, then a terracotta figure of a woman and a ball is also offered along with the terracotta ball. She explained that a horse itself is man, ghoro marad kevay. Even for a housewife the horse is so important that if her husband has not ridden a horse she might say 'oh my timid worthless husband, you do not have any rights over my body' (Maniagar, n.d.).

Terracotta offerings are made either individually or collectively. The occasions when they are used as offerings are as follows:

i) at different stages of the crop's growth;

ii) for the well-being of an individual or village;

iii) to protect against ill health, or to avert evil from men and animals;

iv) to assist or protect during a disease-curing ritual;

v) when installing the spirits of the dead (clay domes and horses are used);

vi) as offerings to ancestors;

vii) when offspring are desired;

viii) to promote the fertility of animals;

ix) when cows or buffaloes do not give milk;

x) to recover property, if there has been a theft.

Sanctuaries

Terracotta figures are usually offered at large sanctuaries in special places away from the village when a specific vow is fulfilled. However, each village also has its own _utara_, or small abode of the god of the area. This _utara_ is a miniature form of the larger sanctuary. When a tribal cannot go to a large sanctuary, he places his offerings at the _utara_ of the same god in his own village (Figs. 16-22). At large sanctuaries the gods have to be approached in the order of hierarchy, from the lowliest upwards. For instance, the _chokidar_, or overall watchman, is approached first, followed by the _nakedar_, or sentry; these in turn are followed by the lower deities, like the smallpox god, _Kakabalia_, until it is the turn of the main god. Of the thousands of terracottas offered to the main gods in a sanctuary, the majority, at any one time, will be seen to be broken. New figures are added to the sanctuaries year after year, producing great heaps of votive offerings. Great care is taken while carrying them to the sanctuary, because before a figure is offered it should not be damaged in any way. The terracottas are brought either in carts or in baskets on people's heads. If a figure breaks or is damaged, it is replaced with a new one. Carrying these figurines, the tribals climb mountains, cross rivers or travel through thick forests. They walk many miles to reach the god's sanctuary, which is always located in a remote place with a ritually-charged atmosphere. The tribals do not install or maintain there any images of the gods. Gods and tigers are close neighbours in the places where sanctuaries are found.

For small offerings, tribals take their chosen terracotta to the sanctuary, along with chickens, incense, flags, rice, coins, wine and coconuts. However, on more important occasions, invitations are sent to friends, relatives and others. People then assemble in one place and play musical instruments. They sing and dance all the way to the sanctuary and continue to do so even when approaching the god. They offer their different gifts, first of all marking them with dots of orange powder. Flags are also offered, and lamps are lit. The bhuvo, or priest, goes into a trance and offers the rice, toddy and the chicken, and invokes all the gods in the sanctuary while chanting and singing. Towards the end of this procedure a man climbs a tree or a high platform and throws rice over the assembled people, which they try to catch and later take home. The ritual is eventually brought to a close with a feast and dancing.

When I see the ritual like the one described, my mind sees the entire Psychic Panorama. I see the white and red flags at the sanctuary, the terracottas quickened by sacrificial offerings, the chanting and the trances, and the crowds of tribals in reverential mood - all mingling one with the other. This ritual, accompanied by feasting and by intense moods, colour, and devotion, is one from which everyone benefits - the terracottas, the gods, the tribals themselves, and the ever-present spirits.

In south Gujarat, for instance, the tribals go to the cowherd god to offer their terracottas and sing and dance at the sanctuary:

> Bharye, nariyele, sindhur, dehu, ma rodali jodi
> Sudio sopario lei lete ma roadali jodi
> Dovadia hovaria vat jove ma rodali jodi
> Dhamania bokde lei lete ma rodali jodi
>
> Pipatye Dhaja Chadhi jahe ma rodali jodi
> Baglya ghoda chadhi jate ma rodali jodi
> Kukda bokda bhog dahu ma rodali jodi

While offering the terracotta horses, they utter:

> I offer this horse to you, the god,
> From today my relief is assured; do good to us.
> May your good wishes prevail.
> May our generation grow!

Note

When quoting from tribal speech the author uses Bhil Garasia, a tribal version of Gujarati. Hence the changes from ghodo to ghoro, chadhava to sadava, etc.

Reference

Maniagar, n.d. Virdo

Stages in making a terracotta horse

Fig. 1 Jethabhai digging clay.

Figs. 2, 3 Preparing a terracotta leg.

Fig. 4 (right) Jethabhai's son joining legs to body.

Figs. 5, 6 (below) Preparing the neck and head.

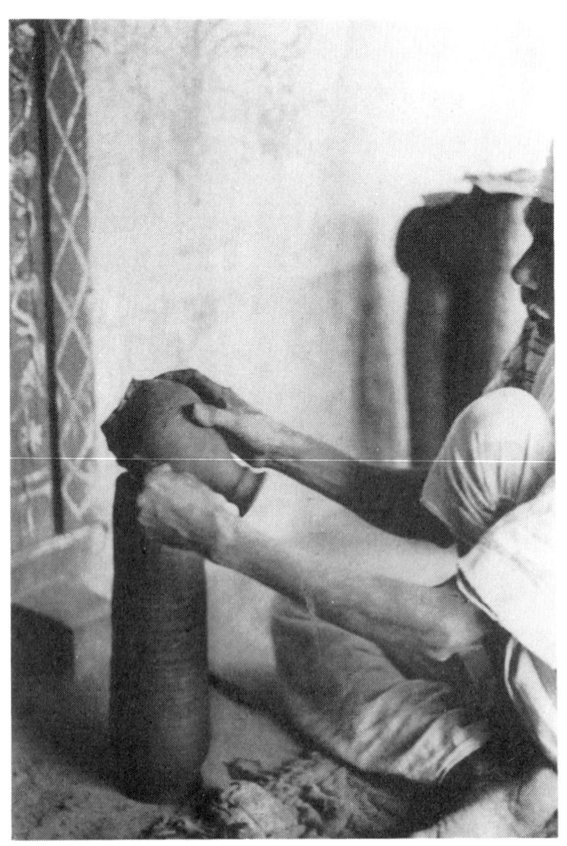

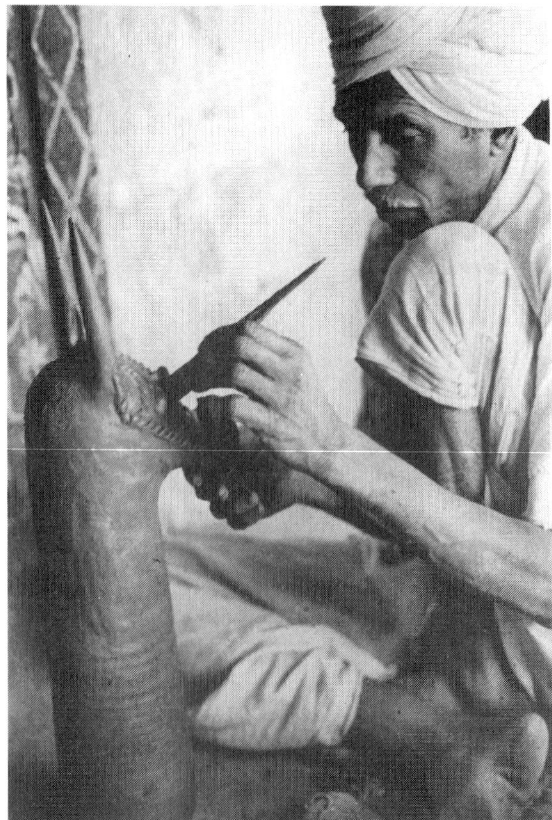

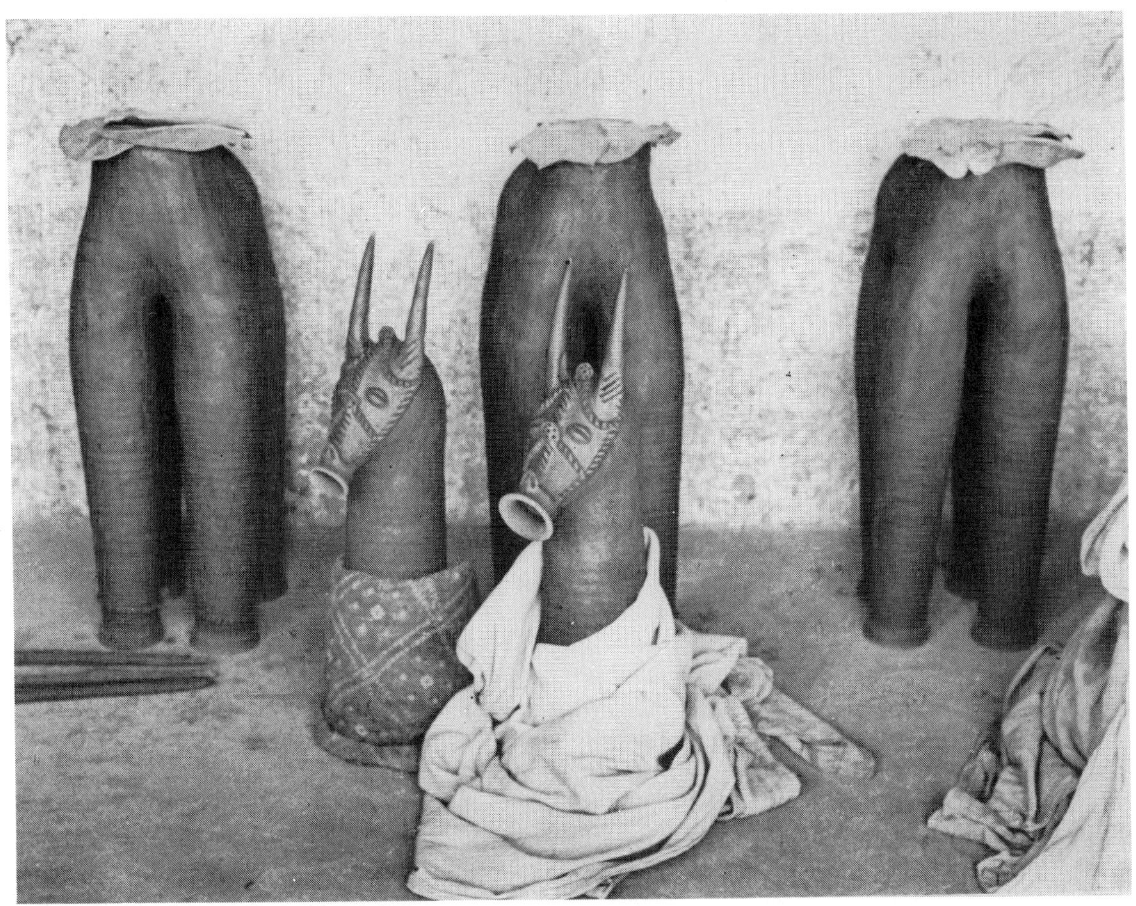

Fig. 7 Heads and bodies left to partially dry.

Fig. 8 The head and neck are fitted on to the body.

Fig. 9 Clay horses and elephants drying in the sun outside the potter's house.

Fig. 10 Jethabhai and his son prepare the kiln for firing.

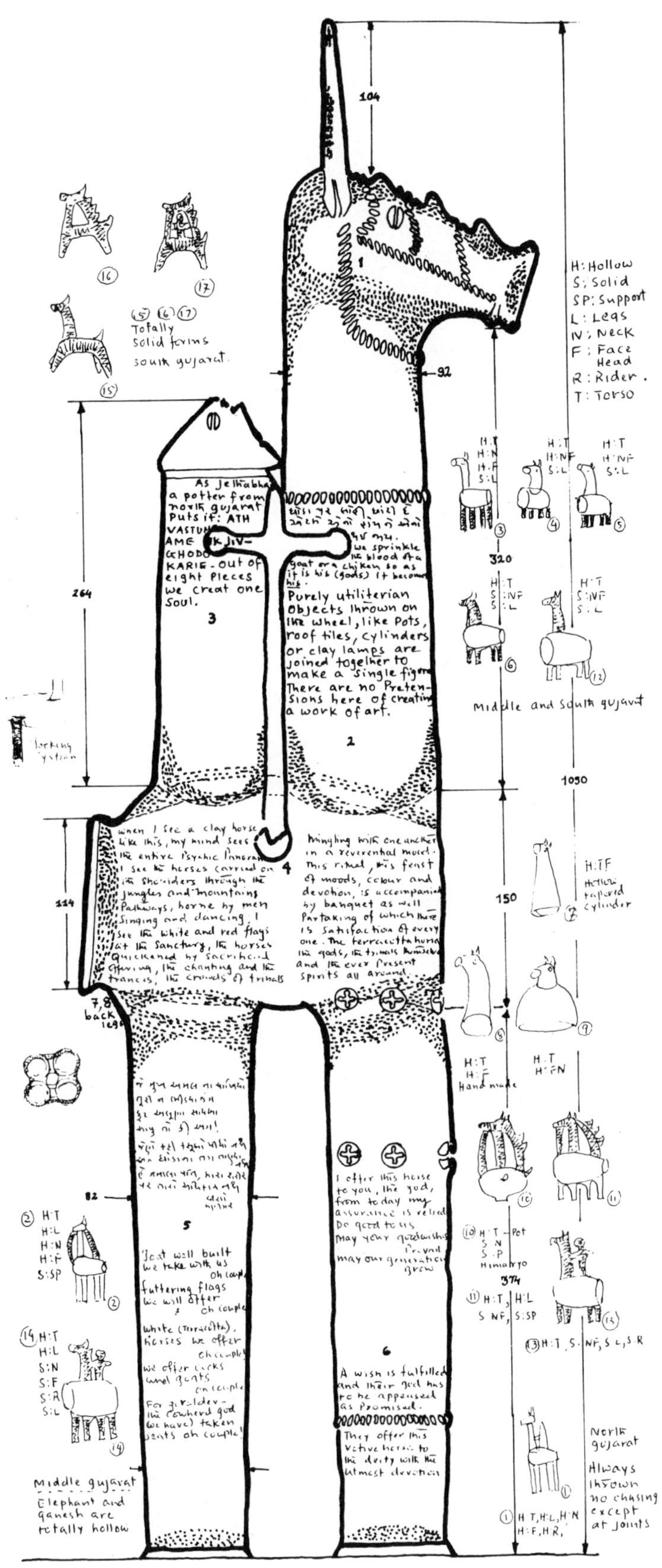

Fig. 11 Proportions and regional variations in design (drawing by the author).

Other terracotta figures from Gujarat

Fig. 12 Hand-modelled figure of a woman of a type made by the Chodhri, Gamit, Kotwalia and Kukua tribal peoples of southern Gujarat.

Fig. 13 Hand-modelled figure of a horse from the same source as Fig. 12.

Fig. 14 Hand-modelled figure of a horse of a type made by the Chodhri, Gamit, Kukua and Dubla tribal peoples of southern Gujarat. Decorated with spots of white flour, such figures may be offered to a village goddess to cure disease.

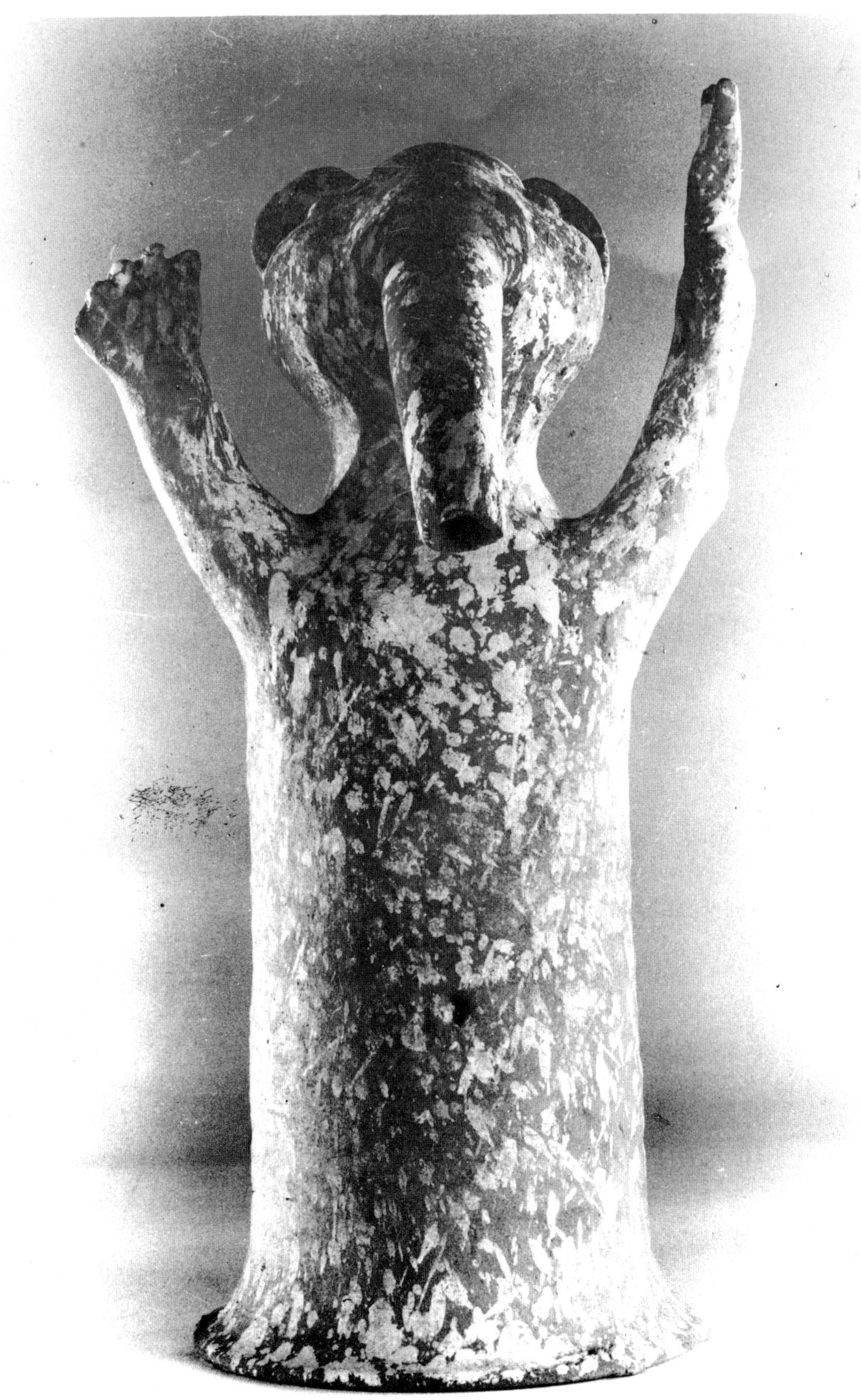

Fig. 15 Figure of the elephant-headed god Gaṇeśa, from the Bhilala tribal people of central Gujarat. The cylindrical body was made on a potter's wheel.

Offering of terracotta horses to the mountain god Tubraj in north Gujarat

Fig. 16 (above) The horses are brought to the god's sanctuary and the sacrificial goat is prepared for slaughter.

Fig. 17 Before the horse is installed in the sanctuary the head of the sacrificed goat is placed upon its own.

The votive use of terracotta figures elsewhere in Gujarat

Fig. 18 A sanctuary in northern Gujarat typical of those where Soklā, Bhīl and Dungrī Garasias tribal peoples offer huge terracotta horses to the mother goddess, Demī dohi.

Fig. 19 In small sanctuaries near villages, the Bhīl of the Panchmahal region offer terracotta horses to the goddess and place a flag alongside.

Fig. 20 Men of the Dhodia tribal group offering various terracotta forms to the mother goddess, Goligadh.

Fig. 21 A tribal man in southern Gujarat marks a human terracotta figure with red pigment before offering it to the deity.

Fig. 22 Wooden figures, khatrī, realistically carved and brightly painted by tribal peoples, are placed in the fields as memorials to the dead, to whom small terracotta horses and vessels are offered.

CONTEMPORARY TAMIL TERRACOTTAS: PRODUCTION AND PURPOSE

Stephen Huyler

Introduction

More than 620 million people in India live in villages, yet the emphasis of most documentation is placed upon urban minorities. In art, the 'refined' products of temples, courts, and cities receive predominant attention while the traditions of innumerable rural artisans are allowed to die unnoticed. Least recognised of this vast array of rural crafts is that of the potter, the maker of both vessels and sculpture. My research focuses on the latter of these two products: terracotta statuary. The large quantities of terracottas excavated in, or found in association with, ancient Indian sites clearly suggest their historical importance. Recently, increased documentation has made the subject more academically acceptable, although it has not yet received its due acclaim. Still little noticed are the contemporary terracottas made by village potters throughout the subcontinent. During the course of fifteen years of extensive travel in rural India, I have discovered low-fired clay sculpture in almost every district. Stylistically they are diverse, but the subject matter and reasons for their production are, in most places, similar, drawing together through ritual imagery such diverse social extremes as tribal people and Brahmans. Full documentation of this vast sub-stratum at least gives some means for understanding the importance of terracottas in ancient traditions and might provide a key for comprehending one of the primary socio-religious roots of Indian art and cultural traditions.

The goal of my research is twofold: to document the production, use and cultural relevance of contemporary terracottas and, through handling and photographing ancient terracottas in existing museums and private collections, to attempt to establish a framework of historic parallels. This latter work can only hope to show similarities in finished imagery, but perhaps through a thorough knowledge of the preparation and importance of current clay sculpture, we can hypothesize about archaic manufacture and meaning. To date I have worked with most of the major terracotta collections in India which have provided numerous examples similar to locally indigenous material. Historically, artisans in the clay medium achieved as high artistic standards as those in other fields[1]. As elsewhere, those results remain unique and could not be said to have close contemporary parallels. However, within those same 'refined' collections and in many others are simpler terracottas, still artistically pleasing, beginning with relics from pre-Aryan sites in the North and Megalithic sites in the far South and continuing through almost every subsequent level of Indian development. These terracottas form an archetypal basis for comparison with contemporary products. In many cases I could place a recent, but weathered, village clay image next to an archaeological one with no apparent differences and only scientific testing to prove which was older.

The other aspect and major corpus of my research emphasizes contemporary terracottas. The only means for gathering information on existing clay sculptural traditions is through comprehensive travel. With the exception of the research of a few scholars working in isolated areas, little has been documented. Within every two or three villages throughout India there is usually a potter. At some point in the year most potters are commissioned to sculpt - sometimes only children's toys, but frequently an image associated with worship, most often as a votive gift. Consequently, my approach is to travel in the rural districts of

India trying to locate shrines containing terracottas and interviewing the potters who made them. Whenever I am able, I document the sculpting technique. When I have covered a given stylistic area I then choose one potter to focus on. I commission his full prescriptive line of images, and, living either with him or in close proximity, document carefully the entire process. In order to make my survey objective, I try to refrain from giving him any advice as to a desirable outcome. As far as possible, I record on tape in his own tongue his impressions of what he is making and his comments, as well as those of his neighbours and his family, as to his status and his craft's place in local society and culture.[2] For my thesis I record these comments first in native script, then transliterated, then translated.

With the advent of aluminium, cheap metals and plastics, the future of pottery in India is precarious. The production of terracotta imagery has always been only a sideline. If the full importance of this massive subculture is to be understood in the future, I feel this form of full documentation is necessary in the present.

This paper is based upon the material from one village, shown in its local context for reference: the finite as an introduction to the generic. Perhaps the most elaborate extant tradition involving terracottas is in Tamil Nadu, where well over a thousand shrines in rural areas are dedicated to Ayyanar.

The earliest terracottas from Tamil Nadu date from the seventh century BC, excavated in Megalithic sites in several districts.[3] These include large hand-built, multilegged sarcophagi (one in the shape of a ram) and numerous small animal and bird figures, as well as a wide range of sculptures similar to those which in the North are referred to as 'archaic mother-goddess' types. Fine terracottas made by both mould and hand have recently been excavated in Madurai, Dharmapuri, and Chingleput Districts, among others, dating from the second century BC to the sixth century AD. The sculptures compare in precision of detail to the better publicized Gangetic terracottas of the same period and are stylistically akin to Satavahana pieces.

The earliest known sculptural references to Ayyanar are in the seventh to eighth centuries AD. The cult of Ayyanar, also called Sasta or Masattan, is clearly similar to the cult of Revanta in the North. His shrines are called Pidari and he is a folk deity with strong classical ties. Dr Frederick Clothi of the University of Pittsburg, who is conducting research on Ayyanar iconography, finds that like Revanta, Ayyanar was first worshipped as a hero before being deified. He is possibly derived from Iyen or Iya, a hero mentioned in early prakrit Jaina and Buddhist texts.

As the son of both Śiva and Viṣṇu, as Mohini, Ayyanar is worshipped today by both sects. He protects village boundaries, provides crop and human fertility and heals the sick and infirm. In return for a boon, a terracotta sculpture (sometimes the image of a child, a donor, a dog, a cow, or an elephant, but usually that of a horse) is given to Ayyanar in his shrine on the village outskirts. The highly decorated sculptures are often quite large, ranging from eight inches to sixteen feet high, the normal height being between two and three feet. Many shrines are surrounded by trees and bushes, the bases of which are densely populated with terracotta horses, some old and fragmentary, others new and brightly painted.

Vaithyalinga Pathar, aged seventy-one when I worked with him in 1980, was the sole remaining sculpting potter in Gudithangichavadi, his village in South Arcot District, 121 miles south of Madras. The population of Gudithangichavadi was 1,872, made up mostly of farmers and factory workers, with no members of the brahman or kshatriya castes. The only other craftsmen were two carpenters and a blacksmith wheelwright. Vaithyalinga's brother, father and grandfather were potters. 'There is not a time when my family were not potters,' he said. 'We have lived in this house for 300 years but before that time my grandfathers lived in Chidambaram.' His father was a farmer who began potting professionally at forty. Vaithyalinga learned to make pottery and figures from both his father and his uncle. He spent two or three years in his apprenticeship, but says it took him ten years to learn his full trade. He married his wife, now known simply as 'Amma', at twenty-five (she was sixteen) and had two sons and a daughter. Amma's father was a weaver, but her maternal grandfather was a potter. Of their sons, one lives eighty miles away working in an automative parts factory, the second died three years ago leaving a wife and two sons. Their daughter died of cholera as a child. In his extended family, only a grand-nephew is learning to throw pots and he, at nineteen, has yet made no sculpture. The wheel is always at the front of the house on the street-verandah, while the firing is done at the back. In the house is a small Shaivite niche in which the principal deities are Murugan, Sivalinga, and Sivakami Amman. Vaithyalinga commented, 'I start my day's work after my regular meditation. Our family deity is Sivakami Amman. During the Tamil month of Thai [January] we celebrate the special puja for her by offering Mavilakku.[4] We also conduct the Karagam festival along with this puja. Karagam consists of devotees dancing with decorated pots on their heads and many garlands on them.'

As a maker of religious vessels and images, Vaithyalinga Pathar, like weavers, blacksmiths and other craftsmen, is a respected member of the Mathizhagan caste. The one graduate in Gudithangichavadi told me that in this village only this Pathar and Jagadesan Pathar (the nephew) make pottery. In spite of their profession and their place in society, these two families enjoy a certain amount of respectability in the village. Vaithyalinga Pathar has studied Tamil classics like Kamban's Rāmāyaṇa and the Mahābhārata. He is considered a scholarly person. People in the village consult him on various matters pertaining to dreams, ill-effects, village life, and so on. He and his wife are invited to all weddings in the village and they participate in all the social functions and festivals.

The average monthly income from all sources used to support the six people under his roof is 150 rupees. The family usually manages one kiln firing each month, the capacity of which is 150 to 300 pieces. A pot measuring six inches by eight inches sells for 30 paise. They only sell on a cash basis. Vaithyalinga said, 'due to the advent of other utensils made in plastic, german silver, or others, the demand for pottery has decreased over the years.'

In response to my request, Vaithyalinga Pathar sculpted the three figures he most frequently makes. Of those three, I will focus here on the horse and rider, Veeran. Veeran is the true guardian of the shrine, riding to battle for Ayyanar to protect the village. He is often represented simply by a riderless horse, also known as Koothukuthirai. These figures are made and decorated on commission to be carried in procession through the village during the Therukoothu festival in June or July. At the climax of the festival the horse figure is placed in an Ayyanar shrine. It is common belief in Tamil Nadu, as similarly viewed in other interpretations in villages all over India, that Veeran rides his horses around the village at night to protect the villagers from evil spirits. In the Therukoothu festival the villagers propitiate both Veeran and Ayyanar to pay them for their services. In a large town fifteen miles away a potter commented, 'the demand has reduced considerably over the years. Ten years ago worshipping was more intense and consequently more devotees were offering horse images. In those days I used to sell fifty horses each year. Now I sell thirty horses per year.' Vaithyalinga Pathar, who can work on as many as six horses simultaneously, now makes only four to six annually.

Once a year he brings four cartloads of clay from a pit half a mile from his house and leaves it in a mound in his back yard. For sculpting he mixes one part chaff to four parts clay with some ash and water until the needed consistency is reached. I commissioned a figure about three feet high. I gave no other instructions, only encouraging him to build it according to his inherited tradition. 'Before starting work I do a small puja for Lord Murugan and meditate for about ten minutes every morning.' Although he does not use the wheel for constructing any part of his Veeran, his approach to it illustrates his basic attitude. He told me, 'our religious belief is that the axis is Lord Brahma, the wheel is Lord Vishnu, and the lump of clay is Lord Shivalinga...the water used for our work is considered as Ganga.'

The sculpting took fourteen days from the mixing of the clay to the receipt of the figure after firing. The first day was occupied with mixing, then making four thin clay pallets about three-eighths of an inch thick and twelve inches square. These were allowed to dry for several hours in the sun before each was separately rolled around with an ash-covered wooden dowel to make four separate standing cylinders. The cylinders were left to dry overnight and each extended at one end the next morning by means of a roll technique, gradually taking the shape of a leg. 'For strengthening the upper portions of the legs I am using a mallet and stone. I hold the stone inside with one hand and beat [pat] the clay against the stone by means of holding a mallet in the other hand.' In the same process, 'I have now joined the legs, thereby forming part of the belly of the horse. I have left a hole about two inches in diameter at the centre of the belly portion for the purpose of proper heating of the inside in the kiln.' The process is slow, as each new section must dry enough to support the weight of the next addition. Vaithyalinga spent the rest of his time each day throwing his normal pottery. On the third day he built up the sides of the body of the horse, as always adding the clay in a large coil before working it into a flattened 'wall' shape. By the fourth day the sides were strong enough to allow for bridging over the back and the slow building up of the neck. While working, Vaithyalinga said, 'the demand for quality of work has certainly come down when compared to my grandfather's days. The customers also do not attach as much importance to the quality of work as in earlier years. Interest in art has come down.' As he started to add the rider's bent legs on the fifth day, he also began to add the first of several garlands (mala) to the horse's neck. The sixth day saw the formation of the trunk of the rider up to his middle torso and the beginning of the top portion of the horse's neck and he began to work on the most difficult step: the horse's head. As the angle of the head must drop down again and not sag, its formation is painstakingly slow, requiring many readjustments. He commented, 'after I started learning to make figures it took me four years to make them to my satisfaction.' On the ninth day the potter was able to support the horse's jaw sufficiently and began to work on the rider's head and arms. For the first time he used other materials to strengthen his sculpture, covering a core of straw and twigs with a surface of clay, and working this appendage on to the stick-supported shoulders. 'With these sticks and straw the head will not become weak. As the clay becomes completely hard in the kiln, the head will remain strong.'

For me the most important day was the tenth when I first felt the artistic merit of the man I was documenting (however subjective that feeling might be): when the amorphous lump on the figure's shoulders was transformed into a sensitive face. Vaithyalinga verbalized that process by saying, 'my mind thinks, my eyes see, my hands perform. Sometimes when I don't get the exact shape, I set it right by adding or removing clay.' The next two days were spent in finishing the horse's head, its eyes, mouth and nostrils, intricately adding on a mane and more mala, and putting the finishing touches to the rider's face and headdress. On the thirteenth day the quite elaborate sculpture was left alone to dry for its final day of firing.

Early in the morning of the fourteenth day, Vaithyalinga spread out behind his house all the items to be fired. This firing included about forty-five pots, six or seven clay cooking platforms, about seventy clay fireworks-housings to be used in an upcoming festival, and the three sculptures I had commissioned. These items, plus all the various fuels used to ignite and maintain the kiln, were left in the sun all morning to warm fully before being assembled to fire. 'This morning I collected dried coconut shells, palm leaves, straw, sticks, casuarina wood, and cowdung cakes and prepared the ground for the kiln. After putting in the Ayyanar figure, cradle-child, Koothukuthirai figure, and a few other items, I made arrangements for lighting up the kiln.' The process of preparing the kiln was aided by his wife, Amma, his daughter-in-law, and eight other neighbourhood women. Amma spent several hours adding water to a small mud-hole near the kiln site, mixing the mud to the desired consistency with her feet and removing all small stones and sticks to make the mixture smooth. On a flat, clean area of plain ground the figures were placed slightly apart while a small dung fire was started close by. At 12.31 p.m. the coals from this fire were divided between several unfired pots which were placed between and around the figures. Some coconut husks and sticks were added as Vaithyalinga and the women began carefully to arrange the remaining pots upside-down, bridging the space between them to form a roughly-shaped dome. These pots were covered and in-filled with coconut husks, sticks, cowdung, and the fireworks-housings. Next the dome was quickly layered with palm leaves, then straw, and finally a smooth surface of mud. This mud was applied by Vaithyalinga at the end of the brigade-line of pots filled by Amma at the other end. Vaithyalinga left a ring of straw nine inches high around the bottom with a fifteen-inch-wide hole at the top, both for ventilation. He then lit the kiln at both spots. The time was 12.50 p.m.. He said, 'even if the weather becomes cloudy after lighting the kiln, no harm shall be done, but if it rains, the whole affair will be a total loss. All the images inside will go to pieces.' It did not rain, as it had five days previously, and the firing was successful. At 3.10 p.m. he began carefully to pull off the dried mud layer. 'What I am using is an iron rod. I am removing the mud to allow sufficient air passage for proper burning of the kiln.' A few minutes later he said, 'I am now opening the kiln in haste as the heat is rather too much and this might spoil the horse figure and others.' Using his iron-tipped rod he gingerly lifted off the top pots, placing them to the side of the kiln, only removing a few at a time to allow the air slowly to cool the figures. As the fired pots were transferred to the ground and tested for cracks by Amma and her daughter-in-law, the image of Veeran on his horse gradually emerged, intact and now red rather than its previous unfired grey colour. The last of the pots was removed by 3.40 p.m., making the full firing just less than three hours long. The finished Koothuthirai horse and rider were ready for use in the festival. Most customers would have had Vaithyalinga paint the figure as well, but the choice is optional and the colours vary according to the devotee's wish. As I was trying not to influence the craftsmen's creativity by interjecting my preferences, it was decided to leave it unpainted.

The terracotta Veeran I had commissioned was not entirely free of my influence. The care the potter had taken with it had given it a finer character than those he normally makes. The terracotta sculptures Vaithyalinga Pathar has made for the last few years are simple and relatively unadorned when compared with the remaining broken ones he and his father made years before. He told me, 'the ability for quality is still there but there is no proper encouragement. We are also affected by stucco and cement sculpture as more and more people turn to that.' The effect of my personal interest in him as a craftsman gave Vaithyalinga an increased sense of pride in his work and his heritage. His sculpture reflected that pride. This example was perhaps not as good as the work of his father, but then it was the first figure he had taken such care with in years. The result was certainly of a fine quality.

In working with Vaithyalinga Pathar I was able to gain some understanding of the position and roles of the contemporary craft and craftsman in his society relative to those of his predecessors. With the thorough documentation of his craft, I am able to both appreciate more fully its quality and have a better perspective for recognizing its relationship to images in other shrines and perhaps in archaeological collections. The focus on one man's work combined with an in-depth survey of the shrines in culturally sympathetic areas can provide a basis for comprehending one of the primary creative forces active throughout the history of Indian civilization.[5]

Notes

1. Remarkably fine terracottas were produced in Uttar Pradesh, Bihar, and Bengal, most especially in the Mauryan, Sunga, Kushan and Gupta periods; and in Maharashtra, Karnataka, Andhra Pradesh, and some in Tamilnadu during the Satavahana period.

2. This documentation in the craftsman's own words is based loosely upon the approach of Fischer and Shah 1972.

3. For further examples see Ramachandran 1980.

4. Flour mixed with clay and given the shape of a lamp.

5. Sadly Vaithyalinga Pathar died shortly after this paper was written. His work is continued by a great-nephew.

References

Anand, Mulk Raj (ed) 1969. Terracottas. Marg, XXIII, No. 1

Biswas, S S 1981. Terracotta Art of Bengal. Delhi, Agam Kala Prakashan

Crafts Council of India. 1981. Terracotta. A catalogue to accompany Kumbha, an all-India workshop-exhibition. Madras

Dhavalikar, M K 1977. Masterpieces of Indian Terracottas. Bombay, Taraporevala

Fischer, Eberhard, Sitakant Mahaptra and Dinanath Pathy (eds) 1980. Orissa: Kunst und Kultur in Nordost-Indien. Zurich, Museum Rietberg

Fischer, Eberhard and Haku Shah 1970. Rural Craftsmen and their Work. Ahmedabad, National Institute of Design

Gupta, P L 1972. Gangetic Valley Terracotta Art. Varanasi, Prithivi Prakashan

Jayakar, Pupul 1981. The Earthen Drum: An Introduction to the Ritual Arts of Rural India. Delhi, The National Museum

Kala, K C 1980. Terracottas in the Allahabad Museum. New Delhi, Abhinav Publications

Kramrisch, Stella 1968. Unknown India: Ritual Art in Tribe and Village. Philadelphia Museum of Art

Ramachandran, K S 1980. Archaeology of South India - Tamil Nadu. Delhi, Sundeep Prakashan

Sankalia, H D 1978. Prehistoric Art in India. New Delhi, Vikas Publishing House

Santra, G 1980. Temple of Midnapur. Calcutta, Firma KLM

Saraswati, Baidyanath 1979. Pottery Making Culture and Indian Civilization. New Delhi, Abhinav

Zaheer, Mohammed 1981. The Temple of Bhitragaon. Delhi, Agam Kala Prakashan